TRAIN TIME

TRAIN TIME

Railroads and the Imminent Reshaping
of the United States Landscape

JOHN R. STILGOE

University of Virginia Press
CHARLOTTESVILLE AND LONDON

University of Virginia Press
© 2007 by the Rector and Visitors of the University of Virginia
Printed in the United States of America on acid-free paper

First published 2007
First paperback edition published 2009
ISBN 978-0-8139-2831-9 (paper)

1 3 5 7 9 8 6 4 2

The Library of Congress has cataloged the hardcover edition as follows:

LIBRARY OF CONGRESS CATALOGING-IN-PUBLICATION DATA

Stilgoe, John R., 1949–
Train time : railroads and the imminent reshaping of the United States
landscape / John R. Stilgoe.
p.   cm.
Includes bibliographical references and index.
ISBN 978-0-8139-2668-1 (cloth : alk. paper)
1. Railroads—United States—History. 2. Landscape—United States.
3. Railroads—United States—Traffic. 4. Railroads—United States—Freight.
5. Railroads—Social aspects—United States—History. I. Title.
HE2751.S683 2007
385.0973—dc22
2007008232

ALL PHOTOGRAPHS BY THE AUTHOR

For Stephen Bartlett and Russell Briggs

CONTENTS

PREFACE

Rumbling faintly in the distance, trains return as the key shaper of the United States built environment. From near oblivion, from a past too long romanticized or simply ignored, trains roll into the attention of those who know how to pause, look around, listen carefully, and see how present events skew the near future. While politicians debate the future of Amtrak and the public reads little of an industry ordinarily newsworthy only when trains derail, consulting firms, real estate developers, and other for-profit enterprises scramble to analyze an industry of once-massive corollary impact.

Unlike so many United States industries, railroads have a fundamental and often ferocious attachment to American soil and to particular regions. Along their tracks, events are unfolding rapidly, generally unnoticed except by rail experts and a cognoscenti attuned to imminent landscape and cultural change.

Away from the coasts, booming freight traffic raises a number of questions about the national economy. Hundreds of trains carry containers emblazoned with the names of Asian shipping companies or Asian manufacturers, mixed now and then with containers labeled in Spanish. In the old Rust Belt, across the High Plains, along the entire Mexican border, across the upland South, rolling freight trains are a reminder that much manufacturing and many assembly-line jobs have moved to the Far East, the Philippines, Mexico, and other foreign countries. This impression is bolstered by Department of Labor calculations that in the 1990s the United States lost 1.5 million manufacturing jobs to China alone.

It might even be said that freight trains swayed the 2004 presidential election. In the American heartland, voters chose a Republican candidate determined to "protect" the nation, not only from containers filled with terrorist explosive or chemical weapons, but—of even more pressing concern to the electorate—from long-term economic dislocation. The growing manufacturing muscle of China so evident in mile-long freight trains conjures images of a

Chinese-dominated automobile industry, a potential economic disruption exceeding any threat posed by the Japanese in the world industrial marketplace. Trains deliver, and increasingly what they deliver rides in boxes obviously from Asia, Mexico, and elsewhere. Those living in United States coastal areas rarely see the long trains that slither inland from ports nowadays isolated, even fenced off from casual observation. High-tech ports opening on world trade, such as Kalama, Washington, are rarely discussed; many otherwise well-informed Americans cannot even locate it, despite its Pacific Rim importance. Yet Kalama and other ports service hundreds of freight trains bound into and across a red-state heartland growing ever more concerned about "homeland security" in ways that are economically protectionist.

Kalama, Halifax in Nova Scotia, perhaps especially Prince Rupert in British Columbia, offer railroad companies exquisitely modern, jam-free access to ocean trade. From Halifax, trains of containers roll west and south across Canada and the northern United States. Halifax now threatens the shipping primacy of Boston, Portland, Maine, and even the clogged, shallow-water wharves of Perth Amboy and Elizabeth in New Jersey. New Jersey has completed a new freight railroad linking its wharves to transcontinental rail lines, partly to lessen truck congestion at the southern end of the George Washington Bridge, but chiefly to avoid the fate of such traffic-vexed Pacific Coast cities as Seattle and Los Angeles. Far to the north, at Prince Rupert, a port city a few hours' steamship time nearer Asia than its California competitors, ultramodern wharves now draw cargo from the Mississippi Valley over a long-decrepit track speculators built a century ago.

Freight trains are at the core of the change analyzed here, but there are other elements involved. Part of the future begins to reveal itself in coastal cities and other urban areas where freight trains share rails with existing and planned passenger service. Manhattan rail commuters cannot fail to notice the lengthening freight trains snaking around new passenger stations at Secaucus and elsewhere. In the harbor itself, the great barges of the New York Cross Harbor Railroad Terminal Corporation float freight cars between New Jersey and Brooklyn. Between 2002 and 2005 car-float traffic has doubled from four thousand to eight thousand cars, as connecting railroads hurried priority cars around jammed yards squeezed by routes already dedicated to passenger service. While New York and New Jersey politicians confront the growing necessity for a freight railroad tunnel under the harbor, a project that already threatens to fracture the Port Authority of New York and New Jersey by shifting transshipment activity back to Brooklyn, commuter rail authorities despair of adding more trains along routes jammed with freight trains. And in rural areas far from New York, Los Angeles, and other ports, burgeoning freight traffic impedes hopes and plans for new passenger service envisioned on New York models. This is already evident in coastal cities and other cities in which freight trains must share rails with new passenger trains.

In late 2004 New Mexico state officials ordered ten new bi-level commuter railcars. Costing $2.2 million each, the cars are intended to serve commuters riding back and forth between Belen and Bernalillo, small communities officials now identify as part of greater Albuquerque. Wealthy people live north and south of the sprawling city, in places that 1970s tourists found quaint and inexpensive villages. Fast commuter service over existing high-quality rails hitherto carrying only long-distance freight trains means that exurbanites will whisk past inner suburbs, truck traffic, and rush-hour traffic jams. Albuquerque might seem an unlikely city to institute commuter rail service, but some of the most aggressive railroad reincarnation happens where city councils suddenly abandon hope in highways. In Atlanta, St. Louis, and other automobile-centric cities, politicians are initiating feasibility studies and rail-equipment manufacturers are soliciting orders. The train is returning, an economic and cultural tsunami about to transform the United States.

A casual survey of railroads and areas where railroads once operated produces multiple discoveries, not all particularly reassuring to observers rooted in highway-based shopping mall culture. Parking lots that once served long-demolished passenger and freight stations host lengthy visits by deep-pocket real estate developers who stare speculatively at adjacent stores and roads, spread old maps across automobile hoods, and make notes on laptop computers. Elsewhere, surveyors park their SUVs next to access points along abandoned tracks converted to nature trails. Sometimes fragments of plastic tape mark their activity, but often surveyors measure adjacent property almost clandestinely. Here and there, usually at rush hour, retail-marketing experts scrutinize the behavior of commuters boarding and exiting trains, walking across retail streets, or driving to and from parking lots; these observers leave no trace either. Around modern warehouses served by rail, logistics engineers test the movement of specialized freight cars or robotic unloading systems. Watching people who watch railroads reveals a new analytical energy, something quiet but brutally powerful happening along railroad alignments. Energy and long-term investment are beginning to gravitate from roads and highways, from suburban and rural land adjacent only to asphalt, and from automobile manufacturers.

Inspectors of grassy, disused railroad tracks often provide the first quasi-public indication that a long-idle mine or manufacturing plant will reopen, or that rail traffic will shift onto a near-abandoned route. Something is about to happen near Etowah and Copperhill in Tennessee, but right now the close-lipped examiners of an overgrown track are the only clue to impending reinvestment. Change less massive but equally indicative of a larger reorientation begins to reshape a bit of western Pennsylvania, where the Rosebud Mining Company, after spending a million dollars in 2004 to repair local roads damaged by its coal-hauling trucks, now debates not only buying the Kiski Junction Railroad but extending it to its Logansport mines. Sharp-eyed observers of landscape note the surveyors, and occasionally, alert local journalists realize something might be about to happen, often in areas where much happened decades ago, before rusting into oblivion.

Everywhere local newspapers record fragments of a larger story seldom reported in the likes of the *Wall Street Journal.* Just as the Wal-Mart and Dollar General retail chains originated and matured almost unnoticed in the Tennessee-Arkansas cradle of Tyson Foods, J. B. Hunt Trucking, and other now-powerful firms reshaping national business and landscape, so railroads and railroad-related industries begin to flex economic muscle, but usually away from coastal areas. Wal-Mart transformed the context of small-store Main Street, shopping malls, and dozens of regional discount department-store chains, and Tyson Foods morphed the agricultural landscape into a well-nigh industrialized zone. Coastal media miss the great changes recently wrought by railroads away from coastal regions.

Anyone who looks carefully will find people studying railroads, both indoors and out. Archivists and librarians note the rising interest in historical railroad documents, from the dustiest and driest of reports dealing with sixteen-hour passenger service between Chicago and New York to information on fast freight operation between New Orleans and Kansas City. Stockbrokers and investment analysts note an upsurge in interest among would-be investors in railroads: the Conrail stock that went on sale in 1987 for $28 a share sold in 1997 at $115. But investment experts often know nothing about profitable companies that serve the railroad industry or that intend to profit from the coming railroad boom. In an age of online stock trading, many investors lack any introduction to the nascent reinvestment already evident in rising railroad company share prices. In 2005, when the first freight train rolled into Dallas over the long-derelict tracks of the former St. Louis, Mexico & Orient, only local newspapers reported the event. Texas Pacifico, Ferroccarril Mexicano, and other subsidiary corporate names suggest the internationalizing of the post-NAFTA border country, but no national news media noted the creation of an integrated transcontinental route between Dallas and Topolobampo.

High-tech industries already serving railroads are sometimes poised to transform them. Rail Power Technologies, a British Columbia builder of locomotives, furnishes low-polluting, fuel-efficient, quiet-switching locomotives especially adapted to urban areas. Its Green Goat prototype heralds a transformation in locomotive design, and its stock prices reflect investor confidence. Other companies, especially those manufacturing railroad cars and making railroad ties from recycled plastic or concrete, surprise even seasoned investors. Shareholders in J. B. Hunt express confidence and satisfaction too, but only those who read annual reports thoroughly know what farm children learn simply by watching speeding freight trains west of St. Louis. J. B. Hunt prospers by moving trailers by rail, not over interstate highways.

Railroad industry annual reports only hint at the much larger subject of this book, the discerning of landscape and cultural change just beginning to occur. The best way of formulating an idea of how the United States landscape will change in the immediate future is to watch the subtle but rapid change so evident around so many active railroad lines. Scrutinizing that change heightens awareness of imminent social, cultural, and economic change otherwise not easily noticed, and usually not noted by news media. Extrapolation is not design, nor is it planning; but it now drives present investment that reflects change and produces change.

Few Americans take notice of developments in the rail industries. Even fewer *realize* them. Comparatively few people ride Amtrak long-haul trains, and often freight trains move in corridors difficult to reach by car. For decades railroads have operated through the skid row sections of cities, skirting the parts of town where middle-income people rarely venture. One train seems much like another. Now and then a freight train stops traffic for a few minutes, but few delayed motorists notice anything particular about the string of specialized railcars rumbling across the road. Tourists in remote areas are likely to express surprise when an Amtrak express flashes across a bridge or emerges from a mountain valley. Urban intellectuals shrug when they learn that trains will return to the abandoned line between Etowah and Copperhill in Tennessee or to the old tracks linking Dallas and Topolobampo or to dozens of other long-quiet routes. Only rarely do they ponder such activity as the effect of wealth transferred geographically and from one set of industries to another. All too rarely, change in rail-centered industries causes change in landscape that passes as unnoticed as a train in the far distance. Making sense of that change describes a scenario of events moving as fast as any express train.

Now a train is often only a whistle heard far off on a sleepless night. But romantic or foreboding or empowering, the whistle announces both return and change to those who listen.

ACKNOWLEDGMENTS

My former students are many now, and the imminent change wrought by railroads intrigues many of them. I began lecturing on railroad-corridor landscapes thirty years ago at Harvard University, and I am grateful for the observations, suspicions, and hunches of alumni who learned to watch the rails. Anonymity often cloaks the enterprise of would-be real estate investors and others; here I maintain the obscurity of people intending to profit from change-in-the-making. Thomas Armstrong, Robert Belyea, Fletcher Hall, Donald House, and Harold Tuttle have all offered valuable insights. Stephen Bartlett and Russell Briggs helped especially acutely, and I am grateful for their friendship and viewpoints. I commend my editor, Boyd Zenner, for her confidence in a book about potential futures. My wife, Debra, deserves more credit than I have words. Not only does she smile when I follow railroads across the country, driving down rutted roads and small-town alleys and into regions lacking good motels, she often notices much I have missed.

TRAIN TIME

Long trains racing over well-maintained tracks everywhere in rural America lure
capital investment away from decaying highways and trucks dependent on them.

INTRODUCTION

Only birds skitter along the high-level platform at Bethel, Maine. Weeds grow among the rails and ties of the track it abuts, and the station behind it sits more quietly even than the quiet town. No automobiles park in the station lot. No passenger trains stop at the platform. No expresses hasten past it. Only one or two daily freight trains rumble along the shiny rails beyond the platform track, linking Portland and Quebec while serving dozens of trackside industries in rural Maine and northeast New Hampshire. The stop at Bethel might be any one of thousands of similar points along United States railroads, except for one thing. The passenger station, the high-level platform, the station track, even the parking lot are all brand new and waiting.

Maine voters and politicians intend that passenger trains will return, and soon. The rationale for the new structures at Bethel proves simple. Three miles away, the spectacular resort of Sunday River offers superb skiing and other snow sports in winter, year-round mountain and forest recreation, and conference facilities. But getting to Sunday River from anywhere, even Portland, can be difficult. Travelers arriving at Portland by air find what all motorists find: two-lane roads winding up hill and down. Neither the Portland airport nor the rural highway system entices visitors to Sunday River, or to Bethel, for that matter. The resort famed for the best skiing in New England deserves something better, and the people of Maine know what: a passenger train.

So with little difficulty, in 2001 the state prevailed upon Amtrak to inaugurate several daily trains between Boston and Portland over upgraded tracks owned by a freight railroad. All the trains, called Downeasters, cover the 116-mile route in about two and a half hours, and all immediately exceeded ridership estimates. At first operating at sixty miles per hour and then at seventy-nine, the trains make commuting between Portland and Boston possible, and between southern Maine and New Hampshire towns and Boston a pleasure. But the Downeasters have a meaning deeper than commuting.

At seventy-nine miles per hour Sunday River is about forty minutes beyond Portland. The state of Maine built a platform, station, and parking lot in anticipation of the start of Amtrak service to Portland continuing under state subsidy sixty-five miles further to Bethel. Such planning and construction are part of a larger transportation vision in a rural state usually considered highway focused but acutely aware that it attracts ever larger numbers of Europeans enjoying six-week vacations and many New Yorkers and southern New Englanders weary of road traffic. In the fall of 2006, buoyed by data indicating that the 330,000 Downeaster passengers represented a 31 percent increase in ridership over the previous year, the governor of Maine issued an executive order to expand service far to the north and west of Portland. In a public address accompanying the order, he emphasized the speed with which the passenger trains had boosted investment in every town in which they stopped.

Few Americans know much about the renaissance of railroads suddenly shaping high-power politics of real estate development, industrial location, and population parameters. Population growth shapes the thinking of decision makers. In 2055 the United States will be home to 417 million people, up 129 million from its current population of 302 million. Most government transportation planning remains based in circa-1960 assumptions derived from a population of about 150 million people. Almost all the anticipated population growth will occur in metropolitan regions already choked with motor vehicle and airliner traffic. As 13D Research emphasized in a private, August 17, 2006, report to institutional investors, "Another Solution to the Energy Crisis: Railroad Equipment," population growth in restricted areas suggests a very strong future for railroads.

Despite feel-good advertising by the automobile, trucking, and airline lobbies, by 1970 most planners knew the futility of building more and wider highways, especially at urban choke points. Almost certainly, advisers to John F. Kennedy understood the futility years earlier. On April 5, 1962, Kennedy sent a terse "Message on Transportation" to Congress, stating what nowadays seems extraordinary for a Democrat of that era. "I am convinced that less Federal regulation and subsidization is in the long run a prime requisite of a healthy intercity transportation network," Kennedy asserted. Moreover, he insisted that until the federal government had solid data reflecting the relationships among transport types, Congress should resist any further tinkering with a transportation industry involving both public rights-of-way, especially interstate highways, and private ones. At some point in the near future, Kennedy concluded, users of taxpayer-subsidized rights-of-way must begin covering the costs of repair and periodic rebuilding, and in the meantime no federal initiative should restrict the innate technological advantages of one transportation type to subsidize another. In the midst of crises involving agriculture, urban renewal, racial integration, Medicare, and the steel industry—but just before the Cuban missile crisis—Kennedy made clear in sixteen typewritten pages that physical realities must henceforth shape federal transportation policy, and that hard data, including demographics, might forecast forces affecting physical realities.

Numbers meant much to Kennedy for reasons nowadays forgotten. The 1960 presidential election proved not only the closest up to that time but the first accurately predicted by computer. Despite a substantial early lead by Nixon, the NBC computer named Kennedy the winner at 8:20 EST, and other network computers followed. After NBC had approached RCA in early 1960 about using one of its mainframe computers to predict the election, RCA quickly divined that election prediction resembled many industrial problems. By 1962 RCA had discerned the simplicity of predicting elections compared with predicting the outcome changes in and among industries, and had become adept at programming scenarios involving electoral effects of issues developing late in political campaigns. But sinister currents swirled beneath much popular reporting of computer-based election prediction because news media experts knew corporations already used computers to predict and analyze trends.

Some of the most respected journalists in the United States, including Eric Sevareid and David Brinkley, insisted that computer-driven scenario analysis might destroy elections. In a 1964 *Popular*

Mechanics article, Clifford B. Hicks outlined journalist fears and then explained the technology RCA used. Before anyone voted in the 1960 election the RCA computer had predicted the outcome almost exactly, based on analysis of polls and regional "political comment."

No one knew better than Kennedy the importance of numbers and scenario prediction, but he glimpsed something more. In pushing the post office to analyze automation, Kennedy envisioned the digitizing of geographic information in ways far more subtle than those used by the Bureau of the Census. In the summer of 1963 the zip code was launched as a way of speeding mail delivery and coding demographic and geographic data. Long before the public learned much about computers predicting elections, astute venture capitalists were using zip-code-based data to track production and consumption flows and to predict the best companies and locations in which to invest.

Computer-driven predictions using zip code and other data merged with other inventions in the early 1960s. In a Baltimore home basement, three freelance inventors won the race to create the videocassette recorder, and by 1965 they were besieged by television network executives and scores of other interested professionals, including school superintendents and golfers anxious for instant video feedback. As Mark R. Levy points out in *The VCR Age,* behind the throng quietly moved another group. Venture capitalists saw not only a massive market for renting video tapes played through television sets, even imagining the tapes rented at specialized stores or delivered and returned by mail, but the splintering of television network hegemony that hired election-result computers. At first, they discerned market areas based on zip code analysis, but quickly at least a few envisioned interactive telephone/teletype/television services linked by cable in ways that presaged the Web and Internet. By 1979 Fotomat had begun renting cassettes from each of its three thousand stores, and within three years a national proliferation of videocassette rental stores proved the correctness of mid-1970s data-driven investment scenarios. Such private-sector scenarios depended on government-collected data, but at first scenario prediction did little to sway federal transportation policy following the Cuban missile crisis.

Foreign policy issues, then assassination, deflected federal interest away from rigorous, scenario-based analysis of transportation issues and from prediction grounded in technological invention. The administration of Lyndon Baines Johnson, mired in both the Vietnam War and expensive antipoverty efforts, avoided the realpolitik Kennedy expressed, perhaps realizing that its social welfare policies could not survive computer-based scenario inspection developed by defense analysts. Just as early computer software required users to type perfectly and in standard English, so late-1960s mainframe-based computer analysis of large-scale, nuanced issues produced results unpalatable to politicians in both parties. Building more urban highways produced a measurable need for more parking garages, for example, and would eventually produce downtowns consisting largely of multistory garages. Retrospect suggests that the Johnson administration devastated not only transportation analysis and planning but urban renewal and rural development despite spending billions of dollars; it ignored the Kennedy understanding that as prediction software became more sophisticated it would shape all public works projects. Its bumbling begat the fast-sprawling metropolitan growth that dwarfed 1950s suburban development, and, more importantly, it stymied efforts by public researchers to predict facets of the growth over time.

Paralyzed by political inaction—especially in large-population states having one or more dense cities sprawling rapidly toward each other—and by fear of angering voters enamored of private motorcars as the key to suburban living, planners said little about the physical impossibility of accommodating tens of millions more automobiles, especially in the vicinity of large airports and harbors. The energy crises of 1973 and 1978 ought to have alerted federal, state, and local planning experts to the futility Kennedy descried, but the official record suggests otherwise. This may be one reason that many left the planning profession for greener pastures in the far more tough-minded private sectors of marketing, real estate development, and site analysis.

In the Nixon, Ford, Carter, and Reagan administrations, federal experts moved slowly toward the deregulation point of view Kennedy espoused years earlier but which the Johnson administration ignored. The most casual investigation of the historical narrative reveals instances of seeming confusion and paradox. The Nixon administration privatized the post office while making rail passenger service the responsibility of the quasi-public Amtrak. The Staggers Act of 1980 effectively removed much railroad industry regulation and produced a far more profitable industry that pleased Carter administration experts and stockholders alike while dismaying labor unions, but railroad deregulation efforts failed to solve the deepening crisis in a national transportation policy still focused on highways. Beyond the radar of government planners, some Americans began moving toward a new vision of railroad-based industrial, commercial, and residential investment. Just as the poultry-farming initiatives of Perdue and Tyson perplexed rural planners, and the spreading of Wal-Mart and Dollar General stores puzzled small-town and then urban planners, the efforts of investors in a railroad-based future now moving from obscurity puzzle and irritate government planners. But remarkably little public discussion focuses on their efforts. The investors might as well be the inventors of the VCR or early investors in Blockbuster Video or Netflix, for they are nearly anonymous and nearly removed from government oversight.

Americans now live in what appears to be the final, sickly sweet blossoming of the automobile and airliner, and the related real estate development. A frantic energy masks the desperation of real estate developers terrified that people will not buy the last of the structures built according to automobile thinking. Recently the California Historic Resources Commission reversed itself by declaring a 7.5-mile stretch of railroad running between National City and Imperial of so little value that it may be built upon. Despite citizen opposition, the commission, under pressure from the governor, stripped the corridor of its Historic Register status in order to expedite residential real estate development favored by the Chula Vista and San Diego Unified Port District Authority. Part of a 21.5-mile portion of the San Diego and Arizona Eastern Railway, which ran from downtown San Diego through Imperial Beach to Coronado, the 7.5-mile stretch raised the specter of a nonautomobile route to downtown. Not often are spaces entered into Historic Registers excised, but in a state still enamored of the motorcar, every existing rail route worries real estate developers still committed to an automobile-focused development model.

That model begins to crumble. In September 2005 national media reported studies suggesting that freight traffic had to move from urban highways to railroads to avoid gridlock. Newspapers tended to frame the scenarios only in local terms. The *Boston Herald* emphasized that shifting a quarter of truck freight to rail by 2025 would save an average of $513 and 32.3 hours a year per metropolitan commuter and reduce Boston-area air pollution by 12,300 tons and fuel consumption by 247 million gallons annually. Few articles note the significance of averages: suburban and exurban commuters would save far more money and time than urban residents. Even fewer noted that the first metropolitan regions to shift to rail freight would increase their competitive advantages significantly or that, in national terms, the scenarios necessitate new models for real estate development.

The argument that follows here rides atop steel rails, sometimes smooth, sometimes rusted and uneven; and what underlies it may surprise, irritate, or anger. At some point soon, many middle-income Americans will no longer be able to afford to live as they live now. They will face difficult choices, including those pitting automobile against home ownership. At present, many find desirable affordable housing only in far outer suburbs. Commuting long distances exacts a toll on automobiles, of course, but it consumes time too—sometimes so much time that it proves unaffordable. Gasoline prices figure in domestic budgeting, but the significant equation involves commuting time and house finance.

Mortgage costs have risen seventy times faster than a worker's income over the past generation, according to authors of the 2001 Consumer Bankruptcy Project. Many married couples, even well-educated ones, now find that both partners must work to earn enough to buy housing in high-quality school districts. However counterintuitive they may be, the findings of Elizabeth Warren and

9

Amelia Warren Tyagi reported in *The Two-Income Trap* seem clear: seemingly successful couples face a far higher likelihood of filing bankruptcy than couples in which only the man works. In 2001 a greater number of people filed for bankruptcy than graduated from college or filed for divorce, and Warren and Tyagi predict that one in seven children will live through a bankruptcy before 2010. What many middle-income couples vaguely feel proves true: even with both people working, often at well-paying jobs, they have less discretionary income than did their parents. Gigantic mortgage costs, spiraling health-insurance premiums, and costs of child care and nursery-school tuition contradict traditional wisdom about success, the good life, and the American dream. As Warren and Tyagi argue, neither news media nor most young or middle-aged adults care to hear that feminism, computerization, and commuting may have contributed to the impoverishment of two generations. Few American families can sustain the actual costs of owning two cars, or of replacing a roof as the oldest child enters college. Despite owning one or more personal computers, almost none can predict their short- and long-term financial circumstances. Many worry about making ends meet, sending children to college, the offshoring of white-collar jobs, and the persistent rumors of Social Security bankruptcy. No politician of any party wants to tell such people that nothing can be done to salvage their lifestyles, and the advertising industry always encourages further consumption. Credit-card indebtedness and middle-class bankruptcy now loom exactly as highway congestion loomed before planners in the early 1970s. What worries middle-income families paralyzes politicians into silence, for the politicians understand the force of scenario analysis.

At some point soon, the grittiness of commuting time, mortgage costs, and rising parallel expenses, including gasoline prices, will reverse suburban sprawl permanently and accelerate staggering spatial and cultural change.

Such change provides opportunity to the forewarned. Some Americans can and do use computers to predict, though running detailed scenarios depends on access to top-notch computer hardware and software, masses of databases, and experts skilled in crunching numbers in geographic context. It requires some knowledge of history too. It was for-profit firm consultants rummaging for that knowledge in the Baker Library at the Harvard Business School and the Loeb Library at the Harvard Graduate School of Design who first alerted me to the tremendous force about to change the United States built environment.

Implicit conspiracy ballasts this book. Conspiracy theorists imagine evil men in office towers or government bunkers manipulating the public or media or economy. Implicit conspiracy requires another sort of imagining. Without active effort, often without knowing each other, individuals—and corporations—may allow something massive to happen because a small part of it benefits them. As Mancur Olson argues in *The Logic of Collective Action,* such unorganized activity often proves immensely powerful but extremely difficult to trace. However forcefully politicians condemned 1960s urban riots, violence and arson produced windfall profits for fencing suppliers, burglar and fire alarm installers, private security firms, and especially for developers of suburban shopping malls, office complexes, industrial parks, and—above all—housing. No one suggests that any of those firms or investors conspired to spark riots or impede efforts to end and prevent civil disturbance. But hindsight offers glimpses of how they and others profited quietly from urban disinvestment and other crises still labeled *urban,* never *metropolitan.*

Implicit or tacit conspiracy often involves nothing more than recognizing a good investment opportunity when it arises and keeping silent about it. Across much of the United States, railroads attract little public scrutiny, let alone sustained historical analysis. In some places—say near North Platte, Nebraska, where the Union Pacific operates a fiercely busy three-track transcontinental main line—rail activity impresses coastal state tourists who chance upon it. Elsewhere, however, railroads seem slightly down-at-the-heels—not quaint exactly, but not high tech. Magisterial works like Carl Condit's *The Port of New York* and Joseph Schwieterman's *When the Railroad Leaves Town* seem pure history. But such books interest investors, management consultants, developers, and others in ways I discovered after I published my *Metropolitan Corridor: Railroads and the American Scene* in 1983. Quietly, always politely, but often intensely, came inquirers. I began fielding questions about the period on which I had focused a scholarly book, roughly that between 1885 and 1939. At first the questions struck me as harmless, the sort every university faculty member routinely receives from the public, usually by telephone. Someone wanted to know about sixteen-hour train service between New York and Chicago. Someone else inquired about express package service. An alumnus, sharp-eyed as an undergraduate and now a venture capitalist, wondered about bright-yellow boxcars with two doors on each side. Another alumnus asked about freight distribution practices across the South in the 1930s, thanked me, and then asked if I would mind not mentioning his inquiry to anyone. Slowly I realized that something other than historical curiosity drove the inquiries, and I began quietly questioning my former students in real estate development. Deep-pocket, long-term investors had begun to think of replicating fragments of the railroad-run past.

In their thinking, and throughout this book, past will be prologue. In the fifty years following 1900 the population of New York City grew from about 3.4 million to 7.9 million. The population of Manhattan scarcely changed, but Brooklyn more than doubled to 2.7 million. As William D. Middleton points out in *Metropolitan Railways: Rapid Transit in America,* almost all New York City growth occurred in the formerly undeveloped sections of Queens, the Bronx, and Brooklyn made accessible by new elevated lines and subways. Added to Condit's impeccable analysis of New York suburban railroad building, Middleton's work becomes a portal through which visionaries might peer. Schwieterman explains what happened when railroads abandoned cities and small towns. What follows here examines what will happen when railroads come back.

When Alvin Toffler published *Future Shock* in 1970, Americans had grown jittery from rapid change, especially the changes in social mores emphasized by news and entertainment media. Free love, political protest, illicit drug use, and other issues now preoccupy most analysts of the 1960s. But retrospect makes clear that much 1960s change worked in subtractive ways: Americans lost many options and opportunities.

In the early 1960s, for example, the Hudson & Manhattan Railroad Company rumbled along in postbankruptcy dirtiness and noise. Its 19th Street station stood abandoned, and few passengers used its stations at 14th and 23rd Streets; its more frequented stations appeared nearly derelict. Commuters between New Jersey and lower Manhattan expected service to cease as other commuter rail service already had, imminently and perhaps with no advance warning. Only an obscure group of visionaries glimpsed the potential in the 12.5 miles of tunnels beneath the Hudson River. Transferring ownership of the rickety system to the Port Authority, which rebuilt and extended it into a swift, reliable railroad, made the World Trade Center towers financially feasible as private development. Analyzing that quiet envisioning of a creaky, derelict, underutilized short-line railroad operating mostly in tunnels as the generator of real estate development across lower Manhattan proves maddeningly frustrating now. In the middle 1960s New Yorkers were scarcely aware of the Hudson & Manhattan trains and tunnels, much less did they think about their potential. But the transformation of the Hudson & Manhattan is only one example from the now-ignored 1960s that demonstrates how much the future shocks when it arrives ahead of schedule. In the wake of 9/11, architectural, urban, and social historians understandably focus on the World Trade Center complex, especially the Twin Towers; but the complex itself depended on the discovery and reinvention of the Hudson & Manhattan commuter railroad, which eventually enabled the concentration of population at the lower end of Manhattan.

Railroads concentrate population. Automobiles and airliners distribute it. Once understood, that simple dichotomy explains not just the new station at Bethel but a spatial revolution in the making, one that is accelerating as many Americans face economic uncertainty and strain.

Railroads will return along routes abandoned to hikers and nature lovers fifty years ago. Already some trails have reverted to railroads again, jarring people who thought abandonment permanent. Since 1997 the Commonwealth of Massachusetts has replaced three entire trail systems with three commuter railroads stretching far south of Boston. Few notice abandoned railroad rights-of-way snaking through the landscape, and fewer still realize the potential of these as transportation corridors. But since the 1950s, as the first chapter will show, some groups have anticipated that the train will come again. Dismissed as nostalgic or cranky by all but deep-pocket, long-term investors, their foresight now shakes the very foundations of politics and economics. *When* the railroad returns, not *if,* it will not only transform the half-forgotten jewels that lie along the nation's obscure operating railroad routes but also re-shape regions far from existing tracks. Return will alter everyday life more dramatically than the arrival of personal computers, Internet connections, or cell phones. Return will remake the United States economy in ways that private-sector savants already anticipate. However difficult it is to imagine a grass-grown railroad track becoming a high-speed, heavily trafficked route, it is still more difficult to imagine grass growing through the pavement of interstate highways. But at least some people with imagination have made the intellectual leap. The built landscape just now is entering a transformation of unprecedented proportions, one as little noticed as the rise of Wal-Mart, the invention of the VCR, or the use of computers to make predictions.

Whether or not they know it, millions of Americans live in an economy waiting for the train. Outsourcing, the offshoring of computer-based jobs, and rising energy prices deflect media interest from a shift in intellectual and financial investment that anyone who looks around can notice and begin to study without much access to research university libraries or think-tank reports.

Small cities, the middle rings of metropolitan regions, very small towns, and much of rural America reward future-focused analysis best. In the 1970s railroads began abandoning their big-city freight yards, selling the acreage for real estate development, and ripping up tracks. In an honest, open way they enlarged existing classification yards in land-cheap locations far from center cities and interstate highways. Low land-use taxes in rural counties prompted railroads to store infrequently used cars on sidetracks along rusty branch lines, and sometimes on the branch lines themselves. Few tourists drive along the dirt roads southeast of Bonne Terre, Missouri, but those who do find strings of automobile-transport cars bisecting farm fields on rarely used track. Decades ago transcontinental travelers would have seen the new yards and stored cars from the windows of passenger trains. Nowadays few travelers see them at all, and few locals think much about them. Far from the gaze of most Americans blooms a railroad industry about to reshape national life and culture. Only recently have national newspapers glimpsed the broad-based economic good times evident in Sioux Falls, Fargo, Rapid City, Iowa City, and other rural cities. As Joel Kotkin argues in an August 2006 *Wall Street Journal* article, "The Great Plains," old images of dying towns, aging populations, and failing ranches remain popular with eastern journalists despite being wrong.

Nothing more definitely indicates mass misperception than the enduring presence of steam locomotives in books and other media aimed at children. The little engine that could still chugs and puffs its way uphill, Thomas the Tank Engine rumbles about Victorian Great Britain, and the whoooooeeeeee of the steam locomotive whistles the longevity of early twentieth-century railroading in contemporary cartoons and music. But only in museums is modern American railroading romantic, smelling of coal smoke, steam, and hot valve oil. Elsewhere it is serious business, far more high-tech than most outside the industry recognize and far more powerful—and capable of rapid change—than almost anyone in or out of the industry is willing to mention in public. In 2005 the General Electric Company ran full-page ads in the *Wall Street Journal* touting its fuel-efficient, low-polluting Evolution Series locomotives as the new "engine that could." In its 2005 annual report, Norfolk Southern told shareholders about its pioneering use of LEADER, Locomotive Engineer Assist Display and Event Recorder, a computer-powered system that advises engineers on the optimum fuel-efficient speed for their trains based on tonnage, topography, and other real-time factors. Children's books, popular music, even railroad museums reflect and encourage a sort of mass nostalgia rooted in the distant past, to the exclusion of contemporary activity and potential.

After World War II, automobiles, trucks, highways, and airliners transformed both landscape and culture, producing the metropolitan sprawl so many Americans condemn while enjoying its amenities. Now, in an era of rising fuel costs and intractable highway congestion, burgeoning metropolitan and diminishing rural population, post-NAFTA manufacturing growth in Canada and Mexico, and perhaps above all a global shift in manufacturing away from the United States, railroads begin to drive spatial and cultural change about to disconcert Americans, especially middle-income people far too comfortable inside their cars. In *Outside Lies Magic: Regaining History and Awareness in Everyday Places,* I counsel Americans to walk acutely, look around, and discover what news media often ignore. Here I suggest they scrutinize railroads to glimpse the signs of large-scale landscape change.

History rides everywhere in the pages that follow, but this book focuses on the near future, not even the near past Richard Saunders brilliantly recounts in *Main Lines: Rebirth of the North American Railroads, 1970–2002.* It emphasizes how subtle change forces more change, despite public outcry or political cravenness. It stresses that physical constraints wield far more power than politicians and media moguls alike, and it emphasizes contemporary change shaped by discerning, future-minded people, often very wealthy ones, who speed such change for their own ends, and only sometimes for the public good. It sketches what will happen in an era when public and private resources prove too scanty to fund alternatives. It glances backward frequently, simply because remnants of past landscapes now function as capital in the plans of people already in the know about future landscapes.

Scenario analysis underlies this book. Such analysis asks a simple question of complex issues and data, and of change: What if? Glimpsing *the* future preoccupies few scenario analysts. Instead they descry possible futures, not so much parallel ones as ones diverging and interlocking, in ways locomotive engineers perhaps see tracks and switches stretching ahead of trains.

Sometimes technical innovation forestalls anticipated technical progress. Technical innovation demands and rewards retrospective scrutiny within any scenario-analysis context. Diesel-electric locomotives use far less fuel now than they did in 1980, a change that dramatically reduced the fuel-saving advantage of electric locomotives operating beneath overhead wires (although widening the competitive gap between trains and long-haul trucks). Railroad locomotives account for only about 1 percent of the national oil consumption, so electrifying tracks has only scant national energy-independence value either. Moreover, locomotive manufacturers actively experiment with liquid fuels derived from coal; such fuel proves uneconomical unless oil moves and remains above forty dollars a barrel. Constructing electrical catenary above existing tracks might interfere with tall freight cars moving new automobiles, double-stacked ocean-shipping containers, and other high cargo; it also might require adjusting the height of bridges and tunnels. But post-1980 electrification experiments have proceeded too, on the Black Mesa & Lake Powell and other little-known short lines, and the nuclear-power industry moves in this realm actively if quietly. The Amtrak Boston–Washington corridor electrification uses ordinary high-voltage electricity from the consumer grid with a success level that pleased electric utilities who envision railroads as new customers. Riders enjoying Amtrak high-speed Acela service know the silent swiftness of electric power, but probably only industry experts and scenario analysts have pondered a 1920 General Electric report authored by A. H. Armstrong, *The Future of Our Railways,* that anticipated Acela and raised an issue ignored for decades.

Armstrong emphasized that electrification sharply reduces rail traffic congestion, since electric-powered locomotives accelerate and decelerate far more rapidly than any others, pull more tonnage at higher speeds, and require little maintenance. Electrification matters not so much when the cost of diesel fuel rises, but rather when railroads reach traffic capacity, as they have *now.* Scenario analysts understand electrification in technological context, in what might be termed "a magic moment," that is, when technological and economic restraints and opportunities coincide, when some decisions are implemented but not others, when computers analyze data and determine only some choices remain, events happen, usually in quickening sequence.

In this book, the magic moment is now. At some point a railroad company must decide to double-track its main line or lose business to a competing line or to trucks, but almost certainly it will not electrify a single-track route. Nevertheless, the first railroad from the Mississippi to the Pacific that electrifies will enjoy a decisive advantage over its rail competitors, and certainly over the long-haul trucking industry, especially if it has already double- or triple-tracked its route. Industry executives know that, and weigh electrification against other variables, including the fact that many ships are too large for the Panama Canal, and the increasing danger that poor maintenance may cause that canal to fail, thus thrusting massive traffic demands on already stretched railroads. They also notice the overtures of the nuclear-power electric industry, which sees the railroad industry as a powerful potential ally in reversing its decline. Might global warming mean more windy days, and higher winds on windy days, producing the sheer that closes small airports? Might inventory- and package-tracing software drive a desire for next-day express shipment service impossible to achieve by truck and highly expensive to manage by air, but tricky to manage even on double-track diesel-powered railroads? Always industry personnel wonder about the rising cost of fuel, the price of real estate along main lines, and ponder the likelihood that automatic train operation may reduce railroad costs below anything highway and airline competitors can manage. In the immediate aftermath of 9/11, one bit of encouraging data emerged: Amtrak handled surging ridership with aplomb. The past partly determines the parameters of any magic moment, and lately the past receives much scrutiny from forward-looking analysts.

At the very close of World War II, just as the federal government began its massive defense-driven subsidizing of the airline industry, railroads contemplated a variety of innovations, especially 110-miles-per-hour passenger trains. In his 1945 *A Railroad for Tomorrow*, Edward Hungerford presciently outlined the intentions. By 1965 only railroad fans recalled the book, and even they paid it little attention: aficionados looked backward, at near-vanished coal smoke. But *A Railroad for Tomorrow* is the sort of book that underlies this one, and puts Jennifer S. Light's *From Warfare to Welfare: Defense Intellectuals and Urban Problems in Cold War America*, Steven W. Usselman's *Regulating Railroad Innovation: Business, Technology, and Politics in America, 1840–1920*, and other new scholarly works into built-environment scenario-analysis perspective. Most of the sources on which this book is founded are available to anyone, but the chief source is the same basic outdoor observation that enriches real estate developers and their consultants. As my Harvard Business School colleague William J. Poorvu points out in *The Real Estate Game: The Intelligent Guide to Decision-Making and Investment,* disciplined looking around reveals a great deal about the context of real estate activity in general, and observation refined by a specific agenda usually leads to profitable discoveries.

Consider an Amtrak Acela rider racing or creeping south from Boston. If the rider holds only an Amtrak timetable, he sees his train in a simple time-space framework: Acela is either on time or late wherever it happens to be. But if the rider holds schedules for the Massachusetts Bay Transportation Authority, Metro North, New Jersey Transit, Southeastern Pennsylvania Transit Authority, and Maryland Area Regional Transit trains, an Acela trip becomes markedly more informative. Even between New York and Washington, the four-track main line operates almost exactly at capacity, especially at rush hour, when trains move on 90-second headways. The inside express tracks require Acela to switch to local-service tracks to make station stops at Metropark, New Carrollton, and other lesser way stations. Switching slows speed considerably, so the high-speed train rarely stops at certain intermediate stations. Analyzing the Amtrak timetable makes it clear that Acela exists chiefly to serve well-heeled business travelers: its intermediate stops vary not only from weekday to weekend but by time of day. Acela races through New Haven but stops in Stamford, and often it scarcely gets up to speed south of Baltimore before stopping at BWI Airport. Acela trains serve both Metropark and BWI, but not both in any one trip; more northbound trips stop at BWI in the morning than in the afternoon (when more southbound trains stop), and southbound Acelas stop often in Metropark in the morning while northbound ones stop frequently in late afternoon. Amtrak timetables demonstrate that Acela targets business travelers and suggest that some people commute via Acela, something Hungerford and others predicted a half-century ago.

On the other hand, very frequently Acela creeps for miles, and any rider holding a regional transit authority schedule soon figures out that Amtrak's premiere train follows a commuter express. Any observer equipped with a watch, several timetables, and a window seat soon realizes that very fast trains pose serious problems to dispatchers overseeing all trains, even on multitrack routes. Regular Acela riders can anticipate the location of delays and thus predict late arrival times with some accuracy. Experience may therefore deflect would-be passengers from Friday afternoon, Monday morning, and holiday trips, or cause them to hop a transit authority express.

Of course, simply watching corridor trains demonstrates how frequently Acela moves slowly, especially between New York and New Haven, and how often it follows a commuter express. Nor is this the case only along the busy Northeast Corridor. Between Walker and Shawnee Junction, Wyoming, the Burlington Northern Santa Fe recently added another eight miles of triple track to its freight line, bringing the route near its planned goal of sixty triple-track miles. Tracks are busy near Baltimore, but busy around Walker too, but far fewer people visit Walker or connect the triple-track route with the rising price of shares. To recognize that overhead electric catenary reaches where the rich and powerful commute, one must first recognize catenary in the built environment. The choice of a rural location may well be influenced by the realization that Walker and other small towns enjoy frequent high-speed international freight service. Deep-pocket investors have no reason to share their hard-won data with anyone, and often corporate annual reports simply ignore the corollary impacts of explicitly mentioned items. Interested observers must notice with care, with the scrutiny of a prospective investor or spy, and then find archival sources that frame what is noticed.

Europeans immediately recognize Acela as different from high-speed British, German, and French trains, but often they cannot specify exactly how they differ. Acela is vastly heavier—something suggested by its locomotive on each end and definitely something apparent in its ride. Federal regulators crafted Acela with a particular wreck in mind, the 1987 collision of two freight locomotives with Amtrak's Colonial in northern Maryland. The conventional express had reached 128 miles per hour when it hit the errant locomotives. The express performed splendidly, in point of fact: the wreck killed 16 and injured 175 of the 622 aboard the ruggedly built cars. But

American passenger trains share rails with very heavy, long freight trains, and engineers have always designed them for potential collisions with freight trains far heavier than any operating in Europe, crafting massive passenger trains that move more slowly than foreign ones. The Colonial wreck shaped the design of Acela, which remains a slow train by European standards. Acela often moves more slowly than the traditional Colonial did in 1987—a fact that may spur investors to consider 128-miles-per-hour "traditional" service to a satellite municipality in which they have interests. The design of Acela indirectly illuminates the rarely mentioned electrification of New Jersey Transit commuter lines and other recent innovations. Acela is not merely an American-design high-speed passenger train intended to operate over tracks once in a while used by freight trains. It is the prototype of trains intended to cruise at 145 miles per hour down long stretches of straight track regularly used by massive coal and other freight trains. Conventional electric passenger trains like the old Colonial will serve metropolitan regions; the successors of Acela will serve the High Plains.

The 1987 wreck accomplished something more dramatic, albeit far from Amtrak tracks. Conrail moved all but local industry freight trains off Amtrak's Northeast Corridor. The old Reading and Lehigh Valley lines became the main Conrail route from the south to metropolitan New York, specifically to a place few white-collar people know, Oak Island Yard, near Newark and harbor wharves. More and more freight trains moved north from Hagerstown in Maryland through Harrisburg, Reading, Allentown, Bethlehem, and Easton, Pennsylvania, and then on through Flemington into Newark, New Jersey. The wreck at Gunpow, Maryland, shifted a massive amount of capital investment away from the Amtrak main line between Washington and New York and refocused it on a weedy route connecting worn-out factories. After Conrail rebuilt the track, abutting factories and warehouses suddenly became valuable. Improved freight train service worked its own magic in Reading, Bethlehem, and other gritty cities. Manufacturing and warehousing enjoyed an infusion of money, service, and, most importantly, multiple potential futures arising from being on a main freight line from New York to the south and west. So many freight trains now roll into the Rutherford yard near Reading that railroad officials have begun considering restoring the double track between Harrisburg and Hagerstown. The wide bridges remain from 1950s double-track passenger train days, making such an improvement financially feasible. Any Amtrak passenger notices the derelict factories and warehouses along the Northeast Corridor, but few see the new structures lining a freight-only route. Few designers or planners identify the rebuilt freight line as the generator of urban design and real estate investment, but it is the equivalent of a new interstate highway slicing a truck-thronged metropolitan region.

Not everything that follows here makes pleasant reading. *What if?* proves hard to face sometimes. Consider the fate of many Americans who own homes near long-abandoned railroad rights-of-way, perhaps routes now converted to nature trails. As traffic increases congestion on active tracks located some distance away, railroads, shippers, and commuters may demand that the nature trail become a rail route once again. Abutters may scream, "Not in my back yard!" just as so many abutters now complain about increased train traffic—and especially grade-crossing whistle noises—but in the end the "greater public good" may demand rail restoration.

But what if only passenger train service operates on the restored rails? Then the municipalities already crossed by the active railroad may find themselves served only by freight trains. Canny real estate developers must analyze such scenarios endlessly: What if most long-abandoned but rail-banked rights-of-way emerge as passenger routes, a sort of parallel rail grid controlled not by a dismembered or vanquished Amtrak but by regional transit authorities manipulated by local politicians? What if they emerge as freight-only routes and passenger trains serve the deteriorated cores of small satellite cities, making them dormitories for big-city service employees? Developers and speculators understand the subtleties of leaving freight trains where they operate now and putting passenger trains where affluent people live—adjacent to nature trails. The well-to-do people will commute swiftly and cheaply, perhaps no longer needing the Chinese-built automobiles freight trains will move inland from ports. On the other hand, moving freight trains from satellite-city downtowns can mean revitalizing and converting much run-down residential and commercial space if passenger trains link the down-towns with center cities.

All that follows here concerns a spatial future emerging subtly, but recognized by many individuals in and close to the railroad industry. *Railway Age* and other railroad industry magazines offer an immediate glimpse into recognition equally apparent in *Modern Materials Handling, Commercial Investment Real Estate,* and similar warehousing, logistics systems, and land-development journals. Chapter 1 analyzes the information sources and the viewpoint that prompted investors to reorient their thinking in the late 1970s. Chapter 2 explains the potential significance of cities like Lynchburg, Virginia—cities now difficult to reach but long ago at the junction of multiple passenger train routes. Chapter 3 deals with the politics that sidetracked the railroad industry in the 1960s, and the creation of Amtrak when "driverless automobile" and other urban transit experiments failed. Chapter 4 explains the myopic view of passenger trains as intercity transportation, then places future passenger service in wilderness recreation areas already populated by the wealthy. Chapter 5 examines luxury train travel in historical perspective as a way the elite strengthened personal and family links and solidified their hold on United States society—something the present-day elite not only remembers or rediscovers but now reinvents. Chapter 6 focuses on how mail and package express shipments once moved extremely quickly, and how such service will return as more and more trains operate above eighty miles an hour. Chapter 7 concerns freight that nowadays moves faster than many mail trains did in the 1950s, and examines the new intermodal cargoes so visible along most major rail lines: boxlike ocean-shipping containers and trucking company trailers. Chapter 8 deals with slow freight trains moving bulk grain, coal, petroleum products, and other commodities in ways that already transform port cities and rural United States regions, and that threaten the hegemony of the Interstate Highway System. Chapter 9 analyzes the failure of government and urban business communities to grasp the imminent urban and suburban difficulties planners recognized as implicit in much 1930s data—data that now suggest that the resurgence of railroads in wilderness and rural locations will transform cities already choked with truck traffic. The final chapter traces the short history of contemporary urban light-rail transit systems built by many cities on disused railroad alignments soon to be needed for regional and long-distance passenger and freight service.

Always the focus here is spatial, not technological and not financial. Railroads now skew landscape change, and the potential of that change forms the core of the argument that follows. Retrospect in landscape studies ordinarily means studying extant artifacts, even entire or fractured landscapes. Looking forward differs from both planning and design. It requires shielding the eye and the mind from distractions without any certain definition of distraction, and it requires a willingness to trust visual apprehension in the absence of quantitative and other sources. It requires seeing what is not in the scene as well as what is, and identifying what is changing even as one looks.

SOURCES: Armstrong, *The Future of Our Railways;* A. Black, *The Story of Tunnels;* General Electric Company, "Can Technology and the Environment Peacefully Coexist?"; Harley, "U.S. Railway Freight Electrification"; Hicks, "They'll Tell You How You'll Vote"; Hungerford, *A Railroad for Tomorrow;* Kotkin, "The Great Plains"; Levy, *The VCR Age;* Light, *From Warfare to Welfare;* Middleton, *Metropolitan Railways;* Norfolk Southern Corporation, *Annual Report 2005;* Olson, *The Logic of Collective Action;* Poorvu, *The Real Estate Game;* Schwieterman, *When the Railroad Leaves Town;* Usselman, *Regulating Railroad Innovation;* Warren and Tyagi, *The Two-Income Trap.*

1

WHISPER

Greenbush waits quietly now. Building after building stands empty. Asphalt and gravel parking lots catch the autumn sun but house no cars. Blue and red machinery stands abandoned, and here and there birds fly in and out open doors and windows. Temporary metal fencing snakes around some lots, its gates punctuated by modest white signs lettered in black. Across the adjacent salt marsh seagulls soar, their movement enlivening the fringes of a district so quiet that their cries echo from inland. Only a rare car cruises Driftway Street. Sunlight strikes deep into the woods at the heart of the industrial area. Much of the undergrowth has been slashed down. Mature trees remain, but for the first time in decades daylight blasts beneath the demolished highway overpass, revealing the soot-smudged granite blocks of its abutments. Old sofas, piles of shingles, lawnmower engines, pallets, and bottles poke above the fallen branches; the boatyard is bereft of boats. Slanting sunlight and frost-dropped leaves reveal paths winding toward the coffee shop, liquor store, and post office beyond the littered woods. The white signs announce condemnation and imminent destruction. The railroad is coming. The railroad is coming back.

Opened almost tentatively in the 1840s, the coastal route of the Old Colony Railroad served towns settled two centuries earlier. Steam locomotion technology supplanted the little packet vessels that connected Hingham, Scituate, Marshfield, Duxbury, and Plymouth with Boston, and it soon supplanted the tiny steamboat too. The parallel coach line along the former highway likewise succumbed, although modest competitors began short-distance, right-angle service linking inland villages with the coast-hugging railroad. Regular rail service altered everyday life, and in time the landscape focused on the tracks. Businesses moved from harbors and estuary wharves to trackside, and as shipping withered, the railroad opened its many drawbridges less and less frequently. By 1900 fishermen growled about spans permanently down, and farmers knew the

Such an unexpected end to the ¶

salt-marsh-crossing railroad as a dike protecting inland fields from gale-driven tides. The railroad seemed almighty, carrying not only commuters and summertime tourists to Cape Cod but almost all the mail and freight that moved along the coast. Its route was more enduring than any public road: it was the *permanent* way.

Twenty years later the railroad company had begun to suffer from the widespread use of automobiles moving along paved roads, and by 1939 it had abandoned the track south of the marsh, ripped up ties and rails, and turned over the weed-grown remnant of permanent way to abutters and municipal government. Greenbush became a terminal, not a way station. The New York, New Haven & Hartford Railroad Company, having acquired the Old Colony by merger, erected a roundhouse, turntable, water tank, and other facilities for turning, storing, and servicing steam locomotives, and built a coach yard south of the overpass it had already installed to alleviate grade-crossing danger. Every evening the yard filled with long trains of dark-green coaches, soon pulled by diesel-electric locomotives that made the expensive roundhouse and most other service facilities superfluous. As late-1950s commuters chose to drive to Boston over newly built highways, the company struggled to maintain track, trains, and profit. When vandals burned an estuary trestle in 1959, the company gave up for good, abandoning passenger service the very next morning. A day or two later the passenger trains rumbled away from Greenbush, making their way to Boston by a roundabout route south and west of the smoldering trestle. For a while a weekly freight train arrived to serve the Greenbush feed mill and a handful of other bulk-commodity industries, before it too disappeared, never to return. No ceremonies marked the abandonment of railroad service.

Weeds and scrub and finally trees masked the railroad right-of-way. Small manufacturing businesses located on the former train yard after the roundhouse burned, but beyond the concrete-block structures and parking lots the trees grew taller by the year. The railroad right-of-way shrank from coach yard and roundhouse site to a narrow strip of land running across the municipality of Scituate and other townships too.

Town governments did nothing with the land acquired by de-

Railroad restoration often begins beneath aging highway bridges, when contractors arrive to start replacement efforts.

why, I wonder ?

fault. Hikers and shortcutting teenagers made a narrow footpath down the center of it, almost precisely halfway between the locations of the long-gone rails. In the early 1980s intrepid mountain-bike riders discovered the right-of-way as a secret route free of interruption and connected with gigantic Wampatuck State Park, itself a former naval ammunition depot once serviced by a spur of the Greenbush route. Cross-county skiers followed the mountain bikers in winter, and joined with bicyclists and hikers to remove the occasional fallen tree that blocked the narrow path. The detritus of railroad operations—switch stands, twisted rails, signal boxes, and other debris—they skirted, and they took special care crossing bridges officialdom neglected. A ribbon of woods ran all the way to East Weymouth, where an active railroad rematerialized at the junction of Conrail and the Fore River Railroad, the latter a short line serving the city of Quincy. At this junction the woods ended, and hiking became trespassing, and dangerous too.

No English word properly designates the overgrowing of the abandoned right-of-way. Such a word might help explain why even users of the right-of-way did not truly see it in a way that made and makes it real. Neither *wilderness* nor *bewilderment* connotes a place overcome by wilderness. Because English lacks the concept Germans know as *Ortsbewüstung,* meaning the re-wildering of a specific place long before shaped by people, the users—and abutters and casual crossers too—did not *realize* the right-of-way any more than did local government authorities. It existed merely as a trail through leaves, somehow distinct from all space and structure through which it sliced, yet also a part of the larger scene.

As memory of the train faded, the path became as well used as the rocky landing in a nearby salt marsh built in the eighteenth century by the prosperous owner of a sailing packet. The packet is long gone from human memory and figures only in obscure local history pamphlets, but the packet landing is now a pleasant fishing and picnicking spot almost universally accepted as "natural." Only the experienced mariner, fisherman, or longshoreman sees its piled rocks as a perfectly sited docking spot, or notices that the tiny pile-driver barge and tug still working the estuaries tie up at it despite its lack of wharf equipment. The packet landing is a good place to touch a workboat to shore, as pleasure boaters sometimes learn when they see a workboat there, or when they need to touch land themselves without problems of tide and current. But so overgrown is the landing that it masquerades as a natural hummock linking estuary, salt marsh, and abutting woodland.

The overgrown right-of-way is bewildered, if one translates the German starkly. *Ortsbewüstung* designates the bewildering of a place, something that jars English speakers accustomed to thinking of people as bewildered by all sorts of circumstances, including being lost in wilderness. Almost certainly a product of the Black Death, the mid-fourteenth-century plagues that killed up to two-thirds of the population in many German-speaking regions, the concept involves nature slowly overwhelming land abandoned by people. Whole villages returned to forest, grass grew in desolate city streets, and well-traveled roads became greenways, used enough to keep down brush but not enough to destroy grass. Generations of

Germans after the Black Death understood nature, and especially forest, as something that only continuous effort keeps at bay. They expected to find ruins deep in forest, and their folk tales often involve children and other wanderers discovering a decrepit cottage or gingerbread house or castle surrounded by dense woods. Despite a terrific death toll from the plagues themselves, the English never formalized a similar understanding. North American colonists accepted the notion that settlement meant carving landscape from wilderness, and that wilderness never overwhelmed the carvers.

Twenty-first-century Americans prove prone to thinking of wilderness in national park terms, or else as something "good" endangered by people. Simple visual encounters sometimes disturb such casual thinking, but rarely for long. Everywhere east of the Appalachians, hikers find stone walls in woods and sometimes cellar holes or still-standing stone and brick chimneys. Obviously people once lived where the hikers hike, but many hikers fail to grasp that the remnants are the detritus of abandoned agricultural enterprise. No one builds stone walls in woods. The walls took form as linear rock piles made by people clearing land for plowing, and proved secondarily useful as fencing. Modern farmers hiking or hunting across such regions can look at the base of the walls and tell from the mounding of soil which side of the wall faced the field plowed last. But most explorers in the woods are not farmers, and they pay no more attention to the mounding of soil along walls than they do to the age and species of trees in the forests, the way brooks flow along channels dug two centuries earlier, or to the traces of a road abandoned a century ago. They cannot even find the well on a long-bewildered farm.

Landscape historians and foresters characterize such territory as afforested, not reforested, meaning that the woods appeared out of neglect rather than by deliberate planting. In the final analysis, however, most Americans care little for such nuance. Only at sundown on a winter night, when the afternoon walk has lasted a bit too long, do the darkening woods take on a wilderness aspect. When big, cat-nourished coyotes appear at the edge of the suburban woodlot, people stare at a raw wildness they decide belongs in some national forest. Genuine wilderness exists everywhere away from the great agricultural regions of the Midwest and High Plains, even if it is wilderness returned.

When pushed, most Americans grudgingly admit they distinguish between woods and forest: the one is defined by well-known surrounding roads and is pedestrian in scale, while the other is amorphous in shape, vast, and penetrable only by well-equipped hikers. They may know that a dense swamp lies beside the interstate highway, but they neither trek across the swamp nor know much about its constituent elements, including the homeless people rumored to inhabit it. Americans tend to think of wilderness in terms of remote national parks; it is unlikely that many spend much time pondering the sharks in urban harbors, or the fact that the eastern states were 80 percent open land two centuries ago and three-quarters afforested now. They do, however, know a gentle walk when they walk it, and railroad rights-of-way, usually almost dead level, make for relaxing walking indeed. In the middle of the nineteenth century, Thoreau commented that he crossed active railroads as though they were cart paths in the woods. By 2000 the Greenbush line had become less wide than even a cart path, and it had become its own woods to boot. Its crossing gates and signals long removed, its highway-crossing rails buried in asphalt, it appeared as a momentary blur of green to motorists speeding across it. Except for old-timers and for a few active walkers, runners, and bicyclists, the right-of-way merged with other forested land, becoming green scenery.

But no municipality designated the Greenbush line as conservation land, recreational space, or anything else. Legally, the right-of-way, all its trees, and the path along its centerline were nonexistent. Abutters encroached upon it, dumping brush and rubbish there, but sometimes extending lawns and gardens into it and even erecting buildings upon it. Municipal authorities, when apprised of such activity, acted suitably if not always aggressively; after all, they knew that the ill-bounded right-of-way was municipal property, if property held for unspecified use. But most of the time, no one but hikers noticed the encroachments into the ribbon of woods, and if they did, few knew the precise boundaries of the old right-of-way.

However, occasionally there walked, among the bikers and hikers and skiers, people enamored of railroad history. Almost always male, usually but not always middle-aged or older, the men often walked in pairs, printed or sketched maps in hand. Their cars left behind at some former grade crossing, or the parking lot of a train station converted into a liquor store or hair-styling salon, they walked slowly, searching for the ruins of the railroad itself.

Everywhere they found them. Some stood out so clearly as to be unmistakable. For example, the salvage companies never removed the six-foot-high metal relay boxes that sheltered signal mechanisms. Spaced at what appeared to be random distances from each other, the silver boxes seemed impervious to rust, and made good landmarks for walkers negotiating the green tunnel. Other ruins lay underfoot. On some, hikers stubbed toes: lengths of rail escaped removal, as did thousands of rail spikes and steel tie plates. Anyone scuffing the leaves on either side of the footwide path almost immediately uncovered something metal, often something heavy sinking into the soil around it. Downslope from the embankment snaking through swamps lay rotting wooden ties escaped from the tie-removal machine, and forty-foot lengths of rail mislaid in the early nineteenth-century track renovation. Skewed at all sorts of angles were fallen telegraph poles, some toppled by the Great Hurricane of 1938 and never retrieved by repair crews erecting new ones. Anyone walking the right-of-way was bound to see some artifacts of rail road.

But only the discerning few noted other ruins. Far out in the salt marsh, where the right-of-way is merely a narrow embankment crowned with poison ivy and other halophytes, the concrete bases of the drawbridge signals remain, swathed in vines. In the dense swamps, the right-of-way embankment broadens where it once supported two parallel tracks, and a few feet from the path lies ballast pitched slightly differently from that a few feet away. In a woods a mile north of the swamps, a massive switch stand lies toppled away from the path, almost invisible in fifty years' worth of fallen leaves. Such ruins attracted the scrutiny of railroad buffs looking for evidence of sidetracks to long-gone industries or junctions with branch lines.

These ruins offered information available elsewhere only in fragmented format. Unlike that compiled by government agencies, railroad company information was and is largely private, and railroad

companies—especially those collapsing into bankruptcy, reorgani-
zation, and nullity—have no legal obligation to keep much of their
documentation. Between the 1920s and about 1980, railroad abandonment and bankruptcy often meant the immediate destruction
of masses of documentation. Long after such destruction, inquirers
found themselves examining physical evidence for answers to questions originating in simple curiosity sparked by bits of information in old newspaper clippings, photographs, or local tradition.
Audubon Society folk enjoyed watching birds along the abandoned
right-of-way, and delighted in piecing together some understanding
of ecosystems, especially avian ones. The railroad historians walking among them enjoyed a similar pleasure, one focused on gaining
a broader understanding of how the railroad actually worked.

Railroad historians bifurcated in the 1920s. By far the more
powerful group continued work begun in the 1860s, perhaps even
earlier. Largely academic and grounded in business schools and
departments of economics, it dealt almost exclusively with the financial end of railroading or with the juxtaposition of railroad finance and government regulation. This group battled within itself,
some scholars arguing in favor of increased government regulation
and others attempting to demonstrate that regulation led to higher
rates, lower profits, and poor service. The group split in other ways
as some writers focused on regional matters, some emphasized the
history of individual railroad companies, and others attempted to
draw international comparisons. Today, economic historians mine
the work the group produced. Almost without exception, however,
the business-focused group ignored the other group, which co-
alesced in 1921 as the Railway and Locomotive Historical Society.

Technological transformation of railroad equipment, physical
plant, and operations occurred so rapidly in the years just before
World War I that a group of interested observers determined to preserve the early technical history of the industry. At first the loose-
knit group focused on the early steam locomotives supplanted not
just by more massive successors but by electric-powered engines.
But then the society quickly began to assemble documents pertaining to the nascent everyday operation of railroads, especially during
the Civil War. Within a few years it had extended its focus to rail-

road building west of the Mississippi and had begun classifying railroad operating information. Around 1930 it began analyzing both
technical innovation and operating procedures.

Until after World War II, the newer group worked essentially aca-
demically too. The society accepted new members only upon sub-
mission of a monograph on some phase of railroad history and two
photographs of steam locomotives. But during the Depression it began to attract a spectrum of other railroad-industry-focused people
ranging from photographers, to collectors of lanterns, telegraph instruments, and other industrial antiques, to those determined to
preserve entire pieces of rolling stock. By the time the New York,
New Haven & Hartford Railroad Company abandoned the line south
of Greenbush in 1939, the society had become a powerful force in preserving documents and artifacts from Depression-era bankruptcies.

The supplanting of steam locomotives by diesel-electrics in
the 1950s brought the second group to national prominence simply by expanding its numbers. However staid and methodical its
core membership might have been, the society welcomed a burgeoning group characterized as "rail fans." Nostalgia for vanishing
steam locomotives suffused these newcomers, almost entirely men
who saw the demise of steam-powered railroading as the end of an
era in which they had come of age. Aficionados may have seen the
steam locomotive as symbolizing values—especially the freedom
to travel—for which they had fought in World War II. The diesel-
electric locomotive often seemed a product of a rapidly changing
economy and a harbinger of excruciating changes in mining, heavy
manufacturing, and other traditionally male-dominated industries.
Thousands of men joined the rail fans in stopping the family car at
grade crossings and dragging little children up to the tracks when a
steam locomotive chugged or blasted past.

The children, especially boys, fit into the larger concatenation of
hope and nostalgia and worry as consumers of toy trains, especially
those made by Lionel and American Flyer. For boys of the 1950s, an
electric train set was the premiere Christmas present, but only retrospect reveals the striking division so apparent in 1950s catalogs of
toy train manufacturers. Every autumn new catalogs featured not
only the latest miniature copies of modern diesel-electric locomo-

tives but the most powerful of steam locomotives, albeit ones developed twenty or thirty years earlier. The entire 1950s panoply of toy trains—the basic train set, the additional cars, the complexities of track and switches, the structures and signal systems, the scenery and the electrical components—all existed perhaps as much for parents (especially fathers) as for children (especially sons). Many of the sons became rail fans themselves, some deeply interested in museum-piece steam locomotives, but most intrigued by the latest permutation of diesel-electric locomotives.

At the beginning of the twenty-first century, the rail fan movement supports multiple magazines, a video industry, perhaps two hundred historical societies focused on extant and long-vanished railroads, and a tour effort that now shapes economic development priorities in remote towns adjacent to high-interest railroad history or contemporary activity. It drives the proliferation of railroad museums and tourist railroads, and even the private ownership of railroad equipment. And it merges with another railroad-focused group, the scale-model railroaders.

Adults who decades ago played with toy trains form the core of the scale-model hobby, a multi-billion-dollar effort that prizes the building and collecting of superb models and their operation in prototypical fashion. Model railroading is more than railroad-model building, although many of its adherents specialize in historically accurate detailing as much as do the modelers of eighteenth-century sailing ships. The operation of models shapes the hobby, which focuses on the layout as the central facet. In clubs and in hundreds of thousands of garages, basements, and special-purpose backyard buildings, model railroaders build layouts that represent a particular piece of railroad at a particular moment, usually the late 1940s steam-to-diesel transition period. They support many of the magazines, artifact-acquisition fund-raising, tours, and other efforts of the rail fans, but since the 1930s have accumulated their own magazines, national organizations, and even museums. Allied with collectors of antique toy trains, and with the burgeoning group of married couples who build large-scale outdoor garden railroad layouts, traditional model railroaders fuel an increasingly intense effort to understand prototypical but long-vanished railroading.

While difficult to measure, the greater railroad enthusiast movement is one of the more muscular popular history phenomena. Perhaps only a half-million families operate layouts: hobby manufacturer associations have uncertain data beyond sales and repeat-sales figures. Each of the larger magazines reaches about a quarter-million readers a month, but many enthusiasts read only special-interest magazines focused on Rocky Mountain narrow-gauge steam-era railroading, or East Coast trolley cars, or contemporary Southern California rail operations. Railroad museums welcome increasing numbers of visitors, but have no way of distinguishing real enthusiasts from general-interest visitors. Surveys suggest that the movement is a cross section of the population, but some components of it, especially the scale-model railroaders, are distinguished by graduate degrees, professional occupations, and high income. Some surveys interpret income in the context of discretionary time: building a model railroad takes decades, and joining a tour to abandoned Rocky Mountain railroad tunnels or Alaskan narrow-gauge rights-of-way takes weeks. In an era when media focus popular attention on sports, all hobbies move beneath most media radar, and even thriving hobbies like those related to the railroad industry get surprisingly little attention.

Railroad hobbyists scarcely intrigued by modeling but rather by collecting photographs, timetables, and other ephemera, or by teasing out the history of a type of rolling stock, a junction, or some stretch of main line or branch track, work almost invisibly. They support journals ranging from national ones such as *Railroad History* to regional ones published by the Terminal Railroad Association of St. Louis Historical and Technical Society and dozens of other quasi-scholarly societies. Moreover, they fuel a very healthy specialized industry that increasingly publishes books by scholars and industry archivists as well as enthusiasts.

Academics and sometimes even railroad industry consultants admire the enthusiast effort and often contribute to it. Sophisticated scholarly work often appears first in *Trains* and competing enthusiast magazines. Michael Bezilla of the University of Pennsylvania and author of *Electric Traction on the Pennsylvania Railroad*—a meticulous history of technological innovation within a business enterprise—explained in a 1978 *Trains* article how diesel fuel prices might cause railroad investors to extend existing electrification beyond Harrisburg to Pittsburgh. Like Civil War, logging, and marine amateur historians, railroad historians enjoy open-air effort. In the 1970s their low-cost hobby blossomed. Magazines began publishing sophisticated and lengthy outdoor-exploration-based articles that in turn engendered others. One on the geology of the Canadian Shield—the 1.8 million sq. mi. rocky, forested region east of Winnipeg—sparked many others analyzing railroad routing and construction nuances forced by topography and geology. An article on the route of the New York, Ontario & Western Railway from Oswego on Lake Ontario south to Cornwall, New York—where it operated over another line into Weehawken, New Jersey—pushed writers to examine how the abandonment of that company subsequently denied specialized rail service to Scranton and to Rome, Utica, and other New York cities. In the 1978 article "The Fun of Finding Yesterday," one *Railroad Model Craftsman* columnist praised the exploration and research effort for producing "feelings of archeological purpose and worth." In the late 1970s, the National Trust for Historic Preservation began advertising in *Railroad Model Craftsman*, having discovered that railroad enthusiasts had a deep interest in material history. Learning about ghost railroads meant stretching mental and physical muscles both, and perhaps producing historical information of some value to succeeding generations. Recently articles have appeared in the *Chicago Tribune* and other large newspapers reporting the strength of the enthusiast movement and linking it to real estate development and other potential change along active and abandoned rights-of-way.

A handful of the men walking the Old Colony right-of-way after 1959 searched for the reality of vanished railroad operation. Understanding the dedicated model railroader as someone every bit as determined as the historical geographer or landscape historian to uncover landscape artifacts or long-hidden documents takes a bit of doing. But a glance at *Mainline Modeler* or *Narrow Gauge and Short-Line Gazette* reveals in-depth articles illustrated with period photographs often assembled over decades, many written by attorneys, physicians, and other professionals. *Railroad History*, published by the Railway and Locomotive Historical Society, remains a scholarly journal, but even its scholar-authors acknowledge the accomplishments of amateurs, especially those who devote decades to chasing paperwork trails. How did it work? Scholars and hobbyists alike often struggle to answer the same question, and sometimes hobbyists trump academics. Determining how a railroad worked in a particular period demands more than skill at archival research: often it requires on-site examination and deep background understanding.

Vanished railroad companies leave behind paperwork. Reports lodged with federal and state regulatory agencies explain financial issues, albeit often in skewed ways. Buried in the mass of regulatory agency documentation, the sheer volume of which deters many academics, amateur researchers tease out arcane data, like the number of trains that arrived late in 1891, or the cost of operating freight service in 1933, or the persistence of United States Post Office distrust of airmail in the 1960s. Much of the research focuses on the collision of engineering miscalculation and subsequent financial disaster. Railroad bridges collapsed repeatedly in the 1890s as locomotives became much heavier; strengthening or replacing thousands of bridges emptied railroad company coffers.

In the 1960s the Pennsylvania, New York Central, and other northeast railroad companies invested heavily in gondola, hopper, and specialty cars serving the steel industry. Within several years that industry collapsed like a bad bridge before moving to Asia, leaving behind a superb but sidetracked fleet of cars eventually sold to China at knockdown prices. From the 1910s through the 1930s, some railroads experimented with electrification. Scholars have difficulty analyzing streetcars that accelerated faster than a contemporary Porsche, let alone hydroelectric-powered locomotives incorrectly dismissed in the 1970s as less efficient than diesel-electrics. While business and economic historians and analysts make some sense of period documentation, other experts explore the realities implicit in working railroads. Their explorations involve the physical artifacts enthusiasts love and sometimes reproduce in miniature, and that frequently lead to on-site examination.

Some exploration leads to fantasies academics might condemn

but investors, especially scenario analysts in large consulting firms, encourage, for speculation by civil engineers, Realtors, and other enthusiasts often begins in data about which professional experts know little. Suppose a railroad company drained of its capital by financial chicanery had instead double-tracked its main line as its earlier ownership intended and announced, and then electrified it. The broader effects of such improvements might have transformed a region. Industries might have expanded owing to more efficient shipping, or suburban growth might have extended along a high-speed, high-capacity route. Such questions intrigue enthusiasts and academics willing to shift contemporary scenario-based spatial analysis away from ecological issues and toward historical ones. Questions about increased speed, frequency of service, and the development of long-distance routing dependent on new motive power beguile inquirers who discover that in 1925 or 1960 railroad management confronted alternate futures. The walkers along the Greenbush line descry more than remnants birders miss. Sometimes they encounter a point where a junction might have been built connecting a planned but never-completed track with another main line: they note the preliminary grading and the lack of any subsequent work. They discern where an extra passing side-track might have increased rush-hour capacity by two additional trains that would have cut 1940 commutes by twenty minutes. From such observation, it is possible to imagine alternative futures now shrouded in mature trees.

Beginning in the early 1970s enthusiasts glimpsed something looming ahead, but not around the curve of the overgrown footpath. Most journalists laughed at their predictions of the tracks returning to the coastal region south of Boston, but a handful of journalists listened and reported on what might be. Since the railroad stopped operating in 1959, the coastal region had become hard to access, especially at rush hour and on summer weekends. The 1960s-era divided highway, so choked with traffic as to become a statewide joke, stymied commuters, Cape Cod–bound tourists, and truckers. While development west and north of Boston mushroomed, the environmentally sensitive rural coastal region to the south enjoyed an eerie peace. Difficult highway access engendered perceptual vagueness: many residents in eastern Massachusetts knew little about the region bordered by the interstate-like highway connecting Boston and Cape Cod. Local residents, especially a new breed working from home offices and rarely visiting Boston, confronted highway engineers vexed by salt marshes, estuaries, swamps, and other half-wild areas that stymied road building, and voiced their disapproval of proposed roads. But in the 1980s archival sources and on-site examination merged into a scenario suddenly viable.

At public hearing after public hearing between 1985 and 1995, all sorts of people began reading aloud railroad timetables from the 1920s, something regional newspapers reported. In 1929 steam locomotives pulled commuter trains at eighty miles an hour. At that speed, living in an environmentally sensitive, beautiful area forty miles from South Station in Boston means a very short commute indeed, scarcely time to read the morning paper. Eighty miles an hour transcends all highway travel: the speed is illegal and, in any metropolitan area at rush hour, a fond fantasy only. But at one public hearing after another, especially those held along the coast and inland near the ends of the proposed revitalized lines, the data from railroad enthusiasts shaped public policy reality almost overnight.

With accelerating speed, the Massachusetts Bay Transportation Authority began rebuilding decrepit freight-only tracks southwest of Boston. Two lines reopened in the late 1990s as state-of-the-art commuter train routes linking Plymouth, Kingston, Middleboro, and intermediate stations with South Station, the Boston terminus undergoing pre-Acela electrification. Ridership exceeded all analyst prognostication. So many passengers thronged the trains north of South Weymouth that conductors could not move through the cars to collect tickets or glance at passes. The transit authority added more coaches, and almost at once they filled. Double-deck passenger cars, the immediate solution to the problem of passengers standing in aisles, seemed at best a stopgap measure.

Transit authority experts admit that adding more trains is tricky without double-tracking the existing lines, but so far that idea has fallen on deaf ears. Within the city of Boston, the single track parallels an interstate highway built on the former six-track railroad main line. Slicing a lane or two from the vehicle-choked Southeast Expressway remains heresy. Perhaps electrification would expedite train movements; perhaps not. But more trains cannot be added now to the renovated routes simply because trains operating from Greenbush will increase traffic to capacity on the single urban track.

At one end of the route, planned for full operation by early 2008, lies a railroad track already maniacally busy at rush hour. Train after train, many with double-deck cars, all carrying standees, sizzle past sometimes as close as five minutes apart, slowed by proximity to terminal platforms. At the other end is only a pregnant stillness interrupted by earth-moving equipment. In Greenbush buildings stand abandoned. Brush cutters have felled sight lines for surveyors, and here and there the wilderness footpath widens into a trail for pickup trucks filled with civil engineers.

No one along the Greenbush right-of-way doubts the trains are coming back. No one any longer believes that restoration of railroad service will please anyone. Abutters who lived for decades next to overgrown walking paths, especially newcomers who bought houses decades ago and paid the rusted rails little attention, often protest and organize against restoration. But their efforts produce mostly blunt response: "When the woman in Hingham moved in sixteen years ago, was she wearing blinders?" asked one 2004 letter to the editor about a still-vocal protestor. "Didn't she see the tracks? Didn't she ask questions?" As early as 1974, the *Boston Globe* published a brief story suggesting the promise in what only railroad aficionados advocated. "The South Shore—200,000 People Within 10 Minutes of an Unused Rail Line" focused on a set of routes reaching far into Cape Cod, and it blew the first faint warning whistle heard by anyone other than railroad enthusiasts. Trains would eventually return because no other form of transportation, even monorails and other science-fiction devices, promised any solution to population growth in environmentally sensitive areas or to rush-hour and summertime traffic jams. But not for ten years did abutters see the first surveyors hiking along the long-abandoned tracks. Only when stakes and orange spray paint appeared in the woods behind backyards did the protests begin.

Elsewhere across the United States, a return of passenger train service strikes most people as folly. But south and southwest of

Boston, observers are beginning to realize something that railroad enthusiasts and railroad historians knew in the 1960s. Underneath nostalgia about glamorous 1930s passenger trains, lonesome steam whistles echoing at midnight, and Lionel toy trains rumbles something vastly more important: the landscape that people created around the railroad may have been better than the sprawl the automobile engenders. Excellent railroad service may enhance our quality of life by reducing commuting time and local road traffic congestion, and by reshaping residential and commercial landscape. A sensible railroad system is a common good, but defining *sensible* is not easy. Replicating the past is foolish, but the possibility of welding the best of the past to the most-choice components of the present makes the study of places like Greenbush well worthwhile.

Real estate developers and investors, and investment analysts, study Greenbush very carefully, not only by examining municipal documents but by speaking with abutters, often asking how to contact property owners who refuse to answer their mail or who might be party to a blind realty trust. The walker trudging inland from the salt marshes on a winter afternoon realizes that the two men looking around so carefully stand near a rental automobile, exactly as Poorvu sketches in *The Real Estate Game*. A few words exchanged about the weather prove enough to verify the hunch. Two Texans stand in the silence of Greenbush, looking for themselves at the face of change. All the walker need do then is remark on how the area functioned when the trains last operated. Then the cross-examination begins, the subtle and not-so-subtle questions that reveal that the visitors work for no railroad or transit authority but for people who intend to profit when the railroad returns to some communities far away from the Atlantic Coast.

SOURCES: Bezilla, "The Electrification That Might Have Been"; Borrone, "Sparking the Globalized Trade and Transportation Connection"; Carstens, "The Shawangunk Carrier"; Ewing, Pendall, and Chen, "Measuring Sprawl and Its Transportation Impacts"; Fifer, "Transcontinental"; Koester, "The Fun of Finding Yesterday"; Menzies, "The South Shore"; Nelson, "Look Again"; Swain, "Scenery of the Canadian Shield"; Wurst, "On Rail's Trails."

In many cities, only freight trains roll where passenger trains once did; too few Americans visualize passenger service supplementing freight service and making downtowns far more vibrant.

NECKLACE

No new regional airport better exemplifies the problems bedeviling small-city airline service than the Lynchburg Regional Airport smack in the center of Virginia. Opened in 1992, the terminal structure faces a 5,799-foot-long runway capable of accommodating midsized jet airliners. But jets no longer serve Lynchburg. Instead a handful of tiny, propeller-driven aircraft flutter back and forth from Charlotte, Pittsburgh, and Washington, D.C. Ostensibly, jet service disappeared in the wake of nationwide financial problems, but something less complex seems a more likely reason.

The new airport is simply too close to other airports. Roanoke Regional is only 57 miles away, Charlottesville is about 60 miles, Piedmont Triad (in Greensboro, N.C.) is 120 miles, and Richmond is not much farther, at 142. Only slightly farther off are two major airports, Washington Dulles and Reagan National, at 166 and 182 miles. Just as nineteenth-century railroad companies once played off one city against another, so now do airlines squeeze Lynchburg. The remaining small-aircraft flights frequently do not operate, especially the last one of the day leaving Charlotte for Lynchburg. Repeated missed connections make Lynchburg residents wary and infuriate regular fliers from distant places.

Lynchburg's 96,000 people form the core of a much larger rural population living in a region known for its spectacular scenic beauty. Lynchburg has a rich history, a multitude of cultural institutions including five colleges; a sumptuous, active downtown of gorgeous period buildings; and a diverse economy based on a sophisticated, prosperous industrial and commercial base. Appomattox Court House National Historic Site, eighteen miles to the east along a state highway, attracts many tourists to the region.

Lynchburg blooms away from interstate highways. I-81 and its parallel cousin, the Blue Ridge Parkway, lie about thirty-five miles west, running north–south. At Charlottesville, some sixty miles north, I-64 runs northwest from Richmond to its T-junction interchange with I-81 at Staunton. Other north–south interstate high-ways run far to the southeast (I-85) and southwest (I-77), but an-gle away from Lynchburg toward Charlotte and other large North Carolina cities. Long-distance motorists simply bypass not only Lynchburg but the entire region that surrounds the city. Lynchburg residents enjoy their distance from dense highway traffic, especially long-haul truck traffic, but they realize the evolving difficulties of driving to airports other than their own. Traffic in Roanoke and Richmond, increasingly heavy and sporadically stopped, makes time-to-airport estimates mere guesswork. The Roanoke Airport is now at least a half-hour longer drive from Lynchburg than it was in 1990.

Highway atlases distort the geographic perspective of travelers and people planning vacation trips. They convert entire regions like the one focused on Lynchburg into perceptual gores, places avoided by interstate routes. Only locals move about on the secondary and tertiary roads removed from interstate highways, and only motor-ists with reasons for penetrating such regions do so. Long-distance motorists are no more likely to wind up in Lynchburg for lunch or for the night than are long-distance truckers. Far more crucially, the road-map mentality blinds most Americans to the long-ago im-portance of cities like Lynchburg in nonhighway topographical and transportation contexts.

Lynchburg lies far enough west and south in Virginia that high-way atlas cartographers depict it in terms of both North Carolina and West Virginia. In most atlases, North Carolina appears only as a quarter-inch-wide yellow margin below the two-page Virginia map, and West Virginia, simply because of the diagonal state boundary, proves an excellent place to insert a half-dozen small maps show-ing Virginia cities against a pale yellow background. No highway atlas attempts to show Lynchburg in relation to the Allegheny or Appalachian mountains, or explains why the Piedmont region is called—in French—"the foothills," let alone makes clear the im-portance of the Shenandoah Valley. No highway atlas explains the relation of Lynchburg to Charleston or Wheeling in West Virginia, or helps anyone understand why Lynchburg Airport has nonstop service to Pittsburgh and Charlotte but not Philadelphia. Highway atlases may be the best-selling annual publications in the country, but they do nothing to suggest, much less explain, why so much population growth remains concentrated in certain areas increasingly choked with automobile traffic.

In 1929 Lynchburg lay about halfway along a direct high-speed rail route between New York and New Orleans. Operated by several cooperating railroads, the Washington, Chattanooga, New Orleans Limited slipped out of New York's Pennsylvania Station every afternoon at 4:50. It arrived in Lynchburg at 3:55 the following morning, bound for Knoxville, Chattanooga, Birmingham, and Meridian. Four hours later, a slower but nonetheless first-class train, No. 25, left New York along the same route, reaching Lynchburg at 8:00 AM. The opposing trains left Lynchburg daily at 1:50 AM and 7:20 PM, arriving in New York at 12:30 PM and 6:40 AM. While not the most convenient service, sleeping cars provided a chance for a good night's rest, even for passengers headed to Washington, where night trains detached Pullman cars so passengers could sleep undisturbed until awakened at 7:15. Trains No. 41, 42, 25, and 26, while not especially luxurious, carried dining cars, drawing-room sleeping cars, and other amenities. They competed, after all, with the Crescent Limited.

That train carried special sleeping cars, a club car, an observation car, and other luxuries, including maid and valet service, showers, and a woman's lounge. It left New York at 8:40 every evening and arrived in Lynchburg at 6:52 the following morning; its opposite number left Lynchburg at 8:45 in the evening and arrived in New York at 10:50 AM. A so-called candy train, it offered luxury travel not only between large cities like New York, Washington, Atlanta, and New Orleans, but between much smaller cities like Charlotte, Spartanburg, Auburn, Montgomery, Pensacola, Mobile—and, of course, Lynchburg. The Crescent Limited touched fortunate small cities with big-city glamour twice a day.

It was not necessarily the fastest way to go, of course, nor was it the longest-mileage train. Twice a day the United States Fast Mail paused in Lynchburg, at 11:00 AM heading toward New Orleans and at 3:50 PM toward New York. Carrying sleepers and a dining car, it offered passengers a first-class if slightly rough ride, for it existed chiefly to hurry car upon car of first-class mail. The Piedmont Limited, the Boston–New Orleans train, paused in Lynchburg too, toward New Orleans at 2:50 AM and toward Boston at 8:45 PM. It too was invested with some urban glamour, but included among its ordinary sleeping cars a special, low-priced "tourist" version operating on to Los Angeles. All joint projects of the Pennsylvania, the Southern, the Norfolk & Western (N&W), and other great railroad companies, the trains operated over tracks of shorter and subsidiary lines carefully noted in master timetables. Cooperation by the Atlanta and West Point Rail Road Company, the Western Railway of Alabama, and the Georgia Railroad made possible the stream of long-distance trains stopping in Lynchburg.

In an east–west direction flowed another set of first-class trains, mostly operating over the N&W, known as the Aristocrats. Advertised as connecting the Midwest with "the Virginias and the Carolinas," the trains originated and terminated in Norfolk, Virginia, and in Cincinnati, where connecting sleeping cars switched onto them for runs west. Pausing in Lynchburg regularly every day and night, the trains connected Winston-Salem, Abingdon, Ironton, and other small cities along a route that opened not only on seashore vacations but on central Midwest connections. All stopped in Lynchburg, in part so that passengers might connect with north–south trains and with the trains operated by the Chesapeake & Ohio Railway.

The C&O trains—the Pocahontas, the Cavalier, and others known by mere numbers—linked Lynchburg and other small cities, and even some towns, with the two east–west C&O main lines running west from Old Point Comfort on the seashore through Norfolk and Richmond to Louisville, Cincinnati, Chicago, and on to St. Louis. The northern main line ran through Charlottesville to Clifton Forge in Virginia, where it joined the southern east–west main line from Richmond that passed through Lynchburg; passengers could choose either route for the same fare. Astride the great lozenge-shaped east–west system linking the nation's capital with West Virginia mountain resorts like White Sulphur Springs and Greenbrier and with major cities farther west, Lynchburg prospered as a junction for transcontinental travel.

It prospered too as a branch-line terminal. Radiating from

Lynchburg stretched secondary tracks that meandered through the hills, sometimes paralleling main tracks a dozen miles away. The C&O operated a curving route from Richmond to Lynchburg by way of Bremo, Warren, and other hamlets, and a northwest-running line to Natural Bridge, a scenic wonder that attracted tourists. The N&W branch line stretched thirty-four miles southeast to Brookneal (where it crossed the Virginian Railroad, a major coal hauler that operated a handful of fast passenger trains too); thirty miles farther on it reached South Boston, a junction on a Southern secondary line, before terminating at Durham in North Carolina. No name trains raced along the branches. But twice a day, at 8:15 AM and 2:20 PM, a train left Lynchburg for Durham, stopping at Rustburg, Gladys, Halifax, and Denniston; the opposing trains arrived in Lynchburg daily at 3:35 and 8:35 PM. Unlike the main-line name trains, especially the United States Fast Mail, the branch-line trains clicked along at about thirty to thirty-five miles an hour. But despite their slowness they made Lynchburg not only a way station on long-distance routes but the hub of a secondary system. And they let long-distance travelers transfer at Lynchburg for trains to Natural Bridge and other tourist destinations.

Twenty-fours a day, seven days a week, a stream of trains paused at Lynchburg, offering residents of the city and its environs a sumptuous choice of destinations and arrival and departure times. For well-to-do riders, the day trains boasted club cars and fine dining service, and the night trains offered multiple choices not only in sleeping accommodations—berths, bedrooms, drawing rooms, and so on—but in ways of spending sleep time. One might board early and rise early at one's destination, or dine late, board late, and sleep late as the train reached New York or Mobile. When the Pullman Company operated most sleeping cars on United States railroads, it functioned as the largest hotel corporation in the country.

Railroad connections mark Lynchburg still. Any visitor to the city marvels at the architectural beauty of its downtown, perhaps especially at the grace of period styles. Something of big-city style suffuses Lynchburg, and not merely in architecture. The Maier Museum of Art has been hosting symposia by New York artists for a century, and the city's historic preservation program rivals anything in Washington, D.C. Yet Lynchburg culture is profoundly regional too: the city is a treasure trove of Piedmont antiquities seasoned somehow by both the Deep South and the sea. Scrutinizing and probing reveals an enduring cosmopolitanism prized by many Lynchburg citizens, belied by the city's lackluster airline service.

Airlines cannot stop cities and counties from building new airports, but in an age of government deregulation they can serve some airports in ways that make them well-nigh useless, while concentrating flights, and hopefully profits, at a handful of others. But perhaps more mysterious forces intend Lynchburg to be isolated.

Cold War worries caused the federal government to build the structure that now houses the Maier Museum of Art at the Randolph Macon College for Woman. Intended as a safe repository for the collection of the National Gallery, the structure opened in 1952 as the college art museum. But behind the single gallery lay rows of sliding metal racks on which curators would hang the national collection evacuated from Washington in time of nuclear threat. Lynchburg lies on the direct route to the Greenbrier, West Virginia, bunkers built to shelter Congress from nuclear attack. Perhaps Congress intended art to arrive by train, for the Military and Interstate Highway System avoids Lynchburg totally. Perhaps Congress intended the Lynchburg and Greenbrier regions to be free of panicked motorists fleeing the East Coast, and so angled highways away from them. But perhaps only bad luck kept the highways from Lynchburg. Or perhaps good luck.

Highways are not air routes, and Lynchburg now pays a heavy price for its honest audacity in building a spectacular airport. Airlines simply expect Lynchburg people to drive one to three hours to airports they consider nearby. Unless one's trip originates in Charlotte or Pittsburgh, almost any flight from anywhere means changing planes at Charlotte or Pittsburgh to fly the seventy-five minutes or so into Lynchburg. Flying to Lynchburg from almost any place within a thousand-mile radius consumes most of a day, even if one lives adjacent to a major airport. Someone who lives an hour or so from a major airport probably spends almost an entire day flying to Lynchburg, given time spent in traffic and security lines. Flying into Roanoke, which has more frequent service, offers little gained time, since one must still drive to Lynchburg. Almost all the flying happens by daylight: by eleven at night the Lynchburg Airport is closed. Savvy travelers and Lynchburg citizens alike now and then wonder about the days when one boarded a fast train in Lynchburg, ate a pleasant meal in the dining car, slept in one's personal bedroom, and awoke outside New York to a shower and breakfast. For that matter, the same people wonder about the fast trains that raced to Washington and stopped in Charlottesville and Arlington.

Lynchburg blossomed as a junction. For a time one of the wealthiest cities in the United States, it prospered as what air travel now calls a hub. Other cities prospered simply because they lay along railroad lines having international significance, as any deep reading of *The Official Guide of the Railways and Steam Navigation Lines of the United States, Porto Rico, Canada, Mexico, and Cuba, Also the Table of Railroads in Central America* demonstrates. In small towns and large, stationmasters and ticket agents thumbed through the 1,800-page tome and figured out how to get prospective passengers to Hamburg, Tokyo, and Havana. For decades, Cuba and the rest of the Caribbean preoccupied station agents in the wee hours of the morning, when only the telegraph sounder clicked for company and they determined how a customer might best enjoy a vacation. Station agents once acted as travel agents, and used the *Official Guide* as their bible.

As the Illinois Central System boldly announced above the pages devoted to its Panama Limited, it saw some of its trains operating "To Foreign Lands Nearby: Cuba, Nassau, Canal Zone, Central and South America." The Panama Limited moved in the company imagination as something like a ship, not only named but operating figuratively across the Caribbean. While railroad employees knew it as No. 7, passengers and onlookers down the Mississippi Valley knew it by name, and knew it carried a ladies' maid, barber and valets, bathtubs, a fine dining car, and only Pullmans, never coaches. Leaving Chicago at 12:30 every afternoon, it raced southward, stopping at a handful of cities only to pick up passengers booked for Memphis and beyond. Only at Memphis did it pause for long: five minutes, to switch out Pullmans bound for Mobile. At 5:40 the following morning it paused for one minute in Jackson, Mississippi, and at

9:30 pulled into New Orleans, 921.2 miles from Chicago. Averaging only forty-four miles an hour, No. 7 ran faster than the New Orleans Special but nowhere near as fast as the Daily Fast Mail, a train that attracted businessmen in a hurry. The Panama Limited existed not for speed but for luxury. Its patrons paid for the privilege of having a buffet car open continuously, and a dining car serving gourmet meals. Such people wanted hot baths before breakfast, and compared forty-four miles an hour with twelve knots.

Buried in the *Official Guide* are secrets that delight careful readers willing to jettison computer software quickness for a far slower mode of analysis. Facts stick to other facts as one consults timetable after timetable, and serendipity shapes inquiries into the history of cities like Lynchburg, Mobile, and Cairo.

While the Panama Limited discharged no passengers at Cairo on its roll southward, other Illinois Central trains, including the Daily Fast Mail, did. An abbreviated timetable in the Illinois Central section advertises a connecting service that made Mobile twenty-three and a half hours from Chicago, via a Mobile & Ohio train, the Gulf Coast Special, operating on the M&O main line between St. Louis and Mobile. At 3:40 every morning, a Pullman filled with sleeping passengers was switched from the New Orleans Limited onto the Gulf Coast Special. Fast freights carrying bananas crossed at Cairo en route from New Orleans and Mobile toward Chicago and St. Louis, but only locals noticed their hurried movements. While frazzled businessmen murmured in their sleep as a switcher moved their Pullmans from one train to another, vacationers bound from St. Louis to New Orleans murmured as the little locomotive plucked their Pullmans from the Mobile-bound train. The banana trains indicated something vague about maritime activity to the south, but the Pullman movements carried explanation printed in timetables and on railroad depot posters.

The railroad companies worked hand in hand with steamship companies, especially the United Fruit Company, which owned the "Great White Fleet." Operating as far north as St. John's, Halifax, and Boston, linking New York, Philadelphia, and Baltimore with Havana, Kingston, and Cristobal, and even connecting San Francisco with Cristobal, the firm provided coastal service from Castilla to Limon and Cartagena. The service between New Orleans and Havana and Cristobal, and between Mobile and Tela, rewards scrutiny in lush ways indeed. The *Official Guide* demonstrates that New Orleans and Mobile bridged the Caribbean region with the whole Midwest and with central Canada.

Passengers aboard the Panama Limited and other trains often expected to continue their journey aboard United Fruit steamers leaving New Orleans for British Honduras, Guatemala, Cuba, the Canal Zone, Costa Rica, Colombia, and Panama. The schedule of the Panama Limited influenced the sailings and arrivals of the small white liners, and the schedule of No. 7 influenced the schedule of connecting trains. The wealth of detail in the July 1929 *Official Guide* almost overwhelms. The fastest way from Champaign-Urbana to Lima in Peru? The *Official Guide* suggests that the business traveler avoid No. 7 and instead take the Daily Fast Mail, then a Wolvin Line ship to Puerto Mexico, then a train to Salina Cruz, then a United Fruit Company ship to Panama, then No. 7 of the Panama Rail Road Company, then a ship again. But vacationers, the *Official Guide* suggests, should work backward from United Fruit Company sailings along railroad routes and schedules. The trains, the *Official Guide* insists, are like the ships: integral parts of the vacation.

A traveler heading south from New York or Lynchburg aboard the Washington, Chattanooga, New Orleans Limited paused in Hattiesburg in Mississippi at 4:33 AM. About two hours later, sixty miles west on a converging route, a passenger aboard the Panama Limited paused in MacComb. About five thousand people lived in Hattiesburg; almost the same number in MacComb. The luxury trains stopped chiefly to take on water and coal, but in southern Mississippi people in two small towns had access to high-speed, luxury travel as well as to ordinary trains spaced evenly all day long. People in both towns lived near the southern end of New York and Chicago to New Orleans routes, but railroad station maps made it clear that they lived at the midpoint of North American–Caribbean–northern South American lines of travel. Neither town was Memphis, not even Jackson or Meridian, but both were infinitesimal jewels on a cosmopolitan string of far larger gems.

The *Official Guide* offers little in the way of railroad maps. Without its companion volume, the 1928 Rand McNally *Handy Railroad Maps of the United States,* it becomes a sort of sorcerer's grimoire, a gigantic compendium of information become arcane. But the atlas makes the grimoire into a sort of alchemical spell book. After an hour or so of intense effort, the *Official Guide* begins to reward anyone struggling to understand the architecture, cultural institutions, and industrial base of Lynchburg and other cities and towns. A bit more study begins to convert the road atlas view of the Republic into another, vastly richer one in which towns now only little known even to well-traveled Americans become prominent. Mac-Comb, Hattiesburg, and Lynchburg float now in the same mists as Tela, Cristobal, Cartagena, and other Spanish Main cities long ago visited by fruit company steamers. But once these three United States places were hubs of regions linked day and night with great cities and small towns.

Between such hubs gleamed other jewels, usually large towns served by single railroads. Like stones on a necklace that become more beautiful together than separately, the large towns partook of urban glamour too.

In 1945 the Burlington Ak-Sar-Ben Zephyr raced across the rural Midwest on a schedule that allowed only one-minute station stops. For example, on May 31 it arrived in Galesburg, Illinois, twenty minutes late from Lincoln, Nebraska, behind twin diesel-electric locomotives named Silver Meteor and Silver Swift, two of the first postwar-specification locomotives delivered to any railroad. The locomotives proved aptly named. Between Oneida and Altona the ten-car train averaged 97.3 miles per hour, its engineer making use of locomotives geared for 118-miles-per-hour maximum speeds. The 31.28-mile trip from Galesburg to Kewanee took twenty-five minutes from start to stop, and the Kewanee stop consumed only sixty seconds. Then the train raced eastward, and beyond Arlington cruised at 105 miles per hour until reaching Aurora, where it paused for one minute, before rolling at around 70 miles per hour into Chicago, where it arrived on time. Ak-Sar-Ben is merely Nebraska spelled backward, and train No. 12, while important to Burlington management, rolled in the shadow of the Denver Zephyr. No. 12 made numerous station stops between Lincoln and Chicago, including many between Galesburg and Chicago, but on May 31 it traversed the 162.2 miles from Galesburg in 140 minutes and arrived on time. Nowadays Galesburg, Oneida, Altona, and Kewanee are all cities lost in flyover land, and many well-educated coastal Americans cannot immediately locate Lincoln on any national map, highway or otherwise. But the two Burlington locomotives pulling No. 12 that day demonstrated that at the end of the war United States railroads intended to further improve rail service not just between the largest cities but between cities and towns nowadays almost impossible to reach by air.

In rural areas, seeing No. 12 charge past at 105 miles per hour meant something markedly different from seeing fast passenger trains thirty years earlier, but not because earlier trains moved more slowly. Something fundamental had happened along the right-of-way.

"Were you ever a boy in a corn field on a hot June day?" asked Sherwood Anderson in a 1904 *Agricultural Advertising* article. "Did the afternoon train, westward bound at forty miles an hour, pass around the corner of the hill and go roaring and screaming off into the strange land that lay over and beyond Brownville?" The ordinary passenger train meant something special to the farm boy, Anderson knew, for he had been that boy himself. "Did something give a savage tug at your heart so that it hurt, as with big hungry eyes you saw all of these people going so blandly and with such careless mien into that wonderful and enchanted land that lay east of Jasperville?" For the typical farm boy, the train meant a momentary glimpse of urbanity: electric lighting, high-fashion attire, newspapers and magazines from far away. As a boy, Anderson knew "such a hungryness to get on that train that he thought he would die of it," and in time the hunger he described so frankly caused him to make his way to Chicago. His column in *Agricultural Advertising* is far more than a potboiler written as he worked on the stories that became *Winesburg, Ohio*, and catapulted him to fame. It is an incisive analysis of why advertising had to reach the entire farm family.

Agricultural Advertising readers produced advertising that appeared in *Ohio Cultivator, Hoard's Dairyman*, and other magazines farm families read carefully. Unless that advertising made farm implements and farm life appear as attractive as the local passenger train and its imagined terminals, upwardly mobile farm children would leave. Anderson warned advertisers that they confronted a powerful adversary in the trains rumbling along the edges of farms, stirring dust and imagination alike. Ever so slowly, farm families acquired what they considered to be urbanities. Rural free delivery brought them daily mail, parcel post offered mail-order shopping and home delivery at lower cost than railway express, telephone lines stretched along poles and fence posts alike, and batteries re-charged by windmill generators powered radios long before elec-tricity crackled along wires to light lamps and power washing ma-chines. The Model T enabled families to drive into town more than once a week—perhaps to shop, more likely to see a Hollywood film—and Rural Electrification Agency efforts had brought power lines to about half the nation's farms by 1941. Historians know the lessening of rural isolation well, and understand television and the interstate highway as ending it. But most know little about the im-pact of train No. 12 in May 1945.

By the close of World War II trains such as the Ak-Sar-Ben Zephyr cruising at 105 miles per hour had become ordinary, something to notice perhaps, but nothing enchanting or exciting. Farm families in prewar sedans and pickup trucks expected to drive at twenty or thirty miles an hour over dirt roads to the nearest station, and there to board No. 12 for Chicago. Many returning GIs had arrived home on No. 12 and similar trains, and the fast train had become only another modern component in lives broadened by travel in Europe and the Pacific. No. 12 and other trains merely reinforced the way small-city, small-town, and rural residents thought of their home places in national geographical contexts. Fast, convenient long-dis-tance travel swept back and forth along nearby rails.

Airliners stripped away that thinking as thoroughly as Allied bombers had laid waste much of Germany, Italy, and Japan. Ameri-cans now think of regions in large-scale terms only: the Midwest, the South, the Pacific Northwest. Terms like *High Plains* and *Mis-souri Basin* mean practically nothing, for vast reaches have become Flyover Land. As airline routes eviscerated railroad routes, cities like Lynchburg and towns like MacComb saw their importance fade.

Most likely, geography vanished as a mainstream high school subject not only because Sputnik-worried educators replaced it with
intensive mathematics and physics but also because large numbers
of Americans had begun flying, and once jet airliners replaced propeller-driven aircraft, they flew mostly between large cities. As regional identity withered, urban sprawl quickened, often at the expense of regions bereft of passenger train service.

Nowadays only geographers, railroad enthusiasts, and real estate
developers care much about the Delaware & Hudson Railroad region. The deep past of the company involves a canal built to bring
coal from eastern Pennsylvania by barge to Kingston on the banks of
the Hudson, and then south to New York City. The company abandoned its canal in 1899, having already pushed north from Wilkes-
Barre and Scranton into the Lackawanna Valley. Tracing the D&H
rails north reveals what geologists emphasize about North American mountain ranges and valleys: they run north to south. From
Wilkes-Barre, therefore, the D&H built roughly north, to Nineveh
in New York, then on through Oneonta, Schenectady and Albany,
Saratoga Springs, Ft. Ticonderoga (with a spur to Rutland in Vermont), Plattsburg, Rouses Point at the north tip of Lake Champlain,
and finally to Montreal. Over the past century, the company has
seen its chief cargo shift from coal to newsprint rolling south from
Canada, but it endures as the armature of much heavy transport
in a region nowadays increasingly focused on international commerce. The North American Free Trade Agreement already reori-
ents the shipping of raw material and manufactured items, but it
promises to transform the Lackawanna Valley and other regions
once tightly linked with Canada as railroads begin moving an ever-
increasing share of new products along old routes. It promises to
reorient some regions away from adjacent large cities as well.

The D&H created a crescent-shaped corridor arcing southwest
from Montreal and moving much more than coal. It linked Saratoga
Springs, Lake Placid, Lake George, and other resorts with large populations at its Wilkes-Barre and Montreal terminals. But far more
importantly, it shaped upstate New York and western Vermont into
a region linked not only with Quebec but with southwestern New
York and central Pennsylvania. It put Albany in a spectacular posi-

tion: the New York capital sat athwart trains operating not only between New York and Boston and Detroit and Chicago, but between Montreal, Binghamton, Scranton, and Wilkes-Barre. Year-round the D&H moved business passengers from the eastern Midwest to upstate New York and Quebec. But in summer it poured thousands of vacationers into a region facing a worsening agricultural situation and relying increasingly on tourism to bolster its manufacturing efforts.

Upstate New York and the so-called Southern Tier of New York—the counties along the Pennsylvania border—grasp today at any business willing to relocate. Difficulties faced north and southwest of Albany originate not in the departure of manufacturing for the American South and offshore so much as in the impact of the airline industry after about 1965. No longer did first-rate rail passenger service weld two regions into one that crossed national borders and offered connecting first-class service from New York City and Chicago. As the D&H faced increased airline competition, its Montreal Limited, Laurentian, and other passenger trains moved less and less swiftly before finally disappearing. By 1970 upstate New York had become difficult to access by rail, air, and automobile, as many vacationers discovered. Its inhabitants, increasingly wary of federal and state efforts to boost the regional economy, began to rue the passing of passenger train service on the D&H, the Rutland Railroad, and other lines that once put small upstate cities on a necklace punctuated by Montreal, Albany, Wilkes-Barre, and other hubs.

If upstate New York and the Southern Tier exist chiefly as flyover land, the Tavaputs Plateau reaching across the Colorado-Utah border might as well be on the moon. Motorists heading west from Grand Junction in Colorado along I-70 move across sparsely settled country indeed. Durham, Mack, Ruby, Utaline, fall into the rearview mirror in Colorado; ahead lie Agate, Cisco, Elba, Brendel, and Green River before the highway heads almost due west into the San Rafael Mountains. Woodside, Grassy, Mounds, Price, Helper, and other tiny towns lie along lesser roads angling toward Salt Lake. For anyone driving the old main line of the Denver, Rio Grande & Western Railroad, towns like Solitude, Sphinx, and Desert focus attention on people who enjoy no public transportation at all and live hundreds of miles from any airport offering scheduled service. Arches National Park is spectacular, but no passenger trains operate from the branch diverging at Crescent Junction to it, or to the town of Potash farther down the line. The seeming desert may not be a desert in precise ecological terms, but it is dry, fiercely hot in summer and bone-numbing cold in winter, and almost empty of people except in the tiny hamlets along the railroad. Even ranchers cannot make a living along the high iron.

After World War II the western railroads operated high-speed long-distance passenger trains across sparsely settled regions like that west of Dodge City. The Atchison, Topeka & Santa Fe Railroad public timetable lists numerous trains moving along the 1,338 miles between Dodge and Albuquerque. In New Mexico the schedule shows some stopping at Springer, Colmor, Wagon Mound, and Shoemaker, and at Las Vegas (New Mexico) and other larger towns too. Ranchers and other high-country residents would not have expected the Super Chief to stop at tiny wood stations painted yellow (the way the Southern Pacific streamliner pauses at the tiny depot in the 1955 feature film *Bad Day at Black Rock*), but they did expect other long-haul trains to provide frequent daily service. From Dodge in western Kansas, across the southeast corner of Colorado, and into central New Mexico, trains across Raton Pass operated parallel with other Santa Fe passenger trains hundreds of miles south. With its subsidiary lines, the Santa Fe operated 13,085 miles of track, crosshatching the vast region between Arkansas and the southern coast of California but reaching northeast to Chicago via Kansas City. Together with its competitors, especially the Southern Pacific, it provided regular long-distance transportation that made Albuquerque a hub. But it made far smaller cities hubs too. Clovis in New Mexico, Pampa in Texas, Kiowa in Kansas, Lamar in Colorado, all enjoyed connecting train service by the same railroad offering multiple routes not only between Chicago and California but also between New Orleans and California. Moreover, the Santa Fe operated fast passenger trains on north–south routes, linking Albuquerque with El Paso, Newton in Kansas with Galveston, and Kiowa with Presidio on the Mexican border. But the terminals and junctions proved less important to thousands of rural people than Sentinel, Lone Wolf, Odell, Crowell, and Rule along the Kiowa–Sweet-water line that terminated in another Santa Fe line linking Clovis with the Gulf of Mexico and steamships.

The finest Santa Fe trains ran fast across vast distances. In the 1940s new diesel-electric locomotives capable of 120 miles per hour amazed onlookers in places that nowadays rarely see a commercial airliner in the sky high above. The demise of frequent, fast, long-distance train service did less to impoverish large cities than it did to isolate small towns and hamlets. In Lynchburg and its vicinity, driving to an airport takes little time in comparison with reaching one on the Tavaputs Plateau or in the vicinity of greater Wagon Mound.

In 2003 financial tremors shook the national airline industry, but news media reported little until the veritable earthquakes of 2004 and 2005. Federal officials targeted the escalating cost of the Essential Air Service (EAS) subsidy program, something that sparked small-town newspaper headlines in Staunton, Virginia, and elsewhere but made scarcely a ripple in metropolitan dailies. Across the United States, the airline industry suddenly confronted a calamity similar to that which afflicted passenger-carrying railroads circa 1970.

Devised in 1978 to subsidize air travel to and from very small regional airports, the EAS program was a response to the aftershock of the creation of Amtrak. In 1971 Amtrak took over responsibility for most long-haul passenger train service, but it did not take over most passenger trains, and not even most routes. Despite government assurances that few people rode long-distance trains and that those who did would find convenient alternative transportation, by the middle 1970s state and local politicians complained to Congress that many voters lived in regions bereft of passenger train service. In 1978 Congress created a program to subsidize the cost per passenger of airlines operating to small, usually rural airports.

Per-passenger subsidies began to rise almost at once. Even discounting what some fiscal conservatives argued in congressional documents was abuse built into the program—Martha's Vineyard airport is considered a rural one, and federal funds subsidize the wealthy summer residents who use the resort field—EAS costs ballooned as more and more counties and small cities built so-called regional airports. By the late 1980s the airports were competing with each other, and with much larger metropolitan ones. The situation Lynchburg faced by the year 2000 was one that developed earlier elsewhere. Rising fuel costs and the increasing price of installing safety-related equipment in very small airliners and at tiny airports exacerbated matters. Between 1995 and 2002 the average per-passenger subsidy paid to airlines serving very small airports in the lower forty-eight states tripled to $229 per flight. In 1996 EAS cost the federal government $22.6 million; by 2003 it cost $113 million. Almost never do transportation experts mention the subsidy program in the context of subsidizing Amtrak. Yet the per-passenger/per-flight subsidy amount varies from $9 at Johnstown, Pennsylvania, to $567 at Lewistown, Montana.

After September 11, 2001, fear of terrorism combined with rising ticket costs to decrease ticket sales at many regional airports. Before the terrorist attacks, many passengers, especially retirees and vacationers with a bit of time to spare, found driving two or three hours to larger airports an attractive alternative to regional airport ticket costs. Airlines entering the subsidy program contract to provide at least two departing flights a day from each subsidized airport. In the twelve-month period ending in June 2002, more than twenty airports reported three passengers or fewer departing per flight. The airport in Alliance, Nebraska, reported a daily average of 2.1 passengers, scarcely more than one per flight. In western Virginia, Shenandoah Valley Regional Airport, a direct competitor with the one at Lynchburg, recorded a decline from 18,947 passengers in 2001 to 6,583 in 2002.

At the current moment, as major airlines struggle to avert bankruptcy by cutting frills and renegotiating union contracts, fuel costs continue to increase and regional airport ridership has failed to return to preterrorism levels. Concomitantly, every United States airport must conform to security regulations. At Alliance, Transportation Security Administration screeners must process four or five passengers a day. What else they do, and how they are paid, is an intriguing question.

Moreover, local airports usually cannot serve groups of passen-

gers, especially on short notice, so groups tend to travel by automobile or chartered bus. The tiny airplanes, many of them carrying
only thirteen passengers, often operate with just enough filled seats
that a family of four must make reservations well in advance. A
sudden business meeting often involves delay for groups of travelers, and even regional sales meetings sometimes force attendees to
drive. Small airliners reduce costs, but in the end eliminate most of
the flexibility postwar Americans hoped air travel would produce.
Some experts suspect that Internet videoconferencing has reduced
business travel at small, EAS airports, but the federal government
now understands that it can no longer subsidize flights into airports
as small as that in Lynchburg.

In 1929 the Chicago, Burlington & Quincy provided Alliance
with quality passenger train service operating between St. Louis and
Chicago and Billings, Montana, and between Omaha and Deadwood, South Dakota; some trains carried Pullmans, dining cars,
and lounge cars, although many provided only coaches. Moreover,
trains operated between Alliance and Denver and between Alliance
and Casper, Wyoming. While the last operated as a roundabout
route away from main lines, it enabled Alliance residents to board a
train moving west and then swinging onto another CB&Q north–
south main line paralleling the St. Louis–Billings main line that
reached east to Omaha and Kansas City before reaching Chicago
and St. Louis. The two parallel "Burlington routes," along with their
east–west lines, created a focused economic region in the short-
grass prairie zone of western Nebraska and eastern Colorado. The
line to Deadwood carried some business people, of course, but its
passenger trains operated mostly for vacationers. Advertised as "the
Black Hills Detour," it connected Alliance and the rest of the nation with Wind Cave National Park, Black Hills National Forest, Mt.
Coolidge, and other resort areas in westernmost South Dakota. Not
every train that stopped in Alliance moved rapidly or operated as
an express elsewhere: No. 303 departed at 2:05 in the afternoon and
did not reach Denver until 10 that night, taking about three hours
longer then than it does to drive from Alliance to Denver today. But
no one in Alliance bemoaned a lack of trains, and in 1929 Alliance
was scarcely on the main line to anywhere. People expected good

service, but not the high-speed service of towns located between large cities.

Nowadays Alliance is a jewel of a little town, but no longer on any necklace. If the EAS subsidy does not rise appreciably, everyone in the area will drive for hours to find an operating airport.

On May 22, 1975, train No. 8 of the Southern Railway System left Lynchburg on its last run to Washington, D.C, scheduled to take four hours and fifty minutes to operate over 175 miles. Reduced to a locomotive and a lone coach rambling at thirty-five miles per hour along the edge of the Blue Ridge Mountains, No. 8 rolled as the wraith of fifteen-car streamliners that once paused in Lynchburg on their way to New Orleans. But No. 8 rolled in an eerie twilight too. Four years after Amtrak took over most passenger trains, the Southern Railway ran its own trains, even the lowly No. 8. Perhaps management saw around the curve of time. Just east of Lynchburg, the one-car train coupled onto some thirty special flatcars carrying truck trailers, and rolled toward Washington. In Alexandria the crew switched out the flatcars and rolled the lone coach into Union Station. Southern No. 8 existed in the twilight of privately operated passenger train service, but it rolled too in the very dawn of mixed passenger/intermodal freight. The Southern had been experimenting for a decade: its Brunswick to Atlanta train carried Pullman cars, but often arrived in Atlanta with a half-dozen red tank cars coupled behind the passenger ones. Management glimpsed something special enough to move it to retain control of passenger trains while it tested mixed consists that might support passenger service. If nothing else, Southern No. 8 revealed the enduring attention Southern management paid to the future importance of Lynchburg. It, Alliance, and so many other towns might become extremely inviting if passenger trains connected them at eighty or ninety miles an hour.

Knowing this now sparks deep-pocket investor support for rails-to-trails programs. Real estate developers grudgingly admit that championing rails-to-trails programs really means "rail banking" rights-of-way. Southwest of Lynchburg, along the old N&W main line on which sped the United States Fast Mail, environmentalists recently heard the governor of Virginia extol the economic advantages of turning abandoned railroad routes into hiking and bicy-

Scotts friend — a setting but — no jewel

cling trails. The mountain region between Lynchburg and Bristol has lost thousands of jobs as tobacco farming failed, then textile mills moved to foreign countries. Already some of its abandoned railroad rights-of-way have become hiking or nature trails, most notably the Virginia Creeper trail between Abingdon and Damascus, on the North Carolina border. Damascus has a population of a thousand, roughly five times its population in the years when branch-line trains connected it to the main line linking Lynchburg and Bristol. The trail brings about two hundred thousand visitors a year to Damascus, which derives about $81,000 per year from taxes on meals and lodging. Indirectly, the visitors support a mountain-bike shop, outfitters, shuttle operators who bring hikers back to cars, and a nascent lodging industry. No one thinks much of the days when N&W trains rumbled to the end of the seventy-five-mile-long line at Elkland, North Carolina. In 1929 the N&W ran only one passenger train a day each way, and the trains took almost five hours to complete their trips, stopping at many hamlets and, for the twenty miles nearest Elkland, moving freight cars along with coaches. Imagining riding trains No. 201 and 202 requires a lot of effort nowadays; it also smacks of heresy. The Virginia Creeper trail is so beautiful and so quiet.

And its northwestern end, at Abingdon, lies adjacent to Interstate Highway 81, a narrow highway so jammed with tractor-trailer traffic that tourists try hard to avoid it. Around the armature of the I-81 corridor spins regional business expressed in motels, gas stations, fast-food restaurants, and discount stores. The rural corridor is not so much suburban sprawl as linear squalor punctuated with brand-new trucking company distribution warehouses. Local business owners and short-distance motorists picture I-81 as it was fifteen years ago, a bucolic, well-maintained highway over which few long-distance trucks operated. No longer do the corridor taxpayers want the highway widened. They want more truck trailers moved by rail, along the adjacent main line of the old N&W, nowadays the Norfolk Southern.

The railroad prospers, and faces new challenges, as its route south of Lynchburg creeps toward track capacity. It can add a second track and take other measures to increase efficiency, all of which make the collateral industrial and commercial real estate potentially more valuable. Meanwhile, twenty miles away from the corridor, people are mostly poor and jobs few—so few that politicians praise the service jobs produced by hiking trails. Anyone driving in the vicinity of Lynchburg, especially southwest toward the historic and scenic Cumberland Gap district, discovers the jarring disconnect between Lynchburg and its satellite towns and the tedious, ugly mess of I-81.

Land-development investors look closely, see the Norfolk Southern routes, and begin to wonder how they might change, and so change the region. Almost beyond doubt, trains will never return to the Virginia Creeper route. But only freight trains hold the promise of sustained economic growth in a beautiful but straitened region, and only passenger trains will make possible the movement of more hikers to trails served by rural, low-volume roads.

Nowadays at least a few investors just ahead of the real estate development curve focus on Lynchburg: local real estate agents admit to more inquiries shaped by the expanding reach of suburban commuter trains operated by Virginia Railway Express, a transit authority. But a handful of national-scale investors think about Abingdon in terms of Bethel, Maine. Rail passenger access to the southwestern corner of Virginia must hinge on trains operating through Lynchburg and Bristol to other cities. Given such rail routes, however, an entire recreational resort economy might be built in a region free of automobile jams and tractor-trailer traffic. An equivalent of the Maine coast or Adirondack Park in upstate New York might enrich its private-industry-based creators in Virginia, and if such an immense park environment developed within easy passenger train access of Washington, D.C., property values in Lynchburg might well skyrocket. The key to it all is managing road traffic and providing an enduring, substantial economic base better than the I-81 corridor mix of motels, gas stations, truck stops, and fast-food eateries. Investors ask consultants to consider such issues. So far only one thing is certain. Another little regional airport will do nothing to advance either the public good or private profit in the region south of Lynchburg. The tracks exist, even if they are very busily moving freight trains, and where the Washington, Chattanooga, New Orleans

Limited once raced, passenger trains may race again. It may be that some would-be land developers, and some landowners, already picture this train of the future as freighted with riches beyond the dreams of avarice.

SOURCES: Anderson, "Business Types"; Boyd, "One Hundred and Fifty Years of the D&H"; Daniels, "From Rumor to Renaissance"; Hemphill, "The Unknown Rio Grande"; Morgan, "Forget the Gods of Old" and "Mr. Pullman Revisited"; New York State Department of Transportation, "A Future for Southern Tier Rail Service?"; "Rising Cost, Falling Ridership"; Stilgoe, "Onshore Force"; Wiley, "Meet the 'Lynchburg Special.'"

SIDETRACKED

High-speed electric automobiles whisk silently along great boulevards while occupants read, play cards, or sleep. At eighty miles an hour, the cars never crunch fenders and never interfere with others converging and diverging. Cars move in great convoys, break into clutches at cities, and cruise individually the last few miles home.

Electronics and snazzy mechanical engineering make such visions serious possibilities. A lot more federal research money now, and metropolitan regions—especially in California—will soon embark on an ecstasy of highway rebuilding. Or so the twenty-first-century visionaries imagine, their hands extended toward grant money.

So they imagined in 1955, and ten years later. The 1973 energy crisis silenced their optimistic pronouncements, but even in the prosperous 1980s they said little. Something had changed.

Nowadays the soothsayers strive for a comeback, basing their hopes on electronic gadgetry and motorist frustration, and on national amnesia. Across Southern California, drivers lobby for electronic toll collection and toll lanes carved from existing arterial highways. People will pay to avoid some traffic and to enjoy some regularity in driving times. People will pay to know a parking space awaits. People will pay to know that miles ahead a massive collision already blocks traffic, and that their itinerary must change. People will pay to apply computer software to making their automobile rides slightly more efficient and perhaps a bit more pleasant. Already first-class airline passengers walk to the head of security screening queues. Why not let first-class motorists drive a little faster and lot more freely?

Swirling beneath the willingness to pay is a deepening vortex of class discrimination, anger, and future energy waste. Astute politicians are wary of high-tech-loving visionaries, whom they may know as warmed-over failures whose new pronouncements can destroy political careers. Something changed in the 1980s that haunts experienced politicians and a tiny cognoscenti—but not most Americans, who remember nothing of it.

United States highway design originated in post–World War II assumptions and in cold war scenario analysis. The Military and Interstate Highway System, to use the official name Americans routinely truncate, reflects Pentagon thinking about the 1930s German autobahns that made blitzkrieg successful. Nowadays few Americans reflect on the late 1930s exchange of German and United States military officers intrigued by highway construction. United States Army officers visited highway building sites across Germany, paying special attention to straight sections useful as fighter plane runways, cloverleaf intersections that sped traffic flow, and rest areas along the limited-access highways that might enable convoys to feed and re-supply rapidly. When Hitler introduced the Volkswagen Beetle, the "people's car" had the beginnings of a unique long-distance highway system on which to operate. German military officers arrived in Pennsylvania to watch the new turnpike under construction on the alignment of a never-completed railroad. Just before Pearl Harbor, the American military realized the significance of a Pennsylvania Turnpike operating with no speed limit. Drivers averaging ninety miles an hour presaged mechanized divisions moving at such speed too. During World War II, when American motorists struggled with wartime fuel-conserving speed limits set at around thirty-five miles per hour, military commanders took the lessons of German limited-access highways and air superiority to heart. They convinced a Congress wary of postwar recession to build a highway system useful in the event of atomic attack. But in the late 1940s—indeed well into the 1950s—the Pentagon envisioned thermonuclear warfare as something dependent on manned bombers, especially the B-52. In its first massive effort to shape the United States built environment, the military understood highways and aerial warfare as integral to one another. Road became highway and runway both, and both became military weapons camouflaged as civilian public works.

Military understanding had changed mightily since the late 1930s. In early 1940, four months after Germany attacked Poland in a blitzkrieg involving air superiority and highway-fed armored movement, the federal government had no coherent plan for stepped-up

In the 1970s, as railroads prepared to discard freight-train cabooses, the cars the public accepted as punctuation marks began showing signs of deferred maintenance.

armament production. Nor did it have any plan for moving men and matériel to embarkation ports. After the war, the head of the War Production Board marveled at a nation that had manufactured 124,000 ships, 100,000 tanks and armored cars, 434 million tons of steel, 2.4 million military trucks, and 4.1 billion rounds of ammunition. Perhaps he should have marveled at the national transport victory, too. Even ship-building material began its seaward progress by rail. But from 1940 onward the board did little to authorize railroads to acquire new locomotives or new cars or signaling equipment. Essentially, United States railroads moved a gigantic increase in freight tonnage and an astronomical increase in passengers using locomotives and cars already in service along tracks maintained in no special fashion. Depression woes in fact meant that many railroad companies had been unable to afford routine rolling stock and right-of-way replacement. Yet from its five-year wartime economic experience, the nation learned a great deal about the flexibility of the railroad industry. The United States military hierarchy learned the lesson much more clearly, and thereafter assumed that the railroad industry would rise to any wartime occasion without much government support or guidance, and would do so immediately. Military academies and war colleges still teach cadets that United States railroads prove a powerful secret weapon because they operate far under capacity and are strikingly flexible transport systems.

Concealment of military bungling still masks the extraordinary contribution of the railroad industry to the war effort. After Pearl Harbor, German submarines began torpedoing oil tankers steaming along the East Coast. In four months the U-boats sank fifty-two tankers, and the navy confessed itself powerless to stop them. Almost all coastwise movement of oil stopped, leaving only enough for the military. Essential civilian needs could not be met, and on May 22, 1942, the federal government rationed oil in the eastern states. Few realized that every sunk tanker meant another 210 tank cars needed. In late summer, far inland from the beaches where civilians found oil-soaked lifeboats, corpses, and debris, trackside observers noticed a surge in railroad movement of tank cars. By autumn, about three-fourths of the oil reaching East Coast refineries moved in fast freights of sixty cars each. From the oil fields of Louisiana, Mississippi, Texas, and Oklahoma, steam locomotives decades in service sped the oil north along sixty-six separate routes on the tightest of schedules. Soon the railroads began moving more such trains back and forth between the oil states and Pacific Coast refineries too. In rural places strings of tank cars roared along at mail train speed, and crack passenger trains took sidings to get out of the way. Only troop trains and freight trains of refrigerator cars filled with fresh produce slowed the madcap progress of the tank trains.

Now only specialist scholars and military scenario analysts know much about the superb success of the oil freights tearing along at passenger express speed. But in July 1943 *Railroad Magazine* published a feature article detailing how 72,500 tank cars moved 900,000 barrels of oil a day (boxcars crammed with drums moved another 21,047); other cars moved gasoline, kerosene, and aviation fuel. Most Americans never learned how close the German navy came to defeating Britain and crippling the early United States war effort. What about the 169 petroleum trains charging north over the Missouri Pacific route from Texarkana to Dupo, each taking thirty hours and fifty-five minutes for a run optimistic experts had scheduled for thirty-four hours? What about the experiences of GIs like C. Grattan Price, who in 1942 clocked the speed of his steam-powered Baltimore-bound Florida Special at 115 miles per hour? It departed Jacksonville an hour late but arrived in Washington, D.C., six minutes early. War produced very fast running indeed, but the precarious military situation produced little published history.

It is possible to learn a good deal from photographs of the last days of steam locomotives. Unlike most prewar images, wartime photographs often show black smoke blasting from stacks. In peacetime locomotives emitted far less smoke. In winter they moved beneath clouds of steam exhausted into stacks to increase the draft over coal and oil fires. In summer they moved beneath a clear haze of hot, shimmering air. No housewife hanging out laundry trackside expected soot to soil her drying clothes, and housewives knew how to complain every bit as fiercely as trackside office workers, storekeepers, and others who expected clean-burning locomotives as neighbors. Railroad companies kept engines in tune, and ordered enginemen to make as little smoke as possible. Failure to comply with smoke-abatement directives meant demerits and discharge.

But in wartime maintenance schedules succumbed to movement schedules, and enginemen grimly determined to make time with extraheavy trains disregarded peacetime emission rules. No one watching a hospital train scream inland from Staten Island or a tank train racing north or west complained about smoke blasting from an overworked passenger locomotive. Then after World War II worn-out steam locomotives seemed suddenly old-fashioned, for all that they routinely moved freight trains at seventy-seven miles per hour and passenger trains far faster. Eclipsed by diesels, they began to vanish, and their whistles became whispers of nostalgia. No one asks today about U-boats operating with impunity off New Orleans, Norfolk, and New York or why the War Production Board restricted the building of diesel locomotives.

In the Depression, European and American railroads experimented with diesel-powered, lightweight passenger trains. By 1939 the German National Railways operated thirty-two such trains that cruised on a variety of routes, mostly west of Berlin, linking Basel, Munich, Hamburg, and Berlin, along with smaller cities. However, Hitler preferred traditional trains pulled by very fast steam locomotives, and his opposition slowed the German experiment. Only slightly different from the German trains, United States experimental trains attracted much attention too, especially the Burlington Zephyr.

In 1934 the Zephyr debuted as the train of the future. Its stainless steel, articulated cars and integral locomotive made it seem like a silver snake. On May 26 it carried passengers nonstop from Denver to Chicago, running a thousand miles at an average speed of 78 miles per hour and hitting 112 for miles at a time. Crowds turned out to witness its streak across the rural region, and many commentators remarked that the streamliner had proved itself. Operating on a railroad of secondary importance, atop lightweight rail ballasted with cinders and slag, the train made a strong impression on railroad officials. Despite its air conditioning, wraparound windows, and other amenities, it proved cheap to operate, even at extraordinary speed. The Burlington immediately ordered similar trains for daytime runs between Chicago and Minneapolis–St. Paul, and between St. Louis and Burlington, Iowa, and more trains to accommodate passengers on the Chicago–Denver route.

Other railroads invested in similar equipment. The Union Pacific experimented with its City of Portland, and the New Haven bought its Comet from Goodyear-Zeppelin, a firm hoping to manufacture something faster than blimps. By 1940 the Union Pacific had invested in more articulated lightweight passenger trains. The New Haven took pardonable pride in its bidirectional Comet, which had an integral locomotive at each end, much like contemporary Amtrak Acela trains. Even smaller railroads such as the Gulf, Mobile & Northern had acquired lightweight experimental trains. The GM&N twin Rebels, modern down to art deco aluminum lighting fixtures, swept through the rural South as harbingers of an impending revolution in intercity travel. Other companies, still not convinced that the articulated trains would succeed, built more lightweight versions of traditional trains pulled by steam loco-motives. In the summer of 1935, the Milwaukee Road operated its orange-painted Chicago–Milwaukee Hiawatha at 120 miles per hour behind a locomotive capable of sprinting even faster. Good times seemed to lie ahead.

America's entry into World War II stopped all such innovation. Railroads desperately needed conventional locomotives and ordinary trains of interchangeable cars. Wartime munitions and other matériel often moved behind passenger locomotives operating on passenger train schedules, and long troop trains and civilian passenger trains moved behind multiple locomotives. But all through the war, railroad companies studied figures suggesting that streamliners, especially lightweight, diesel-powered trains, had reversed the Depression-era decline in passenger revenue precipitated by the rising ownership of automobiles.

In 1920 United States railroads enjoyed the peak of peacetime passenger rail travel. Nine years later a third of the riders had defected to automobiles. By 1933 ridership had shrunk by another 40 percent. Government and industry statistics demonstrated that by 1933 railroads carried only 42 percent of the passengers they had carried in 1921, even though many Americans could no longer afford automobiles or the cost of long road trips and instead took trains.

Railroad company innovation and an improving economy reversed the passenger decline in 1934. By 1938 it had become apparent that modern trains, lightweight or not, pulled by ultramodern steam locomotives and the first multipurpose diesel locomotives would prosper mightily because they pleased the public. Two years after the streamlined Silver Meteor began operating over the Seaboard Railroad and Atlantic Coast Line between New York and Florida in 1939, the companies had added four similar lightweight trains. A year before Pearl Harbor, railroad companies cooperated in establishing Midwest-to-Florida trains like the City of Miami and the South Wind. Full from the start and earning a 50 percent return on investment, such trains prompted only duplication and triplication within the industry. Company after company abandoned the earlier articulated, single-unit, lightweight trains for ultranew but more conventional, often streamlined interchangeable-car consists pulled by diesel locomotives. In 1940, as war seemed inevitable, railroad companies found themselves facing a new problem. Adding cars to the articulated trains proved difficult, and growing passenger traffic meant the necessity of adding cars. So new diesel locomotives capable of operating in multiples pulled the City of Miami and other streamlined trains that grew longer and more frequent by the year.

While wartime necessity stopped the building of additional high-speed streamlined trains, it encouraged railroads to plan postwar expansion of fast passenger equipment. Companies that entered the war with superb steam locomotives learned to expect more than their designers had anticipated. In 1944 the Santa Fe operated its Grand Canyon Limited and Scout between Kansas City and Los Angeles, 1,788 miles, without changing locomotives. Such unexpected and hard-won triumphs caused railroads to inform locomotive manufacturers that diesel locomotives had to perform considerably better than wartime steam power. In 1946 railroads began taking delivery of passenger locomotives geared for 118 miles per hour. In so doing they precipitated what scholars call a colossal federal government blunder that produced almost unimaginable adverse impacts nationwide.

In 1947 Congress voted to restrict passenger train speed to seventy-nine miles per hour except on track equipped with automatic train control (ATC). Despite railroad industry arguments that ATC did not work correctly and would prove prohibitively expensive on long runs, and despite the railroad industry's superb wartime safety record, Congress condemned Americans to slow-speed rail travel. The United States became the only nation in the world to deliberately limit the speed of its passenger trains.

Five years later the Italians successfully tested the new electric-powered train its builders christened Rapido. Not every component worked perfectly. In one instance, one of the pantographs connecting the train with the overhead electric wires flew apart at 149 miles per hour. But only seven years after the end of World War II, the

Italians achieved speeds envisioned in wartime Germany but by then forbidden in the United States.

Hindsight proves both 20/20 and blind. ATC never works correctly, even now. Urban subways operate with updated versions, and the subway serving Harvard University enjoys such frequent ATC failures that most passengers fail to notice the whooshing of air brakes stopping trains between stations, especially in icy weather. To notice the unscheduled stops, most reasonably smooth, is to wonder why the motorman has run past a red light. Of course the motorman has not. The ATC sensor aboard the train incorrectly processes data and stops the train. In 1947 the railroad industry correctly denounced a device that seemed as likely to precipitate derailments through sudden stops as it did to prevent rear-end collisions. Mentioning that Congress insisted on the technology stops much transportation debate today.

Three industries lobbied against 118-miles-per-hour rail passenger service. The highway, trucking, and automobile industries knew within two years of the end of World War II that the Pennsylvania Turnpike could no longer handle cars averaging 90 miles per hour, let along trailer trucks. The mix of cars and trucks led to disaster, and neither civil nor mechanical engineers could envision highways for motor vehicles capable of cruising at 118 miles per hour. The future of the aircraft and airline industries lay in luring passengers aboard long-distance flights, but most intercity travel involved journeys of less than five hundred miles, something likely to prove extremely unprofitable. But the military clinched the deal. Without a massive civilian subsidy in the form of airport building, airmail tariffs, and, above all, passenger- and mail-carrying airliners, the aircraft industry would charge the direct costs of developing new military airplanes, bombers especially, directly to the military. Taxpayers might not support the postwar air superiority the Pentagon envisioned when they understood its cost. After the Soviet Union obtained the atomic bomb and the cold war began in earnest, the military used the specter of atomic attack to energize the building of the Military and Interstate Highway System. The interstate system in turn subsidized the trucking and automobile-manufacturing industries, and promised to solve the airline industry's problem of the short-distance flight. Americans would drive at 60 to 75 miles per hour to the nearest airport and then fly—but only if Congress slowed passenger trains.

At first, only railroad management and railroad company stock-holders complained, along with the builders of high-speed trains; later they were joined by manufacturers confronting the slowing down of fast freight and other time-sensitive railroad service. In the late 1950s and early 1960s a chorus of complaints rose from rural regions, small towns, and small cities concerned about the imminent collapse of railroad service. The Interstate Commerce Commission, caught between dealing with an industry that had acted in monopolistic ways a half century before and a surfeit of new data impossible to process in the years just before computers, bumbled larger issues involving both service abandonment and profitless service maintenance. Federal and state regulatory agencies simply could not imagine the national rail system withering under government-subsidized competition. Agencies processed data so slowly that circumstances had usually changed by the time they rendered decisions, but as early as 1948, when Charles R. Cherington published his densely argued *Regulation of Railroad Abandonments,* a few analysts understood not only the untenable position in which Congress had placed the industry but also the trap encircling the Republic. The trucking industry and the airline industry combined could not meet the demands of a fast-growing economy, let alone a major war.

Deterioration in railroad passenger and freight service might restrict more than GNP growth, analysts argued. As *U.S. Planning for War in Europe, 1963–1964* and other documents recently released by the National Security Archive make clear, they feared it might hamstring military effort in future wars. After the Korean conflict, defense analysts began worrying about a large-scale ground conflict in Asia, especially one involving the Soviet Union or China or both. Their worries led to a fierce military commitment to air power and quick-time, short-term warfare.

Nazi-era German designers had not only produced the auto-bahns and high-speed, lightweight trains but also imagined larger-scale railroad equipment. While traditional in many respects, the envisioned trains would dwarf all others anywhere. With a track gauge of four meters, sumptuous cars seven meters high and six wide, gigantic locomotives, and extremely gentle curves and grades, the futuristic railroad, it was posited, would operate between Paris and Berlin—and perhaps deep into a vassal Soviet Union—by 1950. Engineers did preliminary studies for an even more colossal system operating on rails nine meters apart, but the four-meter gauge seemed technically feasible. A nation already wedded to superhighways had reimagined rail vehicles at the scale of zeppelins. During the early years of World War II, with Germany apparently poised to rule over Europe forever, the broad-gauge railroad did not seem out of the question.

But as wartime tankers evolved into contemporary supertankers, ocean liners matured into cruise ships too wide for the Panama Canal, and propeller-driven cargo planes became Constellations, then 707s, then 747s and Concordes, both railroad and highway vehicles retained nearly wartime dimensions. Whereas contemporary railcars still seat people four abreast—or two or three in first class—no traveler aboard a 747 thinks much about being crammed nineteen abreast in what seems like a miniature movie theater. A railroad boxcar is about ten feet longer than it was in 1940, and Amtrak Superliner cars are taller than all but the streamlined dome cars of 1940, but surprisingly little else has changed on tracks or highways. Eighteen-wheelers are longer and a bit wider than the articulated trucks that irritated motorists blazing down the Pennsylvania Turnpike in 1941, but they are not much bulkier, although tractors now often pull two small trailers. Had Congress embraced the high-speed passenger trains railroad companies had ordered in 1946, perhaps the next stage would have been railroad technology borrowed from the nation that invented limited-access highways, jet airplanes, and rockets. German scientists spirited into the United States to develop missile weapons and space exploration rockets were not joined by German railroad designers. After Congress limited passenger train speed, no one bothered with Nazi-era German engineering studies every bit as realistic as those that produced the VW Beetles scurrying all over late-1950s United States highways. As late as 1955, the Association of American Railroads convened a committee to study atomic-powered locomotives, but the federal government offered strikingly little help, even though it was funding an atomic-powered merchant ship.

The first oil-gasoline crisis, in 1973, alerted millions of Americans to the simple fact that they were almost wholly dependent on automobile travel to reach work, to shop, to vacation, and indeed to get much of anywhere within five hundred miles. The second crisis, six years later, only deepened national anger over gasoline shortages and rising heating and cooling costs. Politicians worried about saving their careers. Petroleum scarcity, rationing, and price fluctuation paralyzed Congress because it had long ago eliminated alternatives that would have mitigated the crisis. But the crises and indignation mask a vastly more serious problem as little studied nowadays as the wartime destruction of the tanker fleet or the 1947 congressional limiting of passenger train speed. Women began working outside the home.

Until the early 1970s, highway planners did reasonably well in anticipating growth rates in motor vehicle use. Only in the largest metropolitan areas did planners make serious misjudgments. In New York, Boston, and Los Angeles especially, new highways opened and immediately jammed with traffic. By the end of the 1960s, planners had begun thinking ahead, trying to design highways that could be built immediately and widened later. Sparing taxpayers the shock of building highways with six lanes in each direction seemed politically wise, since many urban neighborhoods had begun resisting so-called urban renewal through highway building. In an age when highway designers seriously considered paving the lanes of limited-access highways in pastel colors so that women drivers might negotiate them without collision—according to Carl Stelling in "Designing for the Ladies," a 1958 article on the challenges women faced on divided highways, "an extra, slow-speed, truckless lane would be provided for women who become nervous at high speeds"—imagining the design of intersections of twelve-lane highways for women drivers taxed male imagination. The idea of building such intersections in urban and suburban areas terrified politicians, who saw them as destroying budgets and neighborhoods both. Then suddenly in the middle 1970s highway planners confronted the skewing and wholesale collapse of all their highway building scenarios. Women moved into the workforce in cars that thronged existing highways and defied traditional routing analysis.

Women who drive to and from work tend to do so differently than men did in the early 1960s. As Margy Waller and Evelyn Blumenberg make clear in *The Long Journey to Work: A Federal Transportation Policy for Working Families,* they are far more likely to make stops at grocery stores and dry cleaners and vastly more likely to drop and collect children at schools and day care. Collecting what planners call "journey-to-work" statistics grew far more complex in the mid-1970s, then worsened as the advent of the personal computer produced a significant number of workers able to telecommute some days and drive others. Moreover, women who hitherto had dropped off and picked up husbands at suburban commuter rail stations no longer did so; men drove, and parked in lots that were suddenly jammed. Planners complained that women working outside the home not only produced a staggering number of multiple-car families and complex trip data but created all sorts of parking issues the public blamed on poor planning.

In the early 1980s highway planners and entire regional planning authorities battered themselves against the reality of highway-widening issues they had imagined facing—or rather, imagined their successors facing—forty years down the road. As ecological concerns widened and deepened, metropolitan planners realized the decreasing likelihood of widening many highways, and the futility of widening highways many commuters, especially women who tended to work in suburbs, did not use. Urban planners and historians of city planning rarely speak for the record about the spatial impacts of women driving to work outside the home. They argue for more studies and more precise data collection, but since 1980 they have been reticent about designing highways that lead where errand-running data suggest they must.

The contemplation of choked urban and metropolitan highways goaded planners toward better prognostication methods. Unfortunately for planner peace of mind, the computer-generated scenarios outlined the highway needs of a growing national population, the rising number of women working outside the home, and time consumed by men and women driving many miles on errands. In 2007 the national population is about 301 million; in 2055 the nation will have 417 million people. Highway planning and design guidelines originated when the national population was about 120 million. At the current rate of growth of tractor-trailer truck traffic across the George Washington Bridge in New York City, *all* the bridge traffic will be such trucks in 2015, since the bridge will be continuously covered with trucks. Such statistics imply that automobiles and buses will be routed elsewhere—an implication that is nonsensical unless a parallel bridge is being designed now and construction planned for next week. A United States of 417 million people will know highway congestion beyond the darkest imaginings of all but a few experts. The vast explosion of population will occur in a handful of sprawling metropolitan regions, while—paradoxically—gigantic sections of the forty-eight contiguous states experience almost no growth at all.

Wheeler County in Oregon is roughly twice the area of Rhode Island but is home to only 1,500 people. A motorist sitting in a Providence, Rhode Island, traffic jam on I-95 might ponder Wheeler County. Why are so many people stopped in Providence, and what will traffic jams will be like five or ten years from now? Will any of it spill into the likes of Wheeler County, or will Wheeler County remain as sparsely populated as it is? Census statistics offer answers, but the answers displease almost everyone.

Such questions preoccupied many Americans in the late 1930s and then again in the 1960s. The Depression-era imagination focused on small aircraft, chiefly the autogiro (a hybrid helicopter/ fixed-wing plane), that would alleviate urban boulevard congestion. The subsequent moment concentrated on a variety of land-based inventions, mostly driverless cars. In time, 1960s dreamers derived some instruction from the 1930s visionaries, and eventually they learned defeat.

Invented in the 1920s in Spain, and perhaps simultaneously in Russia, the autogiro is best glimpsed now in the film *It Happened One Night*. Essentially a hybrid of airplane and helicopter, it featured a large propeller overhead and a second giving horizontal thrust. The United States licensee produced only about thirty of these aircraft. In the 1930s a few of the United States autogiros carried airmail, but most achieved prominence when used by journalists hurrying to important news sites. The *Detroit News* used one for aerial photography, and in 1931 Amelia Earhart reached 18,415 feet in one as a stunt. Highly maneuverable and, most importantly, capable of landing and taking off almost vertically, for a short time the autogiro seemed a commuter's dream come true. In the end, however, they used too much space in landing.

After World War II military interest shifted to helicopters. A few inventors tinkered with gyrocopters—one-person, vertical-takeoff-and-landing machines tricky to fly reliably. Another civilian contingent tried to perfect one- and two-person traditional airplanes that offered possibilities to people with large backyards but not enough acreage for runways. By the late 1950s the tinkering had shifted focus to rural places, and by the 1960s it had devolved into *Popular Mechanics* and *Popular Science* cover stories entitled "Build a VW-Powered Plane for $600" or "Build This 4-Place Cabin Plane for $3500." Despite early 1970s interest in James Bond–like tiny automobiles that sprouted wings, propeller, and rudder to become two-passenger airplanes, the 1973 energy crisis shifted interest toward ultralight, purely recreational aircraft. While many rural Americans, especially professionals, depend on privately owned airplanes using private runways or tiny county or municipal airports, the slow death of 1930s autogiro thinking emphasizes a single salient fact: no inventor could explain how a flock of autogiros or other tiny aircraft might converge on a city at rush hour without daily collisions. Nor could any inventor or any government expert explain how or where all the incoming aircraft would land or how flocks would take off simultaneously. In the face of these obstacles, interest in autogiros and similar flying machines waned and finally died.

Highway traffic jams began refocusing inventor attention in the 1960s. Some of the inventions merely tweaked earlier ones: the monorails at the Seattle World's Fair and at Disney theme parks represent nineteenth-century devices much improved. In 1910, for example, an electric-powered monorail system operated from Barstow in the New York suburbs through Pelham Park to Belden's

Point on City Island. The fifty-foot-long, cigar-shaped cars cruised at thirty miles per hour along the three-mile route, providing reliable enough service until one, carrying a hundred people rather than its usual fifty, twisted the overhead rail and wrecked. Long forgotten by the 1960s, such prototypes scarcely shaped the flow of federal research money to institutions like the Cornell Aeronautical Laboratory. As researchers discovered the unwillingness of Americans to tolerate noisy helicopters and sonic-booming airliners, they turned toward imagining a future of driverless (more or less) automobiles having some aircraft characteristics.

Popular Science featured the "Urbmobile" in a 1967 cover story illustrated with an image of bubblelike cars sweeping above a traditional interstate highway. Long on fantasy but short on facts, the story sketched an automobile that might or might not have flanged steel wheels, that might or might not be able to drive directly to guided highways, and that might or might not be powered by subwaylike electrified third rails. Working from the simple facts that an interstate highway lane chokes at around three thousand people per hour and that a traditional rail line chokes at around forty thousand per hour, the visionaries behind the Urbmobile fantasized about necklaces of bubble cars buzzing along at sixty miles per hour while drivers read or napped. If one car develops mechanical problems, magnetic devices will kill power to the third rail and slow the entire necklace to a safe stop. But near the end of the article researchers admitted that the system would only be possible for Los Angeles, Denver, Houston, and other sprawling cities. In New York, Philadelphia, Boston, Chicago, and similar cities "with really dense central cores," the Urbmobile system simply will not work, since no space exists to park the bubble cars. The system, experts agree, "doesn't approach the efficiency of a commuter train." Possibly bureaucrats at the old Department of Housing and Urban Development glimpsed the futility of the Urbmobile research effort: funding stopped. Given the rapid growth of cities, the rising number of women working away from home, and the developing density of automobile traffic, the visionary dream of a 1985 debut lay shattered by demographics in 1975.

In 1972 *Popular Science* reported that Department of Commerce bureaucrats were aware of the mounting catastrophe facing the interstate system. That year the whole forty-one thousand miles of the original system would be finished, but motorists in urban areas, already fuming about traffic jams, would confront worsening driving conditions. Engineers envisioned a futuristic Century Expressway running between Boston and Washington, D.C., as a 150-miles-per-hour route open to ordinary automobiles but not trucks. In 1965 studies had already revealed motorist dislike of trucks, especially big trucks, and engineers planning a highway that, in the words of one *Popular Science* reporter, will "separate the men from the boys" asserted that no trucks would irritate drivers merging from 80-miles-per-hour lanes into the high-speed, long-distance ones. But for commonsense questions the experts had few answers. Fog and snow would cause "beauts" of accidents, in the words of one Century Expressway designer, and no one really expected Detroit automakers to invent engines capable of sustained 150-miles-per-hour operation. By 1968, when the New York State Department of Motor Vehicles allied with the Republic Aviation Division of the Fairchild-Hiller Corporation to produce its prototype "safety sedan"—complete with rearview periscope—most government and industry experts realized that traffic jams meant the end of high-speed highway hype. They shifted their attention toward safety issues, and subsequently toward fuel-saving ones.

But year after year, automobile and mass circulation magazines focused on futuristic highways, for after all, automobile manufacturers advertised heavily. Manufacturers emphasized fast, high-powered cars in campaigns aimed at young blue- and white-collar men. Throughout the late 1960s and into the 1970s, *Motor Trend* featured stories on "sports personal" cars nowadays called muscle cars: Mustang, Camaro, Barracuda, Javelin, Cougar, Firebird. Such cars needed open roads and high speed limits to satisfy their owners, especially those who used them as family cars. Advertising brochures show that similar cars, the 1970 Dodge Coronet for example, competed with "sports personal" models. "Long, one of the longest in its field," the Coronet merely contributed to the downtown parallel-parking crisis and to the growing fervor for high-speed driving.

Only occasionally did reality check the advertising effort. In 1967

Popular Science ran a cover story suggesting that heavy-duty heli-copters might diminish traffic jams by lifting damaged automobiles straight up. Tow trucks simply took too long to reach accident scenes and remove wrecked cars. Gradually both general magazine and federal government interest in traffic jams shifted toward very light duty, urban mass-transit gimmicks like the Personal Rapid Transit system—a sort of semiautomated dial-a-bus operation—*Popular Science* profiled in 1971. Such systems seemed somewhat useful in sprawling airports and in theme amusement parks, convention centers, and resorts, automobile magazines admitted grudgingly, but they offered no hope for even suburban-scale travel. But the 1973 energy crisis forced even muscle car magazines away from fantasizing about superfast cars, highways, and ninety-mile-per-hour commutes. A 1974 *Popular Mechanics* feature story suggested putting a highway atop the Alaska oil pipeline, but afterward editors shifted emphasis to fuel economy, and then to the current mix of fuel economy and safety that makes many Americans view muscle cars and SUVs (which evolved from sports personal vehicles) with mixed emotions. No visionary could get past simple issues of traffic flow or deal with parking problems. Even Congress asked for ideas that would speed automobile traffic. But almost no one replied.

Off the record, trucking industry executives wanted commuters aboard commuter trains, preferably lightweight, delicate, trol-ley-car-like "people-mover" trains operating on rails too flimsy to support freight cars. Rush-hour traffic jams had begun to seriously discommode trucking companies, which responded by increasing efficiency where they could, mostly by operating ever larger trucks but also by installing devices few outside the industry know. The so-called jake brake saves brake-pad wear by diverting exhaust gas into diesel-engine cylinders suddenly free of fuel. But jake-brake exhaust screams from tail pipes, and many communities ban their operation except on fire apparatus. Longer, streamlined trailer trucks, jake brakes, then tractors towing two trailers at a time proved useful on rural long-distance runs, but far less so in cities. Almost all trucking innovation annoyed automobile drivers, and sometimes pedestrians as well, especially in cities. When confronted in the late

1960s by a Congress trying to dampen complaints, the trucking industry admitted what the automobile manufacturers agreed to be true—the passenger train had to keep rolling.

Amtrak originated in 1971, just as motorcar fantasizing was skidding to a halt. This is more than coincidence. Computers had begun to predict motor vehicle traffic growth, and the predictions worried politicians, who in turn harried design professionals. Practicing planners, intent upon preserving not only their self-respect but also their jobs following the disaster of urban renewal, turned against another generation of highways, automated or not. Highway designers confronted not only issues of snow, rain, and fog but rising public ire at traffic jams, long, speeding trucks, and fatal accidents. They fixated on traditional, incremental improvements and complained bitterly, among themselves, then in print, especially in Federal Highway Administration long-range scenarios, about the adverse impact of large trucks on cities and inner suburbs, especially on New York and other very densely populated areas. Even mechanical engineers hopeful about small-scale, onboard-computer-driven equipment that might operate traffic lights shifted focus to creating safer, more fuel-efficient automobiles. Despite continuous generalized lobbying by the automobile, trucking, and airline industries, especially by car manufacturers, Congress created Amtrak simply because the so-called Northeast Corridor seemed unlikely to function without railroad passenger service.

Congress merely spread the cost of a regional railroad service bailout. By creating a handful of long-distance railroad routes along with Northeast Corridor ones, Congress hoped to convince all taxpayers that the quasi-public Amtrak operated a national network. Despite immediate and continual complaints that the bulk of Amtrak funding and vision went to the Boston–Washington corridor, and despite its original assertion that Amtrak would operate no commuter or short-distance trains, Congress persevered in its dual vision of high-speed, frequent service for one densely populated section of the nation, and slow-speed, one-train-a-day service for the rest. If Wheeler County saw two Amtrak trains a day, fine. Providence mattered more: it needed fourteen so that I-95 traffic jams did not destroy access to nearby cities and to adjacent airports.

As early as 1969, the editor of *Popular Mechanics* glimpsed the commuting value implicit in the Penn Central Railroad Metroliner service offered between New York and Washington. While he lamented that faster trains operated in Japan, he saw the United States electric-powered trains as a step toward a sensible, overarching transportation policy. People commuted on Metroliners that reached speeds of 110 miles per hour. Within three years the handful of experts knew a simple fact still rarely cited by historians. Amtrak had to survive simply because regional commuter rail operations had become interstate in scale. Without some federal structure, any one of the regional commuter systems might succeed in ways reminiscent of the 1934 Zephyr. That success would immediately cripple all federal automobile, trucking, and airline lobbying by dramatically increasing real estate values within one region people and news media would see as prototypical. Once the United States motorist glimpsed land travel without traffic jams in one large metropolitan region, airline travel would become long-distance only. The three powerful lobbies understood the failure of the intercity bus industry, and in their corporate memories perhaps recalled the failure of the trolley car industry too. A least a few of their employees knew something of German ideas about colossal railroads. Amtrak represented a simple, indeed elegant means of keeping railroad innovation under the control of a Congress controlled by road and airline industries—and by the military.

But Amtrak notwithstanding, the regional transit authorities began to flex muscle. The Southeastern Pennsylvania Transit Authority (SEPTA) snaked its tentacles out from Philadelphia; the Massachusetts Bay Transit Authority (MBTA) reached southwest from Boston into Rhode Island; the California Transit Authority (CalTrans), if not exactly interstate, sprawled along its own ocean-front corridor; Metro North (a commuter train authority) linked New York City with Connecticut. Other, often smaller systems began expanding too. While Amtrak's Northeast Corridor service began functioning as a commuter line—bringing commuters to and from Trenton and Princeton in New Jersey to New York, for example—many states hitherto not served by Amtrak or served by only a pair of trains daily began seeing opportunities beyond those offered by Congress.

Maine moved surely but steadily in a way that presaged efforts elsewhere. After decades without Amtrak service, it suddenly demanded Boston–Portland trains. Despite much squabbling with the freight railroad that owns the tracks, government agencies made the operation a reality in 2001. But not just a pair of trains connects the two cities. Instead three trains a day each way link the cities. The Downeasters surpassed ridership estimates immediately after beginning service, and despite initial fluctuations in ridership, they pleased passengers: the trains have 96 percent on-time rates and 95 percent customer-satisfaction rates. Many riders commute the 116 miles: the first train leaves Portland at 6:05 and arrives in Boston at 8:50. Many others commute between Boston and intermediate stops, especially Exeter, New Hampshire, seventy-seven minutes from Boston, even at rush hour. But the service is linked to the commuter rail lines Maine is beginning to reactivate around Portland. And it is linked as well to the high-level passenger platform at Bethel, a mile or so from the Sunday River resort.

The Maine effort rewards sustained scrutiny. Unlike earlier efforts by other states, it succeeded in convincing Amtrak to operate multiple trains, not one daily train each way. Moreover, the Downeasters connect—albeit indirectly, Boston having two terminals and having built a gigantic, expensive highway tunnel system while determining to forgo building a rail link between the two stations—with the high-speed Acela trains. A state that advertises itself as "vacationland" at home and in Europe implemented a meticulously scheduled plan while Amtrak struggled to get Acela rolling. Suddenly Maine became far more accessible, but the Amtrak trains serving it connect at Portland with a nascent regional rail network intended to increase property values and help wealthy taxpayers not only commute to Portland but connect for points south.

Very astutely, Maine never asked Amtrak to operate north and east of Portland, perhaps on a route into New Brunswick and Nova Scotia. Maine does little to provide passenger rail service deep into its north woods, although it pays close attention to the condition of freight tracks potentially useful for it. Instead Maine emphasizes, in the quietest way possible, a regional commuter-like railroad that is essentially a recreational-region railroad only partly dependent on Amtrak.

Maine planners were far ahead of most state planners throughout the 1980s and '90s. They knew they needed at least six trains a day to make their concept work, and they convinced Amtrak to provide the trains. What they learned now attracts attention in Virginia, the Carolinas, and even on the Georgia coast, and throughout the Pacific Northwest.

Maine vacationers just looking around glimpse the end of the sidetrack of which Maine residents are so well aware. Maine worked around Congress, finessed Amtrak, and pioneers a new vision of regional passenger railroading derived from historical record. Intended to serve wealthy Maine residents and boost real estate values in environmentally sensitive regions, the Maine vision is not so much focused on urban rail commuting as it is on a resort view of the future.

SOURCES: Burr, *U.S. Planning for War in Europe, 1963–1964;* Cherington, *Regulation of Railroad Abandonments;* Cole, *The Road to Rainbow;* Doughty, *New York Central and the Trains of the Future;* Fales, "How You'll Drive 120 MPH Legally"; Gunnell, *An Atomic Powered Railroad Locomotive;* Hubbard, "Nine Hundred Thousand Barrels a Day"; Lambert, "More Long Islanders Looking to Move Out"; Mischke, "Pages from the Past"; Morgan, "Ninety Miles an Hour Aboard a 4-6-4"; New York State Department of Motor Vehicles, *The Safety Sedan;* Price, "I Remember"; Smith, "The Diesel from D to L"; Stelling, "Designing for the Ladies"; "Super-Highway"; "Testing 6 Sports-Personal Cars"; Thompson, "Definition of a Redball"; Waller and Blumenberg, *Long Journey to Work.*

RESORT

No passenger trains stop at Bethel, Maine. Not yet. But the glistening new station and the high-level platform suggest that leisure may breed more long-distance passenger train experiments than business or commuting.

Cape Cod too!

By the end of the 1950s the airline industry had begun devastating long-haul passenger train service, and coaches and first-class cars grew shabbier every year, with the exceptions of a few railroads determined to make their trains succeed. Railroad companies had abandoned dozen of trains, and the pace of abandonment quickened throughout the 1960s. Urban rioting and crime produced a suburban exodus from downtown residential areas convenient to train stations. Nowadays anyone reading mainstream media stories of passenger train failure will observe the odd morphing of *long-distance* into *intercity*. The change in usage strongly suggests that public-policy argument advanced in skewed ways. When Congress established Amtrak in 1971, most discussion focused on linking cities, not suburbs. Wilderness and resort regions merited scarcely a mention. That clean, fast, friendly passenger trains often lasted longest in the Far West merited none.

Throughout the 1950s and 1960s, vacationers accounted for much passenger train travel, as they had for decades. Trains operated regularly or seasonally between cities and to or through places of leisure, often collecting passengers during one-minute stops in small towns. By no stretch of imagination could anyone call Glacier National Park or the Maine coast *cities*. As airlines purchased more and more news media advertising, however, the media began ignoring how Americans—especially the wealthy—typically traveled. Disneyland became the premiere family vacation, and Disney and the airline industry combined to make flying to California convenient and affordable, the airlines by offering reduced fares, Disney by advertising its park. In time, advertising made Disney World even more desirable among children, and families found discounted ticket prices between most cities and Orlando. National parks became first automobile accessible and then automobile choked, and many resorts, especially those catering to the wealthy, disappeared, often deliberately, into the obscurity the wealthy love.

Most American workers are limited to the standard two-week vacation, in contrast to the six weeks their European counterparts enjoy. So long as Americans must hurry on vacation, air travel holds sway on the long-distance routes that prove most profitable. To most Americans, transcontinental train travel is a joke, not only because they know little about how it once worked or might work in the future, but perhaps also because it offers a half-conscious reminder of how little leisure time they enjoy.

Long-distance driving becomes hectic when undertaken at speed. Many vacationing families discover that the interstate system is really an intercity system that bypasses cities, scenic wonders, and first-class resorts alike. Air travel becomes proportionately necessary as available travel time decreases, but few airlines operate between wilderness areas, national parks, and classy resorts. Well-to-do people escape to places once served by train, many still difficult and expensive to reach by air. Rail travel once offered alternatives to the Disney-type vacations: alternatives involving national parks, forests, grasslands, and other places many taxpayers now find difficult to reach. Parents learn that driving from any coastal city to any one national park, enjoying the park, and driving home is possible in a two-week vacation, but visiting more than one or two parks becomes a frantic chore.

Nonetheless, people try. Often the family car shares the same secondary and tertiary roads as campers, motor homes, agricultural machinery, and other slow-moving vehicles. Often when vacationers approach major parks they find urban-scale traffic congestion. Very frequently, unless they have made reservations well in advance, they find no place to camp and sometimes, indeed, no place to park.

The National Park Service, the United States Forest Service, and other federal agencies despair over the masses of automobiles and other recreational vehicles jamming parking lots. Not surprisingly, they build more lots and more roads, trying to spread visitors over a broader area. As the building of lots and roads continues apace,

The hiker surprised by a freight train realizes that railroads often cross wilderness areas remote from roads.

whole wilderness parks teem with vehicles that destroy any semblance of wilderness experience and any hope of relaxation. Consultants struggling to solve the motor vehicle conundrum may fail to examine the complicity of news media, airlines, and automobile manufacturers as a contributing factor. In desperation they think about a monorail system for Yosemite National Park.

Yosemite once had railroad access, as did most long-established national parks. Part of traveling cross-country on business frequently involved spending a day or two in a national park, and railroads strove mightily to make these minivacations convenient and enjoyable. Business travelers who spent a day or two sampling a park frequently returned on longer vacations, often with family and friends, or timed their next business trip around fishing, hunting, or skiing seasons. Very often, both business travelers and vacationers arrived and departed in first-class style, aboard trains with dining and Pullman cars, but many others made do with inexpensive, so-called tourist sleeping-car accommodations and even coach seats. Trains brought people to Yosemite and other parks, and the Park Service directed people from edge stations into wilderness devoid of automobiles.

When Yosemite opened in 1890 its western edge lay at the end of a two-day stagecoach trip from the San Joaquin Valley town of Merced. The town was situated on the main north–south lines of both the Southern Pacific and Santa Fe railroads. "Midway between Stockton and Fresno" meant little, but "on the main lines between Oakland, San Francisco, Los Angeles and about every point north, south, and east" certainly did. The Yosemite Valley Railroad began operations in 1907, running from Merced to El Portal, on the boundary of Yosemite, where it built a wilderness-style station and a sumptuous lodge. Almost immediately, the two transcontinental railroads began dispatching Pullman cars from Oakland and Los Angeles to El Portal via the Yosemite Valley branch line. First-class and coach passengers boarded wagons, and later open-top motor buses, for transport into the park interior. By 1916, however, more visitors were arriving by automobile than by train, and Yosemite began suffering the first throes of automobile congestion. Train conveyance steadily declined until 1945, when scrappers tore up the rails of the abandoned Yosemite Valley Railroad.

Short lines connected other resorts with main-line railroads. The Lake Tahoe Railway started in 1900 as a narrow-gauge line running south from the east–west Southern Pacific main line over the Donner Pass at Truckee. Twenty-five years later the Southern Pacific bought the line, made it standard gauge, and operated Pullman service from Oakland. Peter T. Maiken reports in *Night Trains: The Pullman System in the Golden Years of American Rail Travel*, that the Southern Pacific timed the night train to arrive at dawn, when the lake seemed almost golden. The company operated a day train from Oakland too, and connecting trains from Truckee for the convenience of long-distance travelers headed for Lake Tahoe, or simply wanting to break their trip in a pleasant place. Until motorists streamed onto its shores, Lake Tahoe was an immaculate gem prized by people who arrived by train and then walked the shoreline or took a tiny steamboat to scenic points around the periphery.

Unlike Yosemite and Lake Tahoe, many other national parks lay far distant from major population centers. Railroads viewed the parks as both long-term destinations and convenient places to break long trips.

In 1901 the Santa Fe Railroad began advertising the Grand Canyon in Arizona as a must-see spot of true wilderness grandeur. That summer it operated the first Pullman cars north along a branch from Williams, a town on its east–west main line. The railroad soon built a splendid hotel on the canyon rim, and quickly discovered that word-of-mouth advertising supplanted the draw of full-page ads in national magazines. In 1929 the Santa Fe inaugurated the Grand Canyon Limiteds, first-class trains between Chicago and San Francisco (with sections to Phoenix) scheduled so that Pullman cars could be detached at Williams and sent on to the Grand Canyon, where they served as temporary hotels. In systematizing what so many passengers already did, the Santa Fe passenger department achieved a service that demanded strict adherence to a custom timetable, since the sleeping cars left one Grand Canyon Limited and joined a subsequent one.

At 10:15 PM on a Sunday, passengers would have left Chicago for Los Angeles and San Francisco, arriving at 10:00 the following morning in Kansas City; 11:45 that night in La Junta, Colorado; and 12:15 the following afternoon in Albuquerque. At 11:00 PM that night the train would pause in Williams to switch out cars for the Grand Canyon. The sleeping cars waited most of the night in Williams, and at 5:40 the following morning began their sixty-four-mile trip to the Grand Canyon, where they arrived at 8:15. At 8:30 that night, their occupants having enjoyed a busy or leisurely day of exploring and dining, the Pullmans rolled back to Williams, where a locomotive switched them onto another Grand Canyon Limited en route to Phoenix via Ash Fork, Prescott, and Wickenburg or on to Los Angeles, San Diego, and San Francisco. While not especially fast, the Grand Canyon Limiteds carried club cars with valets, maids, barbers, bathtubs, and, of course, dining cars, along with a variety of Pullman cars configured with accommodations for single travelers, married couples, and families with children.

Devising a timetable that explained a service terminating in three cities with part of every train stopping over at the Grand Canyon taxed the ingenuity of Santa Fe employees. Passengers could book berths and rooms aboard the Grand Canyon Limiteds in sleepers not detached at Williams, of course. At the Grand Canyon they might want to meet friends aboard the opposing Grand Canyon Limited, which left San Francisco at 10:15 at night; the railroad thus arranged to have both trains switch out sleepers at Williams at about the same time. Finally, passengers might want to go to the Grand Canyon from Chicago or San Francisco not for a day (as a bonus on a business trip, perhaps) but for an extended vacation. In the final instance, the timetable directed their attention to other trains, perhaps the California Limited. But since any passenger aboard any Santa Fe train routed via La Junta–Colorado–Albuquerque might suddenly conceive a desire to visit the Grand Canyon, the company operated two daytime trains, Nos. 11 and 14, between Williams and the Grand Canyon, in addition to the night trains moving sleeping cars. However contorted the 1929 timetable, Santa Fe advertising made clear the proximity of the Grand Canyon to many of its transcontinental trains and the usefulness of a wilderness resort to all sorts of long-distance travelers.

Not surprisingly, other transcontinental railroads soon began to look on the national park system as something that might increase passenger revenue. The early examples of Yosemite and the Grand Canyon transformed coast-to-coast rail travel as coach and first-class passengers alike began choosing destinations based on intermediate wilderness stops.

Glacier National Park is a national park because the Great Northern Railroad saw its potential as a tourist attraction. In 1910 Congress created the park, using the Great Northern main line as its sixty-mile-long southern boundary. The company in turn built all sorts of lodgings for the visitors who stepped from trains operating through what it called "the scenic wonderland." Pullman cars dedicated solely to Glacier National Park service left from Chicago, Kansas City, and Omaha, arriving at Glacier Park station as their destination. Other cars stayed with trains but discharged passengers at a station linked directly with hotels.

Understanding the role of Glacier National Park in 1920s United

States railroading means seeing coast-to-coast rail passenger service in terms not merely of scenery but also of stopover experience in a region still sparsely populated today. Moreover, it involves a consideration of the North, especially the Canadian North, in east–west frameworks. In 1929 the Great Northern Empire Builder departed from Chicago at 9:00 PM, left Minneapolis twelve hours later, paused in Minot in North Dakota after another twelve hours, and four hours later stopped at Glacier Park, twenty-eight hours and 1,100 miles from Chicago. Dozens of towns, each meticulously noted in the 1929 *Official Guide,* slipped past. Read today, the timetable staggers: it extends for three full pages of fine print. The Empire Builder scarcely slowed at Gunsight, Sundance, and Spotted Robe before it stopped at Glacier Park; nor did it stop at Bison, Singleshot, or Hidden Lake after. But slower trains did.

Glacier National Park sat at the junction of a great T. South from it to Kansas City ran Great Northern trains that paused at Great Falls, Billings, Denver, Lincoln, and St. Joseph. The Great Northern operated through Pullman cars from Omaha and other cities far south of the park. But the main line of the Great Northern extended not only southeast from the park to Minneapolis and Chicago but also north (from Crookston in Minnesota) to Winnipeg and east to Duluth. In northern Wisconsin, near the western edge of Lake Superior, the Great Northern touched the territory of the Soo Line, controlled by the Canadian Pacific. From Minneapolis and St. Paul the two railroads operated Pullman service east to Montreal and, by the Boston & Maine, to Boston. Thus a New Englander might travel north, across the top of the Great Lakes, then swing southwest, then take the Empire Builder on to Glacier National Park.

New Englanders might have visited Yellowstone almost as easily, traveling west on the Northern Pacific. For all its fame as the first national reserve—created by Congress in 1872, immediately after the establishment of the first transcontinental railroad—Yellowstone still suffers from identity problems. Part of it extends into Montana and Idaho, but its bulk lies in Wyoming and, like the Grand Canyon, off main-line east–west routes. The Northern Pacific simply built a spur south from Livingston in Montana to Gardiner and, like its competitors elsewhere, erected a wilderness-style log station on a great loop that turned Yellowstone trains back onto the line to Livingston. Thereafter the company advertised itself as the "Yellowstone Park Line," in the hope that harried coast-to-coast business travelers might leave its premiere train, the North Coast Limited, for a minivacation at Yellowstone. Many did, but the suddenly accessible park itself attracted longer-term visitors from across the nation.

Eventually the Northern Pacific operated three gateways to Yellowstone. Gardiner remained extremely popular. In the 1920s, just before the season opened, entire trainloads of college students arrived to work in the lodges, and thereafter a stream of regular and special trains poured into the loop. The company subsequently opened a second gateway station at Cody in Wyoming and a third at Red Lodge, Montana; neither offered the convenience of the Gardiner, but both were more convenient for eastern travelers. In the late 1920s Northern Pacific service included the Yellowstone Comet operating from Chicago. The train split at Billings: one section operated over Chicago, Burlington & Quincy tracks to Cody, and the other went on to Gardiner. The Comet stopped only at St. Paul, Minneapolis, and Fargo before reaching Billings, and it carried what vacationing Americans had come to expect in the way of amenities: dining, buffet, and observation cars, sleeping cars, and bathtubs. From Livingston to Gardner it carried an additional pleasantry: open-air observation cars that made approaching Yellowstone an unforgettable sensory experience. Unnamed special trains, Nos. 3 and 4, operated between Yellowstone and Seattle via Tacoma, Portland, and Spokane, and other trains, even the plodding stop-at-every-town coach-only locals offered connecting service at Livingston.

Park visitors might avoid the Northern Pacific altogether, however, and ride the line that the Union Pacific opened from Idaho Falls to the western edge of Yellowstone. Trains to West Yellowstone carried Pullman cars switched from Union Pacific east–west limiteds at Pocatello and, of course, coaches. While the Yellowstone Express and Yellowstone Special built transcontinental traffic, West Yellowstone soon lay at the northern end of a new route originating in Salt Lake City. Midway between Idaho Falls and West Yellowstone lay the junction of Aston, from which the Union Pacific built a line southeast to the base of a mountain pass more than two miles high; on its far side lay Grand Teton National Park. Union Pacific service to Yellowstone prospered in ways that mystify anyone now turning the pages of old timetables, magazine advertisements, and travel diaries. In the mid-1920s a dedicated Yellowstone Pullman sleeper left Jacksonville in Florida via five railroads before the Union Pacific switched it onto a train at Kansas City. From the south and southeast, and from California, park visitors used the Union Pacific gateway, often without encountering visitors arriving at the northern and eastern gateways operated by the Northern Pacific.

Advertising maps from the 1920s illuminate the importance of the western national parks in rail passenger travel. Would-be tourists and even small children staring at posters in tiny depots might send for brochures from different railroads about wilderness vacations. Union Pacific maps and booklets emphasized that the railroad not only linked cities, small towns, and connecting lines with individual parks but linked the parks with each other. A traveler might want to visit Yellowstone along with Zion National Park, Bryce Canyon, Lassen Volcanic, Crater Lake, Sequoia, and Yosemite. Small-town depot masters and big-city travel agents pored over the *Official Guide* and figured out how would-be customers might enjoy a fast or a cheap ride to one park, then convenient rides to others. In a precomputer age, customers, stationmasters, and travel agents collaborated on many decisions. Passengers who went by the Denver, Rio Grande & Western through Colorado enjoyed detraining during the scheduled ten-minute photography stop in the Royal Gorge of the Arkansas River. Passengers who liked to eat favored the Great Northern and Northern Pacific, both famed for potato and fish cuisine. Others, especially schoolteachers on a budget but with many weeks of summer vacation, might favor slower but far less expensive coach and tourist sleeper trains, as well as "budget tours" of certain clusters of parks. College students bound for summer jobs in the national parks often favored the cheapest long-distance services of all, sacrificing not just luxury but even comfort in coaches rolling toward exquisite summer opportunity. More than most groups, undergraduates in tiny college towns like Galena in

Illinois appreciated the long-distance trains that paused to collect young people en route to wilderness summer jobs.

Vacation travel by rail involved far more than the western national parks, yet nowadays this is difficult to reconstruct. Recent patterns created by interstate highways and airline routes blur the fine distinctions that once reflected important decisions. Many city dwellers moved to particular suburbs not only because they offered convenient commuter train access to central cities but also because long-distance trains bound for vacationland paused at those suburban stations. The Oranges in New Jersey enjoyed summertime Pullman car service direct to the Maine coast, while commuter suburbs a few miles west did not. Choosing a year-round suburban home, and sometimes considering a job offer in a distant city, involved a precise evaluation of work and pleasure rail links.

No long-distance resort rail service better demonstrates the importance of home-base location than the summertime service to northern New England. Convenient connections from downtown New York, Hartford, and Boston meant that fathers might spend long weekends with families away for the summer. Equally convenient service from suburbs meant that families might make several short vacation trips to the same place. Just as few contemporary Americans consider the historical impact of the two-week vacation on highway congestion, airline travel, and resort choice, so do few understand the invention of the corporate executive as enabling the wealthy to vacation at length.

Executives execute orders. In the late 1950s corporate culture overwhelmed much United States thinking and skewed understanding of workplace hierarchy. Few Americans consider the directors who act through executives, let alone trace the creation of executive positions back to the perfecting of long-distance telephone technology. Not only did the telephone allow senior management to move away from factories, mills, and other manufacturing sites, in time creating the office avenues of New York and other cities. It also enabled directors and, far more importantly, owners of large and small businesses to remain in daily contact with trusted employees left behind during business and pleasure trips. To their employees, executives often look like senior authority, but to their employers, often individuals who remain in the background of business culture, they are merely the trusted keepers of order and the executors of new directives. Telephones and the executive class made possible season-long vacations for business owners after the 1890s. Schoolchildren learn about Alexander Graham Bell but little about people other than teachers who enjoy long summer vacations and stay in touch by long-distance telephone. By 1915 the wealthy had perfected the remote resort accessible only by long-distance train.

Year-round passenger trains operating north of Boston to Maine and to the Canadian Maritime Provinces began carrying summer-time tourists in large numbers by 1880. But many of the trains did not operate through Boston, simply because the city lacked—and still lacks—a direct rail link between its two terminals, South Station and North Station. Instead, Pullman cars moving from Washington and New York rolled north along the present Amtrak seacoast route, but diverged in Connecticut at New Haven or New London on a route through Worcester in Massachusetts and Nashua, New Hampshire. North–south travel skirting Boston produced not only a gigantic station in Worcester (now converted into an arena) and a nine-track one in Portland, Maine, but deep fears in Boston. While the city enjoyed heavy commuter train traffic—in the 1890s South Station boasted of being the busiest terminal in the world—and train-to-ship transfer, by the first years of the twentieth century long-distance trains, especially ones carrying very wealthy people, bypassed it. The State of Maine Express operated from Washington over the Pennsylvania, New York, New Haven & Hartford, and Boston & Maine railroads. Serving both Concord in New Hampshire and Portland, the train's summertime consists expanded until "the train" meant multiple sections of first-class cars filled with wealthy people intending to summer in Maine.

Resort travel reinforced techniques railroads learned at Christmastime and, later, Thanksgiving time: trains had to operate in multiple sections to meet demand. A train advertised to depart a terminal at four in the afternoon might operate with several "advance" sections that left earlier; alert newspaper readers watched for advertisements announcing such sections. Then the train departed at the appointed time, followed by several subsequent sections running as closely spaced as signaling systems allowed. Holiday operations became seasonal rushes by the 1920s. The Santa Fe frequently operated its Chicago to Los Angeles California Limited in seven sections each way, each separate train carrying not only the name but eleven sleeping cars, diners, and observation cars. On one occasion, the train operated with twenty-two sections westbound. Railroad companies disliked turning away would-be passengers, especially vacation-bound passengers not in a tearing hurry, since such people tended to find routes on competing carriers. Even the Boston & Maine, which controlled most north–south travel in Maine, ran multiple sections of its summertime trains.

For almost sixty years after its debut in 1902, the Bar Harbor Express journeyed north from New York through Worcester to the Maine coast. Operating over the same or roughly parallel routes rolled the so-called camp specials of as many as twenty Pullmans each carrying children to summer camps in Maine and along the Connecticut River. The New York, New Haven & Hartford Railroad created the Bar Harbor Express, differed with the Boston & Albany over its handling of the train, and finally ran it over its own rails to a Boston & Maine connection. In the summers of the 1920s it frequently operated in three sections, bringing Pullman cars from Washington and New York to Mount Desert Ferry and Ellsworth, and running the remaining sleepers to Rockland. The train carried private cars belonging to the rich, and one day operated, in addition to its regular sections open to the public, three sections only for twenty-one family-owned private cars. Long-distance telephone lines, the creation of an executive cohort, and the Bar Harbor Express made the northern (or eastern) coast of Maine into an exclusive summer resort.

The Bar Harbor Express left Washington, D.C., at 1:00 every afternoon in summer and arrived at Portland at 4:24 the following morning, its passengers still snuggled in berths, compartments, and drawing rooms. At Portland the train split. One part rolled on to Kineo and Waterville, where it arrived three hours later. Another went to Rockland via Bath, Wiscasset, Waldoboro, and Thomaston; it too terminated about three hours after leaving Portland. Another went westward to North Conway, Crawfords, Bretton Woods, and Fabyan, and still another on to Kennebago. The final part left Portland for Ellsworth, Mt. Desert Ferry, and Bar Harbor, arriving at 11:45 in the morning. The express left Bar Harbor at 2:00 every afternoon; departures from other resorts were scheduled so that Pullmans would collect at Portland's Union Station and be fed into several southbound sections. The companies respected the wishes of passengers from different resorts who wanted to visit en route based on their home or resort destinations. Consequently, Philadelphia-bound passengers from the deep woods of Maine merged into the flow of Philadelphia-bound passengers from the coastal resorts; that train became a subset of the larger one and carried the name Philadelphia–Bar Harbor Express. Except for the interruption of World War II, the companies enjoyed tremendous success with a train that operated between large cities and the tiniest of wilderness and coastal resort stations.

The Boston & Maine learned from its successes and tailored other trains and even lone Pullman car service to individual resorts. Rockport, a tiny Massachusetts harbor town north of Boston, developed an artists' colony that made it attractive to seasonal visitors in the 1920s. In June 1930 the Boston & Maine experimented with a sleeping car switched from an express train running north from New York via Worcester. Within days the service had burgeoned into five Pullmans and a baggage car departing Rockport at the end of the July 4th weekend. The following year a Pullman dedicated to Rockport left Washington, D.C., on a 4:10 afternoon express; it arrived at the quaint harbor terminal at 7:29 the following morning. On Sunday evening it rolled south at 8:36, after dinner. In the Depression the Boston & Maine launched a new profitable service based simply on the commonsense understanding that passengers had to sleep somewhere and might just as well sleep comfortably en route to a wilderness or resort destination, not to another city.

The smallest of wilderness stations, which ordinarily saw only a couple of coach and freight trains a day, hosted Pullman cars during the summer season. Finding deep-woods Maine resorts like Kennebago and Kineo today is difficult, even with a good map, but they remain resorts dedicated to people who often stay the summer. As Acadia National Park chokes the whole Mount Desert Island region with motor vehicle traffic, the inland resorts in the north woods keep a low profile indeed.

Only people devoted to fly fishing, canoeing, camping, hiking, and other relaxing pursuits in deep forest know much about a vast section of Maine peopled every summer by upper-class families "from away." The sleeping-car service that long ago linked Boston with Minneapolis and St. Paul via the Canadian Pacific also linked the canoe country of Maine with the boundary waters canoeing region of the Upper Peninsula of Michigan, northern Wisconsin, and Minnesota. The Pullman service is long gone, and the tracks to Kennebago are too, but the people who prize their resort areas have kept sprawl at bay in both canoe-focused regions. Just as wealthy, powerful families have kept Washington, D.C., sprawl from swamping Middleburg, Upperville, Warrenton, and other communities along I-66 west of the city, so people who love Kennebago have stopped what most politicians think is unstoppable. When Pullman service to Kineo Station failed, families drove north from Washington, Philadelphia, and New York, and east from Syracuse. Such drives made two-week-long visits rather difficult, but the families asked for neither improved roads nor airline access. Instead they learned how to spend whole summers away.

Such places lay only a little distance from the old Canadian Pacific main-line tracks between Montreal and Halifax that slice east–west across northern Maine. Quebec and New Brunswick lay beyond the Bar Harbor Express, but not beyond the reach of the State of Maine Express. The year-round train connected at Portland with trains bound for New Brunswick and Nova Scotia, and with trains operating to Caribou and Van Buren in far northeast Maine. It crossed tracks with far less elegant Boston & Maine trains like No. 111, which left Boston every morning at 8:30 and arrived at Kennebago eight hours later. No. 111 split in Portland; another part arrived in Rangeley at 5:20 that afternoon. Getting to Kineo Station meant leaving Boston at 1:00 in the morning for a train trip nine hours and forty minutes long. But No. 103 chugged a bit further than Kineo Station in 1929, poking another fifteen minutes through the woods to the Mt. Kineo House, bought in 1911 by the Maine Central Railroad as the way to bring people to Moosehead Lake. Six miles north of the

Canadian Pacific route, Kineo station is barely halfway from the southern border of Maine. North of it lies mostly forest traversed by the Bangor & Aroostook in its long run to Frenchville. And Canada.

Canadians came south on vacation. People from Montreal took Pullmans south to Kennebunkport and Old Orchard Beach in Maine and to Cape Cod. Other Canadians swept south on trains from Quebec and Montreal along the Canadian-owned Central of Vermont, and south through Buffalo. Often, like tens of thousands of Americans, they headed for Florida. In winter the Pullman Company shifted sleepers no longer needed by trains bound for the national parks and the woods of northern Maine, Michigan, and Minnesota to the burgeoning Florida and Cuba markets, and to the steamships leaving New Orleans and Mobile.

The history of Florida as a holiday destination demonstrates the immense power of rail passenger service. The tourist industry boom can be traced back to 1887, when the Atlantic Coast Line Railroad opened the Ponce De Leon Hotel in St. Augustine as a destination for its Florida Special. The Florida East Coast Railway built a line from one Florida island to another until it reached Key West, where it connected with steamships. The combined Havana Special and steamship service offered passengers a forty-four-hour journey from New York to Havana; the Spanish culture, Prohibition-free liquor, and casinos of Cuba attracted thousands of passengers. The fierce competition for speed and luxury of service that developed between the Atlantic Coast Line and the Seaboard Air Line produced both hundred-miles-per-hour trains like the Orange Blossom Special and the Seaboard Florida Limited and a plethora of resort hotels on lines radiating south from Jacksonville.

Travelers wanting to get to a warm climate quickly, enjoy it quickly, and get home again quickly during the busy winter manufacturing and commercial season forced railroads east of the Rockies to create a number of high-speed routes from St. Louis, Omaha, Chicago, Buffalo, and places due north of Florida. Many of the high-speed trains came west across southern Georgia through Bainbridge and Valdosta to Jacksonville. Few snaked along the Florida Panhandle, something that explains why Pensacola, Panama City, and Apala-

Some like it Hot!

101

chicola remain less developed than Miami, Palm Beach, and St. Petersburg. The Florida boom enriched cities such as Atlanta, Memphis, and Nashville, and such smaller cities as Montgomery and Birmingham in Alabama and Evansville in Indiana. The quest for trackage rights to Florida resorts preoccupied many Midwest-based railroads. The Illinois Central viewed the Florida boom as a threat to its Panama Limited–focused territory, and in 1909 bought the Central of Georgia a year after getting rights to a route into Birmingham. Its Seminole train offered year-round sleeping-car service from Chicago to Florida, and during the 1920s land boom it also ran the luxurious Floridian in the winter months. Traveling salesmen and other frequent riders quickly tumbled to the impact of Florida development. In wintertime they saw Pullmans painted for the Bar Harbor Express racing south from Chicago. Cincinnati, long a north–south junction, boomed as the Louisville & Nashville and the Southern rolled trains diagonally across the New York–to–New Orleans routes.

Well into the 1920s, no one would have considered these Florida-bound trains *intercity,* although most terminated in places developers called cities. The trains linked a new sort of resort, mostly hotels and long, sandy beaches, much as others provided service to the western national parks and the deep woods of northern Maine or Minnesota. Business began to slow after the 1920s land bubble burst, and it slowed again into the Depression; but it picked up remarkably in the middle 1930s as more and more Americans, especially retirees, discovered that Florida lay not very far at all from Asheville in North Carolina or Evansville in Indiana, and from hundreds of other small cities and large towns where long-distance luxury trains paused for a minute or so several times daily. Ever so slowly, Florida became the midwinter destination of choice for people who lived as far away as Detroit and St. Louis, but it became easily accessible and very desirable for people who lived much closer.

Until the 1950s, many Americans planned two annual vacations, a short wintertime one to Florida (rather than a longer one beyond New Orleans via ship) and a longer summer one, often to wilderness regions. Not owning a car often meant having the funds for more than one vacation, especially if the vacation destination was a city with superb public transit or a wilderness area in which the presence of automobiles seemed to run counter to the intended and expected experience. Gradually, however, both Florida and Southern California fell victim to sprawl produced first by automobiles, then by coastal international airports that connected domestic flights with overseas ones. But elsewhere, wealthy and powerful people protected the seasonal turf they loved as children. When train travel ended, they improved few existing roads and built even fewer new ones, and they built almost no airports. For four decades after World War II they enjoyed an enviable seclusion for weeks and months at a time in places that rarely advertised to attract newcomers. When sprawl threatened, they quietly embarked on restoring what their parents and grandparents once enjoyed.

Into the 1950s ski trains operated frequently in New England, California, and the Pacific Northwest, as well as within the Rocky Mountains. Railroads provided bar cars and dance cars, and sold tickets that put two people in berths for an extra dime. Usually the rowdiness remained good-natured, and travel to and from ski areas seemed far more entertaining than driving—and sometimes skiing. Especially in New England and in the Rockies, the ski trains offered dependable schedules in bad weather and freedom from automobile trouble. Like many concepts from the halcyon days of railroading and their 1950s afterglow, the details of ski trains and resort trains have faded from national memory. They have not, however, escaped the consideration of the real estate developers. Moving skiers from city to ski resorts via fast trains produces little in the way of negative local impact. The skiers sweep in, ski, spend money, and sweep out, no more bothersome to the local inhabitants than were the tens of thousands of visitors who once detrained at Glacier, Yellowstone, and other national parks in the 1920s. In Maine, especially in northern Maine and along the entire seacoast, the powerful residents see rail passenger travel as the solution to the automobile traffic ruining Acadia, Yosemite, and other national parks. North of Portland, rail passenger service will prevent such traffic from destroying Baxter and other parks.

Elsewhere in wilderness regions, similar ideas are taking hold. Residents of Teton County in Wyoming know the ability of trains to order the flow of tourists into adjacent Yellowstone National Park. In 2004 the Internal Revenue Service ranked the county first in per-capita income nationwide; in 2002 its average adjusted gross household income hit $107,694. Perhaps wealthy people living adjacent to a spectacular and increasingly popular national park envision lifestyle deterioration more clearly than others. In any case, they tend to act when they observe a burgeoning threat. Passenger train service would control the flow of park visitors in ways far more effective than more highways or larger airports. Conversely, the trains would give the privileged park abutters convenient access not just to far-off cities but also to other wilderness enclaves likewise inhabited by the wealthy.

Wilderness is closer to many would-be vacationers than many would-be vacationers think. Muddled now by traffic jams, too-short vacations, cheap airline fares to Orlando but not elsewhere, the hazards of driving all night, unpredictable interim motel availability, and the difficulties of transporting canoes, kayaks, and other wilderness equipment, Americans find it awkward to analyze wilderness-as-resort thinking. But adding hundred-miles-per-hour train travel to the perceptual stew clarifies matters, especially if the long-distance trains serve suburbs and offer comfort along with speed. The train itself would be a resort.

SOURCES: Maiken, *Night Trains;* Marshall, *Santa Fe;* Runte, "Yosemite Valley Railroad"; Shaffer, *See America First.*

THRESHOLD

Exclamation points sometimes punctuate the ends of Amtrak trains. Private cars recall an era when the rich traveled in a style far above first class, and savored travel as leisurely but invigorating progress. Lingering on the threshold between places, they enjoyed the immense private rail yachts that still ply North American railroads. Nowadays the wealthy charter cars for weekend or summer-long jaunts, and lucky clients of corporate owners sweep to the Kentucky Derby or Super Bowl, or to wilderness hunting preserves, atop twelve steel wheels. "Travel as travel was and should be" runs the unassuming advertisement, meaning: double beds, showers, chefs and stewards, and a plate-glass proscenium on the passing scene. In Brunswick green, maroon, royal blue, and sometimes burnished stainless steel, the cars trailing Amtrak trains jar the observer into wondering about travel the day before yesterday.

As World War II neared, heiress Barbara Hutton and actor Cary Grant made love aboard Japauldon. Built in 1926 for F. W. Woolworth, the car served the entire family of the dime-store-chain founder, but perhaps pleased his granddaughter most. When she inherited fifty million dollars in 1933 at the age of twenty-one, newspapers lionized the debutante who knew private cars intimately. Her father, Franklin Hutton, cofounded an investment firm with her uncle E. F. Hutton; together they roamed the country in sumptuous private cars. E. F. Hutton had the car Hussar built in 1922 by American Car & Foundry in St. Charles, Missouri, following his marriage to Marjorie Merriweather Post, heiress to the Post cereals fortune. Hussar transported Post clients in extraordinary style, but more often whisked its owners from New York to a palatial home in Palm Beach, or deep into the Adirondacks to a wilderness retreat at Topridge. In the north woods, beyond the end of the Raquette Lake Railway opened to provide swift access for the Vanderbilt, Durant, Huntington, and other railroad financier families, Topridge included sixty-eight buildings. But none surpassed Japauldon and

Hussar in elegance. Japauldon welded the best design money could buy with a Hollywood flair of which the Hutton and Grant pairing was the perfect emblem.

Today Japauldon rolls out of Atlanta under the name Survivor, elegance available for charter. Eight-five feet long, with a railed observation platform gracing its observation lounge end, the car contains a master bedroom with double bed, a double bedroom with upper and lower berths, a fold-down Murphy bed, a convertible sofa, a marble bathtub with shower, electronic gadgetry galore, and full meal service provided by onboard staff. Paneled entirely in wood and fitted with museum-quality furnishings, Survivor is a palpable ghost of Roaring Twenties luxury. Like hundreds of other private cars swaying at the end of Amtrak trains or rolling in trains of their own, it operates under the public radar.

Other charter cars sleep more people in elegance. Amtrak charges private-car owners roughly ten first-class tickets to move a car from point to point at the end of an Amtrak train; five couples each paying first-class fares plus a bit more thus get private accommodation, fine dining, and a taste of luxury about which most Americans know nothing. More importantly, they get superb on-site accommodation, at the Kentucky Derby, at the end of some wilderness spur track, or far along the Oregon or Maine coast. Union Station in Washington, D.C., maintains a special sidetrack for citizens who arrive aboard their own hotels. Those who still travel in their own cars know what a handful of merely very wealthy people know too: not only do the cars make travel exceedingly pleasant, they become private hotels and offices once they reach their destinations. Chartering a private railroad car mandates an intriguing calibration of first-class fares against five-star hotel fees. Folding hotel and restaurant costs into fare calculations transforms any evaluation of total cost into a window opening on another way of visiting cities, national parks, and small towns.

In the early 1980s a number of newspapers, including the *Wall Street Journal*, wondered at the resurgence of private-car ownership. In a 1984 *Wall Street Journal* article entitled "Expensive Toys," Daniel Machalaba interpreted it as being akin to owning ocean-going yachts or isolated islands. He suggested that individuals and

Private-car opulence endures on private sidetracks and in private warehouses; the opulence speaks of a time when the very wealthy understood luxury travel as private.

firms chartering such cars were merely responding to the renewed glamour of the Orient Express in Europe or simply aping the behavior of Old World aristocracy. But many very rich people had always understood private railroad cars as vehicles that enforced relaxation. Newcomers who bought derelict private cars for as little as five thousand dollars and then spent two hundred thousand more on renovations learned what "old money" had known for generations: private-carriage travel relaxed, refreshed, and somehow encouraged wide-ranging meditation, perhaps on the passing scene as potential real estate development. The sumptuous, eighty-foot cars nurtured the rarest of leisure.

Airlines nearly vanquished such leisure in the 1960s. Business travel became harried, and news media focused on the so-called jet set as the new travel celebrities. Both groups shared the same aircraft with economy-class passengers, and despite VIP lounges and a handful of other airline amenities, egalitarianism and brevity swept away older train and steamship distinctions. Jet airliners deified the two-week vacation. No longer could business travelers justify taking passage to Europe, South America, or Asia aboard a fine ocean liner, or enjoying a fine train across the country. As expense-account thinking transformed media notions of expendable wealth, business travelers lamented increasingly frenetic schedules. Vacationers emulating the jet set accepted the compression of two weeks into twelve days bounded by flying time. Only hippies hitch-hiking across the country experienced traces of the leisure that once rode rails. Everyone else found themselves trapped in the binary prison: drive or fly. Neither driving nor flying proved conducive to the peculiar leisure and opportunity for scenario-analysis thinking that typified the private railcar travel experience.

The rise of automobile ownership became synonymous with "modern times." Just as the jet airliner shattered the dominance of traditional, time-consuming modes of travel, so automobile ownership deflected personal wealth away from other goods and services. Few American adults away from New York, Boston, and other cities boasting good public transportation networks can imagine life without automobile ownership, let alone analyze its costs and benefits. Automobile advertising supports newspapers; perhaps not coincidentally, few journalists investigate the long-term ramifications of seventy-six-month auto loans, insurance premiums elevated by collision and other riders mandated by lien holders, and the depreciation of vehicles no one expects to last a decade. Half-consciously, automobile owners compare the costs of driving five hundred miles against buying an airplane or Amtrak ticket: unless time impinges, they usually drive. After all, whispers the back of the mind, the car is ready. It should be. It is already owned, even if financed. Do high school or college students ponder what they might do with the personal wealth they will lavish on automobiles, insurance, maintenance, excise taxes, and even gasoline? Probably not. Before Henry Ford popularized the horseless carriage, millions of Americans devoted similar attention to horses (which reproduce in ways automobiles do not), carriages, oats, and baled hay, but with a significant difference: any overland trip more than twenty miles involved a train. Period.

Railroad company advertising before about 1920 consequently jars the contemporary reader, and not just because first-class trains appear so luxurious. The passengers seem so *young*. How did thirty-year-old couples afford travel aboard the Santa Fe de-Luxe? Beginning in December 1911, the de-Luxe operated once a week between Chicago and Los Angeles. The train left Chicago every Tuesday evening at 8:00, and arrived the following Friday morning at 9:00; the eastbound de-Luxe left Los Angeles every Tuesday at 6:10 in the evening and arrived Friday morning at 11:10. The company charged a fare premium of twenty-five dollars; it had learned that young people would pay extra for a good time.

Since inaugurating its California Limited in 1892, the Santa Fe had discovered that first-class service involved far more than high speed. A train operating over 2,265-mile route—a longer journey, the company delighted in pointing out, than that of the slower Orient Express—had to function as a resort. As the Limited barreled over the California border, a flower boy presented every woman onboard with a bouquet of roses, lilies, violets, or other in-season blossoms, and gave every male passenger an alligator wallet. But the key to any successful resort lies in its guests, as the Santa Fe well knew. "On a long journey it is pleasant to know that no over-crowding is permitted, and one's traveling companions are of a desirable class," proclaimed one brochure. "Persons you like to meet—successful men of affairs, authors, musicians, journalists, 'globe trotters,' pretty and witty women and happy children—these constitute the patrons of the *California Limited*." Collecting such passengers proved easier than the company imagined, for as word spread, the passengers selected themselves. The Limited came to be known as a stylish train indeed, and not necessarily because of the new Pullmans, dining car, and buffet-smoker. The "traveling companions . . . of a desirable class" were the real draw.

Creating the de-Luxe involved building on the success of the Limited but angling marketing toward younger people, especially those traveling on business but able to pay the surcharge from their own pocket. Many travelers want only comfort, announced a gold-paper, embossed 1913 brochure, dismissing ordinary first-class cuisine and fellow passengers. Others want all the comforts, plus luxuries. "They are in somewhat of a hurry. They like, too, to be a bit exclusive." The Santa Fe understood that speed might yield precedence to luxury and to the right mix of people sharing luxury across a particular region. Anyone needing the fastest Santa Fe train between Los Angeles and Chicago could grab the Fast Mail or the mail trains operated by competing companies. But for those—especially the young—desiring luxury and good company on an excursion through a sun-washed region, the de-Luxe was an obvious choice. In 1913 *fine train* no longer meant the fastest, at least for the sixty people aboard the de-Luxe.

In one full-color illustration after another, the pamphlet depicted luxuries being enjoyed by people in their late twenties and early thirties. The train carried only compartment and drawing-room Pullmans: no one slept in a berth behind curtains. Each bedroom had its own bathroom, most had doors that opened on the others—making possible travel en suite—and the drawing-room units offered both double beds and foldout beds. The club car provided a smoking and reading section for men. Positioned at the head of the train where no women ever needed to walk through it, the male preserve provided a shower and tub bath, a barber and a porter assigned to clothes care, current magazines, stock market and other telegraphed news reports snatched from cranes in front of depots, and a fully stocked buffet. The train carried a manicurist, a maid to help women bathe and dress, and perhaps more importantly, care for young children, who at night slept in the foldout sofa beds provided in bedrooms. A stenographer took dictation of important mail, typing it directly into letter and telegram format; chefs and waiters provided sumptuous meals in the dining car, and passengers congregated in the observation lounge car at the end of the train, served by stewards. If they chose, they sat or stood on the open-air platform and watched spectacular scenery, or they sat inside, enjoying a luxury newer than electric lighting: air specially cooled and cleaned. The pamphlet in the end proved almost unnecessary; word of the train spread everywhere, and young people delighted in riding it. Travel on the de-Luxe meant one had joined the beautiful young people moving across a discrete region toward a modern, sun-kissed location.

Until the end of passenger train travel, Santa Fe premiere service both created and reflected the glamour of Southern California, and especially of Hollywood. The de-Luxe stopped operating in World War I. In 1926 the Santa Fe created the Chief to relieve pressure on the ever-popular California Limited, and in time the premiere train became the Super Chief, a luxury train still associated with Hollywood stars. Throughout the Roaring Twenties the company upgraded the Chief, changing decor in concert with changing trends, installing indirect lighting, and otherwise integrating ultramodern design with very traditional notions of luxury. In the late 1930s the Santa Fe replaced the train with a streamlined one pulled by diesel-electric locomotives that sliced almost sixteen hours from the steam locomotive schedule. Sunlight reflected from its stainless steel exterior nearly blinded New Mexico onlookers. Inside the cars, Ceylonese satinwood, English sycamore, Makassar ebony, and other rare woods veneered surfaces to relieve eyes watching sun-drenched scenery flash past. Most of the cars carried hand-crafted ornamentation made by Navajo and Zuni artists, and turquoise motifs harmonized the decor from car to car. Passengers reveled in the totally designed environment, while farmers, ranchers, and small-town inhabitants saw the speeding silver trains as slivers of Hollywood fantasy, racing at up to 115 miles per hour.

Dining aboard the Super Chief became a national marvel. In 1936 the dinner menu opened with "Romanoff Fresh Malossol Caviar," hearts of California artichokes, and antipasto; proceeded through swordfish steaks, salmon, and several varieties of steak, accompanied by side dishes ranging from fresh corn on the cob to fresh asparagus; and concluded with a variety of American and foreign desserts. Strawberry shortcake coexisted with English Cheshire cheese and a variety of hot drinks. In the depths of the Depression, some passengers were dining well indeed.

Obscurity nowadays masks many American class distinctions. Electronic media constantly extolling equality subtly convey the message that most people are middle-class, and that the poor and the very rich are few and far off. Yet Americans recognize that catastrophic illness and subsequent job loss almost invariably lead to poverty, and many blue-collar families compete against welfare families for housing. Despite the surfeit of advertising to the contrary, the specter of downward mobility shadows much long-term thinking, perhaps especially when stock-market downturns weaken retirement accounts. Dramatic upward mobility, outside of lottery jackpots, seems far less real as a possibility or probability. But most of the time ordinary living confronts Americans with no more evidence of class distinction than a Jaguar caught in a traffic jam next to a Ford.

The Super Chief, on the other hand, offered a blatant display of class entitlement. Its Depression-era dining car menus surpassed all but a few fine restaurants, and those mostly in New York City. Cuisine historians unravel their significance only with difficulty. The Santa Fe served better meals en route aboard the Super Chief than passengers could obtain anywhere else between Chicago and Los Angeles.

But the Super Chief carried no private cars. The ultrarich attached their cars to lesser trains. The Super Chief served a segment of the population nowadays very difficult to define—Broadway and Hollywood stars, radio celebrities, and political figures—mixing them for days and nights with wealthy people also still hard to characterize. Some of the other travelers merely wanted extremely pleasant carriage over two thousand miles. Others specifically sought casual or intimate contact with the famous, the rich, and people on their way to fame and wealth. In the dining car the chief steward distributed guests among the tables, sometimes precipitating good conversation, short- and long-term love affairs, enduring friendship and business relationships, and quarrels. People mixed beyond the dining cars: in lounges over drinks, in observation cars before plate glass, in barbershops, and—after the war, when the Santa Fe replaced the trains with newer, more sumptuous ones—in second-story, glass-roofed dome cars. They had time to get to know one other.

A great many Depression-era Americans had time on their hands, but comparatively few had time and money both. In the great run-up to the 1929 stock market crash, radio frequently reminded listeners that time is money. But as Douglas Rushkoff points out in *Coercion: Why We Listen to What "They" Say*, Americans unwittingly turning to media as children turn to parents soon stopped think-ing logically. If time is money, then money must be time. But can money buy time? Or can money perhaps only carve one type of time from another?

Nothing offers a better portal on changes in American leisure than the marketing of Santa Fe premiere trains between 1900 and 1971. When Amtrak took over most of national long-distance pas-senger train service it confronted vexing issues of class. Should a democratic government provide passenger rail service in multiple classes? Should the taxpayer subsidize caviar and strawberry short-cake? Would Americans mind not having a shower before bed, or in the morning before breakfast? Avoiding and answering such ques-tions consumed thirty years, but the Santa Fe and other companies knew the answers decades earlier.

Ostensibly, exclusivity and ostentation belong nowhere in the Republic. Exclusive suburbs, country and yacht clubs, and universi-ties by definition exclude, sometimes by race or gender or standard-ized test scores, but far more frequently by class divisions media ignore. Ostentation belongs nowhere in a nation founded on equal-ity, but ostentation drives the entire entertainment industry. Airline travelers sometimes dismiss the great center of the nation as *flyover land*. Immense jets land at St. Louis and Denver, but to many coastal residents, only the coasts matter. In the sparsely populated central states, especially on the High Plains, airliners move so far aloft that no one sees or hears them. But the de-Luxe and the Super Chief moved in plain view, at high speed but almost within touch. At a lonely Kansas or Arizona grade crossing a boy or girl might look up at the silver blur and see Kirk Douglas, Katherine Hepburn, or Marilyn Monroe gazing back.

Once the media created celebrities—the evanescent cohort of people gathered from the stage and cinema, music, fashion mod-eling, and a variety of subsidiary industries—the traditional rich slipped into a most comfortable obscurity. In the 1970s, when bur-glars discovered their usefulness, even local newspapers stopped publishing the social notes that informed readers of local luminar-ies traveling away from home. Birth and anniversary notices dis-appeared, engagement and wedding announcements appear only in abbreviated format on Saturdays, and obituaries alone memorialize an earlier era focused on people who now never appear in the entertainment pages. Children who somehow elude the grasp of television find almost nothing in print media about the people earlier generations expected to read about daily. The rise of the corporate executive made possible the summer-long vacations by business owners who took the Bar Harbor Express with their families and disappeared for months. Similarly, the rise of the celebrity has made possible the near-perfect disappearance from public view of wealthy people who value leisure and privacy.

Long-distance luxury train travel enforced a state of being utterly different from the so-called *dead time* all but novice air travelers experience. Time aboard the de-Luxe, Chief, and Super Chief moved differently than time aboard lesser trains and—beyond the plate-glass windows—in small towns, great cities, and mountain chasms. In the Roaring Twenties, the heyday of private railroad cars, the rich reveled in downtime only scarcely more luxurious than that others enjoyed aboard luxury trains. For that matter, even schoolchildren reveled in comfort, if not luxury, aboard trains nearly as sumptuous as the de-Luxe.

But those children were preppies. Their existence haunts Fitzgerald's 1925 novel *The Great Gatsby* in ways that give public high school teachers fits: the fictional characters strike contemporary high school students as preternaturally mature. "One of my most vivid memories is of coming back West from prep school and later from college at Christmas time," the narrator recalls, remembering Union Station in Chicago at six in the evening, when "the murky yellow cars of the Chicago, Milwaukee, and St. Paul railroad looking cheerful as Christmas itself on the tracks beside the gate." Unlike the chaperoned children riding trains between East Coast cities and the camps of northern New England, the prep school students rode as adults. Twelve years and older, they rode to and from New England with élan. In those days, children traveled alone and luxuriously, aboard the Pioneer Limited at Christmastime.

The Pioneer Limited north from Chicago has remained Train No. 1 in the memories of many who rode it or saw it flash past as a flagship train of the Milwaukee Road. Leaving Union Station at 6:30

for Minneapolis, it paused at Milwaukee and thereafter only at Red Wing and a handful of other towns. Through what *Gatsby*'s narrator calls "the lost Swede towns" the train raced without stopping, its sleeping-car shades drawn as its passengers slept. Thirteen hours later, its passengers having breakfasted aboard or slept in, it reached Minneapolis.

As early as 1898, when the Milwaukee Road took delivery of new equipment for its new train, local and trade-industry journalists marveled at the experience of traveling in luxury. Interior decor harmonized from car to car in ways one writer decided had never been experienced by many passengers. Women preferred to visit in each others' compartments, but men often chose to gather in the lounge to read, enjoy a smoke and a drink, and sometimes the company of royalty. In 1902 Prince Henry of Prussia took passage aboard one section of the Pioneer Limited, by that time illuminated with electric lights seldom seen outside great cities. Competition forced the Milwaukee Road to constantly upgrade the train: seven trains left Chicago around dinnertime for Minneapolis. The Milwaukee did well in the battle for passenger goodwill by offering convenience, speed, and luxury. By 1914 the Pioneer Limited left Chicago most evenings with fourteen Pullmans, a lounge car, and a dining car.

Five other railroads offered service between Chicago and the Twin Cities. The Soo operated the Twin City–Chicago Milwaukee Express; the Minneapolis & St. Louis–Illinois Central ran the Twin Cities–Chicago Limited, and the Chicago Great Western provided its Great Western Limited. The trains paced the North Western Limited and the Burlington's Minnesota Limited. Overnight travel between Chicago and the Twin Cities proved so heavy and constant that many of the trains operated in multiple sections. The first section of the Pioneer, carrying mail cars, baggage cars, and coaches, departed five minutes ahead of the second, which carried luxury cars only.

Sleeping cars like the Oconomowoc, fitted with three drawing rooms and six compartments that could be connected privately for large families and "parties of friends," made some travelers choose the Pioneer. Minor amenities such as electric clocks, fans, and bedroom doorbells enhanced the deep, genuine luxury of beds, sofas, and private baths. Lone passengers, especially tall men, enjoyed the single rooms and private baths of another car, the Minnehaha, which provided beds six and a half feet long with deep box springs, thick mattresses, and silk spreads. The Minnehaha included an observation lounge with outdoor platform (for viewing the 140 miles of Mississippi River summer travelers enjoyed seeing before or after dinner), writing desks, and an enclosed, intimate women's lounge. For passengers not so interested in the passing scene, club cars like the Chicago, described by Arthur Dubin in *Some Classic Trains,* featured deep, leather-upholstered chairs for thirty-two people, a bookcase of novels and nonfiction facing its "library" section, writing desks, and a "lounging room beyond the buffet from which a steward served snacks and drinks." In the so-called public cars friends and regular travelers gathered, and strangers met other strangers. To encourage such encounters, designers made all furniture except sofas movable; stewards arranged chairs in clusters as groups formed, and separated them as people drifted off to bedrooms or to the dining car.

Food service meant food both extravagant and simple, as well as extraordinary personal service. In 1927 the Milwaukee named a new dining car Dan Healey, in honor of a longtime dining car steward who had died a year earlier. Healey had become an institution in himself, not only for serving nine presidents of the United States but also for remembering the tastes of regular passengers and providing free food to passengers whose taste he deemed needed broadening to include game, European delicacies, and regional fish. Healey and the Milwaukee Road prided themselves on meals besting any served in Chicago restaurants and hotels, but only by providing free side dishes could they convince many serious-minded travelers to experiment. Healey probably knew that many travelers confronted his menus with awe and chose the simplest entrees to be safe. His courtly service put everyone at ease, and his offering for free what he was sure passengers would like in addition to what they had ordered reshaped the palate of many travelers forever. Great Northern stewards and waiters were famous for introducing passengers to potatoes cooked in myriad ways, but Healey and his counterparts and staff focused on a wider range of dinner cuisine—served at ninety miles an hour.

Sleeping-car porters focused on everything else. In ordinary Pullman cars they made up the berths that folded out and up and down from large seats, hung the curtains that provided privacy, and during the night attended to passengers' wants, beginning with shining shoes. On luxury trains they turned down beds, brought food and drink from kitchens to passengers wanting privacy, and performed a thousand other services, from dispatching telegrams to bringing aboard flowers deposited at stations by florists following long-distance instructions. They watched over children and teenagers traveling alone, and often they looked the other away as participants in lounge-car romance strolled back to sleeping cars.

Until well after World War II, luxury train travel continued to advertise stark class division. In 1948 the Milwaukee Road replaced its earlier Pioneers with streamlined, all-room sleeping cars and diners, and into the 1960s the ever-faster train remained profitable. Travelers paid for luxury despite options of fine motorcars and highways and despite far faster airline service. But from the Depression era onward, luxury became increasingly difficult to advertise.

In the 1950s railroads discovered that luxury trains swept through a darkening tunnel of dislike. Motorists delighted with new Oldsmobiles or Lincolns refused to compare apples with oranges, and instead glowered at the streamlined trains racing past. In the postwar years when a new car and a small house on a small lot became what advertisers called "the American dream," the luxury train slithering through the distance smacked of old-money elitism, mass-marketing trickery, or both.

Racy pulp novels like Frederic Wakeman's 1955 *The Fabulous Train* slyly shifted settings backward into the 1930s. Hal, an underemployed college graduate in a Kansas small town, grows desperate to find a good job or enter graduate school. Selling Fords proves almost impossible in the Dust Bowl region, and local women seem less than glamorous. "Ph.D. or Rhoda?" Hal wonders as he waits for customers at the quiescent dealership. Then one day the Santa Fe Chief makes an emergency stop in a town through which it ordinarily passes at more than a hundred miles an hour. While its engine

crew works feverishly to repair the locomotive, the passengers detrain to walk along the platform in blistering heat. "There ain't one
chair car on her. You either treat yourself to a Pullman or you stay
home. And honest to God, two dining cars. And wait'll you see the
observation car, where they serve drinks and play cards," a friend
bursts in to tell Hal. "And the babes. Hal, there's one blonde walkin'
up and down the platform, you can see all the way down to her
belly button." The young men drift down to the dusty depot, stare
at the passengers, and then, ashamed of their own desperate curiosity, look in the windows at immaculate tables, roses in bud vases,
and food they learn is "black bass and cantaloupe sherbert," the rarest, juiciest steaks, "exotic French sauces composed of mushrooms
and herbs and butter and divers unpronounceable ingredients," and
bowls of black Spanish olives and red raspberries resting on beds of
cracked ice set in crystal bowls. Hal and his friends, all college educated and all unemployed or underemployed in a dusty town, gape
at "the cargo of exotic humanity."

After the Chief departs, Hal slips into a depression that deep-
ens by the hour, until the following afternoon he considers fling-
ing himself under the westbound Chief. He jumps sideways at the
last minute and gazes with longing at a little girl, watched over by
a nanny, playing with long paper streamers on the observation car
platform. The little girl waves and Hal determines to try his for-
tunes away from his dusty little town and brand-new Ford automobiles. No automobile will ever match the luxury of the Pullmans.

Like many other authors of 1950s racy fiction, Frederic Wakeman left the advertising industry but never forgot what he learned.
The Fabulous Train focuses on the abyss between ordinary people
like Hal and the people aboard luxury trains. It also emphasizes the
staggering power of the close-up view. So long as it speeds through
town at a hundred miles an hour, the Chief is scarcely real to onlookers. But when it stops, the whole town seems more grittier than
ever by comparison. Everything, even V-8 showroom Fords and
pretty girls, fades before the exotics strolling the platform and enjoying themselves in air-conditioned luxury. Advertising, Wakeman
knew, might make a Ford desirable, but not if the Chief paused

across from the showroom. The stopped train offered a vision more powerful than television.

Four years later Alfred Hitchcock released his box-office hit *North by Northwest*. Nowadays the thriller disturbs undergraduates who view it in film study courses or film festivals, even if they already know it in video format. Cary Grant and Eva Marie Saint still shock the sensibilities of young people. Their affair begins as effortlessly as the streamlined Twentieth Century Limited laps the miles from New York to Chicago. Close examination reveals that censors made Hitchcock dub lines: Eva Marie Saint is clearly telling Grant that she never makes love on an empty stomach, but the voice-over substitutes "discuss" for "make." Who is this confident, sexually free woman aboard the pre–feminist era luxury train? Why does Grant play an advertising man versed in "expedient exaggeration" but never lying? Such questions nag young viewers if they struggle past their awe at the set. Many do not. Too much happens in Room E, Car 3901.

Refitted in 1948 with lightweight cars that retained the splendor of past incarnations, the 1950s Century operated with all the luxuries serious travelers expected and many more. A train secretary, shower, lounge with bar, and other amenities remained after 1948, but radiotelephones, fluorescent lights, and automatic, push-button doors emphasized modernity. Nevertheless, luxury sixteen-hour overnight service between New York and Chicago, even when timed to connect with the Santa Fe Super Chief, no longer appealed as it had in the 1920s, when the Twentieth Century Limited often operated in seven sections chasing other named trains on the same route and preceding many more. As *North by Northwest* opened, the New York Central took the astonishing step of adding coaches to its finest train: the style Hitchcock depicted had begun to fade.

But neither automobiles operating on interstate highways nor competition from airlines instigated the decline of United States luxury trains. Instead, the culprit was the electronic media, especially television. Railroads and government regulatory industries kept long-distance passenger train service operating, but luxuries disappeared. First the barbers and valets vanished, then the ladies' maids, then whole varieties of cars. Tracing the disposal of luxury cars demonstrates that by 1960 luxury cars were migrating from railroads operating in television-rich regions to railroads operating in regions still lacking stations and reception. Millions of Americans stayed home and stared at screens, rather than experiencing glamour, adventure, and the exotics Wakeman described aboard the Super Chief. The New York Central sold Lake Shore and Atlantic Shore lounge cars from its Century to the Rock Island in 1959. No longer could the Central justify barbers and showers and lounges with bars in its premiere train, but the Rock Island running southwest from Chicago to Tucumcari, New Mexico, determined that it might. Television glamour had not yet spoiled the little Kansas towns of *The Fabulous Train* for enjoying luxury train travel. Where television came late, Americans continued to actively enjoy experiences; but eventually they too became passive, sofa-sitting watchers of the blue-light screen.

Television advertising began to subtly shift national priorities in the 1950s. Television skewed not just wants and values but the ability to analyze worldviews objectively. Network television lured more and more Hollywood cinematographers into making television shows: for two decades studios wondered whether movie-going would collapse as quickly as had luxury and long-distance train travel. Local cinemas survived the television onslaught only by shrinking seats and cutting amenities.

The television-Hollywood alliance quickly became a New York–Los Angeles one that stressed and then destroyed older regional ties, especially the north–south advertising link between Dallas and Chicago. Through the 1950s into the early 1960s, sunbathing women readers of racy novels like Wakeman's often wore risqué bikinis designed in Texas and marketed throughout a region reaching north to Chicago. Texas ranching and oil wealth produced self-confident, wealthy people who looked north to Chicago and Canada for recreation and business connections, and to Mexico and the Caribbean for fashion. But such older cultural axes collapsed in the face of New York–based network television news, entertainment, and advertising. Television extolled itself as travel while unconsciously defining real-world travel as short-distance, short-time effort. As media moguls based in New York and Los Angeles worked to ever tighter schedules and accepted transcontinental flying by necessity, television ignored situations it could not penetrate, luxury trains included. The makers of fast-paced television programming succumbed to a fast-paced, homogenized lifestyle that television glorified. Railroads lost not merely passengers devoted to regional style and even regional cuisine but also people who savored time, thought, relaxation, and a few hours or days swathed in luxury.

By the late 1960s America had become home to a vast middle-class peasantry easily led by advertisers. When the peasantry traveled, on business or pleasure, it often drove, using its own labor. If middle-class Americans flew, they carried their own luggage and accepted plastic tableware and microwaved meals, then sandwiches, then finally only snacks. And they hurried, always they hurried. Sometimes they hurried to Rocky Mountain ski resorts and other glamorous places developed with airline industry help, just as they hurried between hotels, and at the end of day stared at the same television shows they watched at home or in the motels at which they paused their cars. In 1970 Reuben Gronau reported in *The Value of Time in Passenger Transportation: The Demand for Air Travel,* that an entire population had learned to value speed of travel over all other considerations.

Advertising supporting the fast-paced programming of television in time made Americans want to speed through their business and pleasure travel alike, especially over long distances. Advertising encouraged Americans, via expedient exaggeration, to spend the time they supposedly saved watching more television, and more advertising. As Douglas Rushkoff explains in *Coercion,* millions of Americans now watch television in the evenings because they work such long hours in such high-stress environments that they are too weary to do anything else. For them, television is a window on glitz if not glamour. Never does the window open on how the rich and powerful really live at home, or how they vacation and travel.

Wakeman's *The Fabulous Train* still resonates today, for all that its raciness now seems tame. Wakeman knew that in tiny plains towns, the mid-1950s did not differ all that much from the mid-1930s. The Chief might still make an unscheduled stop and thrust exoticism onto Main Street; the Ford still had a V-8. By 1980 the Chief was gone, and nowadays small-town people have only televised images of glitz to replace the train's vanished glamour.

Nevertheless, they might watch the rails. Private cars still trail Amtrak trains and sometimes even freight trains. Some people still appreciate the leisurely mode of travel and understand the benefits of having time to think, to get to know business colleagues or would-be lovers—even to see the country. Few observers seem to really *see* Amtrak trains: to notice the private cars at their ends, off-limits to Amtrak passengers. But sometimes the people inside these private cars are looking over a region, often over a period of several days: contemplating how to change it to fit their personal interests, whether that means preserving it from sprawl or limiting access by common, automobile-driving tourists. Along tracks winding through scenic regions, rare observers understand that private-car occupants may want to know how the region looks from the rails, not from local roads.

As of old, private cars and luxury trains still offer the chance for prolonged interaction among like-minded groups and strangers. Americans no longer realize the energizing impact of prolonged chance encounters simply because they rarely enjoy them. The upper classes maintain exclusivity at yacht and country clubs, at private urban clubs, at hunting and fishing camps, and now and then ordinary middle-class Americans learn of these redoubts. But as anyone onboard Amtrak Acela trains may observe, people in first class seem to introduce themselves easily and to fall into conversation. Such encounters happen in first-class sections during international flights, of course, but even large aircraft offer little room for physical movement, and the noise of their engines is not conducive to conversation. The ordering of railroad space is subtly different, perhaps because it exists within a more measured temporal framework and offers a window on the passing scene. Just as ordinary commuter trains produce a relaxed camaraderie over years that helps individuals find new jobs, secure capital, sell houses, and so on, so the luxury train operating not just between cities but between cities, small towns, and wilderness resorts will provide something special for which some people already pay handsomely.

Will provide. Exclusive trains, if not exactly luxury ones, already roll. Acela offers an intellectual feast to any sociology-minded passenger, especially in first class. The train is relatively expensive to ride and its food service exorbitant, for all that the food tends to be good. When the train is not full, business-class passengers drawn to each other by visual cues—similar books, Blackberries or other wireless devices, even upscale shopping bags or European newspapers—often strike up conversations; they may change seats or walk to the snack car together for muffins or sandwiches or wine. The alert eavesdropper discovers that seat changes often lead to the exchange of telephone numbers or business cards. Certain recurrent phrases float through conversations, usually relating to the decided superiority of Acela trains over ordinary Amtrak ones or the freedoms offered by unassigned seats. Strangers remark to one another how discerning Acela passengers are, something that matters more and more as the sun goes down and windows become mirrors that reveal much about what money buys. Perhaps making connections among like-minded others matters a great deal to passengers in their twenties, not only in terms of career or business but socially. Acela rolls like a private club, its tickets the price of entry, and hosts a definable cohort of well-dressed, upwardly mobile men and women in their late twenties. Often they and other passengers voice their fervent wish that Acela operated on other routes as well: to Hyannis on Cape Cod, north to Portland, or southwest to Charlottesville or Williamsburg in Virginia, deep into the North Carolina mountains, or far into the Adirondack Park in upstate New York.

Acela service amply rewards close scrutiny. In the final analysis the trains move only marginally faster than the Metroliners the Penn Central Railroad operated between New York and Washington in the early 1970s. Only near Mansfield in Massachusetts and in western Rhode Island do the Acela trains reach 145 miles per hour; elsewhere they travel at little more than 110 miles per hour, just as the Super Chief and so many other trains did circa 1950. What proves intriguing about Acela has little to do with speed, but with exclusivity and frequency welded to comfort if not to luxury. Most Amtrak cars feature tiny windows and other airliner-like characteristics because 1980s industrial designers intended that trains resemble aircraft. Designers abandoned such thinking when they created Acela: the giant windows, the plate-glass partitions between cars, the wide seats and comfortable footrests, and other amenities immediately make passengers aware that the high-speed trains define a change.

Acela service is not Metroliner service extended beneath catenary to Boston. It is the first evidence that wealthy people might be willing to abandon both automobiles and airliners for high-speed travel over distances between about four hundred and five hundred miles, especially between suburbs, the precise distance Gronau discerned in 1970 as critical in air-travel marketing. Such people will not ride in ordinary trains moving at 125 miles per hour, but will nevertheless be drawn to amenities eerily reminiscent of those boasted by early 1950s streamliners, themselves based on upscale Depression-era trains. The large windows, indirect lighting, and extremely wide seats with generous leg room strike the young as a vast improvement over both ordinary airliners and Amfleet passenger cars. Design historians—and the elderly—recognize these features as 1950s retro despite the electric outlets installed for laptop computers. As metropolitan highways clog, and shuttle-service airline passengers complain about bus-service-in-the-sky inconvenience and rudeness from airline employees and Transportation Security Administration guards alike, marketing firms focus on people who *will pay extra* for short-distance rail services prototyped by Acela. Marketing research shaped the design of Acela equipment, right down to the extension of electrification from New Haven to Boston. Articles in the *Journal of Travel Research* and other periodicals emphasize the growing attraction of amenities other than speed. The attractiveness of rail-based comfort and luxury may chill both automobile manufacturers and airline-industry management: automobiles can scarcely cruise at 110 miles per hour, and airplanes, especially small commuter-type aircraft, can offer no luxuries at all.

Having separated their vacation regions from ordinary places, the rich now savor the exclusivity of some trains and begin to taste other advantages implicit in high-speed, extrafare, relaxing railroad travel. The widening gap between rich and poor in the United States is rapidly becoming a chasm, but most middle-income people prefer to ignore it, believing themselves established on the affluent side

of the divide. They seldom question why the United States government directs Transportation Security Administration officers to
move first-class airline passengers to the head of security lines, past
hundreds of ordinary passengers who pay taxes too. Such favoritism allows the rich to arrive just before flights, rather than two or
more hours early, and at busy airports now congests security operations. But airline coach passengers stand mute, defeated by wealth.
On toll highways in New York, Massachusetts, and elsewhere, most
motorists wait in long lines to pay tolls, while the more affluent use
electronic devices to pay as they speed through reserved lanes. The
rich have satellite phones, middle-income people have cell phones,
and the poor discover almost no public telephones anywhere, even
in cities. Just as Wal-Mart squeezes out stores catering to moder-
ate-income people, leaving behind abandoned main streets and the
empty boxes of its bankrupt competitors, while very profitable, upscale niche retailers prosper in wealthy communities, just as prices
for ordinary single-family houses force more and more middle-income families into buying far out into exurban hinterlands, so Acela
demonstrates that the rich and the expense-account-equipped business traveler have shoved Amtrak toward elite service.

Acela links places owned or visited by the rich and, through the
Downeasters and other ordinary Amtrak trains, connects the rich
with exclusive resort areas. Acela makes real estate developers wonder about high-speed, very comfortable, quite expensive trains operating to the Hamptons on Long Island and to dozens of other
wealthy enclaves, even to the Maine coast, exactly as many Acela
riders envision. State economic development officials admit, often
on Web sites such as those devoted to the Downeasters, that real
estate developers and passengers have begun to produce a revolution of rising expectations. Acela prompts scenario analysts, especially those retained by the California High-Speed Rail Authority,
to imagine regional commuter rail transit authorities beginning
to operate express, extrafare trains, and to rummage through old
documents about the parlor cars once attached to Long Island Rail
Road expresses. Railroad companies and taxpayers will upgrade
existing rail lines and reopen abandoned ones, at first for regular
freight and seventy-nine-miles-per-hour passenger service. Then—

and only then—will the first-class trains appear, deluxe in every-thing but name. The attack on Amtrak must always be understood in part as an attack by people committed to improving rail service regionally, not nationally. State and regional rail transit authorities might be cozened into using taxpayer dollars to restore rail routes of particular interest to the wealthy—and to those who intend to develop real estate for the small but growing number of young peo-ple becoming wealthy and wanting something other than televised glamour. *Building a High-Speed Train System for California*, a 2000 report by the California High-Speed Rail Authority, makes it clear that the envisioned ridership differs from that riding urban mass transit.

Interested observers in Vermont, New Hampshire, New York, and California have already realized this and have begun to map the old routes they want to restore for electrified service. Soon their counterparts in other states will discover that on the east and west coasts the rich have already begun abandoning highway travel for Acela and other fast trains. Perhaps the California High-Speed Rail Authority plans are the furthest developed of any state or regional entity, but the triumph of Acela and the documented successes of older luxury trains now come together in tightly argued scenarios. Clogged highways, straitened airline service, and an economic di-vide combine to make fast, luxurious trains something well-to-do people begin to desire.

SOURCES: W. J. Black, *Santa Fe de-Luxe;* California High-Speed Rail Authority, *Building a High-Speed Train System;* Dubin, *Some Classic Trains;* Gronau, *The Value of Time;* Machalaba, "Expensive Toys"; Morgan, "Ninety Miles an Hour Aboard a 4-6-4"; Rushkoff, *Coercion;* Wakeman, *The Fabulous Train.*

EXPRESS

At first a far-off speck of light, then a dark mass surrounding a probing headlight, the train hurtles along the main line toward the small-town depot. Its whistle begins wailing far off, warning that the train will not stop. The post office employee hurries back from one end of the platform, glancing over his shoulder at the small crane from which he has just suspended a large, rugged pouch. He makes sure no bystanders linger on the far end of the platform. The whistle wails, and wails again. Slowing only slightly, the gigantic steam locomotive slams past, and from a specially built railcar behind it, action blurs.

For a moment a man stands framed in a open doorway, a holstered revolver strapped to his waist. Then he heaves out a pouch identical to the one suspended from the arms of the crane. With a single fluid motion he swings up a great curved hook rotating on hinges. As one mail pouch slides along the platform the hook grabs the mail pouch from the crane, and the postal transportation clerk yanks it inside the car as the door rolls shut. It is 1891 or 1928 or even 1951, and this is how first-class mail moves. Swiftly.

Inside the car designated a railway post office, one or more of the thirty thousand railway mail clerks employed by the United States Post Office (now the Postal Service) in 1951 opens the collected pouch and begins sorting its contents, along with through mail from distant places and letters picked up a few miles back. As the train surges on, its engine men concerned only with safety and speed rather than passenger comfort, the mail clerks deftly sort the letters into pigeonholes, then grab and band letters for the next town ahead and stuff them into another pouch. The whistle screams its warning and alerts the mail clerks. The door slides open once again, the clerk leans outward against the safety bar and hook, and launches another pouch into small-town America as the great hook flings another inboard from another mail crane.

In West Texas and Kansas, in 1935, postal patrons expected rapid,

Restored small-town depots across the United States showcase the special doors and platform package wagons integral to express service.

acutely timed delivery of first-class mail. Unlike the local freight and passenger trains that stopped at every tiny town and water tank, unlike even the fast through freights and the long-distance luxury limiteds that usually paused only in large cities, the train most railroad companies and onlookers nicknamed the Fast Mail or the Mail and Express rarely stopped. Many rural dwellers never saw it stopped, or even slowing. The mail clerks aboard it sorted mail as it raced along, and Americans valued the regular, high-speed mail service it provided. Beyond that, it was usually a headlight, a passing roar, and a pair of red markers disappearing in the distance, and perhaps a whiff of coal smoke in the air.

In the depths of the Depression the fast trains demonstrated not only an efficiency that stimulated economic recovery but a nationwide evenhandedness. Across the High Plains, in Midwest farm country, in the timberlands of the Pacific Northwest and the Deep South, in the north of New England, small-town people appreciated the local significance of the mail trains linking great cities and tiny hamlets. The post office hurried for everyone, not just for the citizens of bustling cities.

When a letter positively, absolutely had to be delivered *the same day* up or down the line, it behooved farmers, storekeepers, and perhaps especially lovers to get that letter into the pouch to be hand carried by a local postmaster or other postal employee to the depot mail crane for pickup. Illuminated at night by kerosene lanterns or electric lights, mail cranes derived from the wedding of post office standards with manufacturing innovation. No amount of tinkering solved some problems caused by letters snatched from a standstill at sixty miles per hour or more (coins inside envelopes tended to break free), but the cranes made extremely fast service possible.

Not every letter arrived a few hours later in another small town further down the line. Many traveled across the continent, and many arrived in small towns aboard other mail trains. But always the United States Post Office emphasized the speed of the mail train. In the side of every railway post office car it placed an ordinary mail slot, so that anyone might post a letter directly into the rolling post office momentarily paused at a depot platform. Enthralled children watched as Railway Mail Service employees jumped down from

some cars attached to passenger trains, dashed across depot platforms and emptied mail from mailboxes, then rushed back to the
post office supplementing the one ensconced in a building a block
or so away. The railway post office car attached to so many mail
trains provided fast service, but as part of high-speed-mail-and-
express-only trains it provided something verging on magic.

Operating as scheduled trains, usually behind high-speed passenger train locomotives and equipped with cars that resembled
passenger coaches, mail trains rolled in quasi obscurity. Postal regulations forbade any railroad employee other than train conductors
to enter mail cars, so brakemen and other train crew rode in lone
coaches attached to the ends of most mail trains. Some railroads
sold tickets to passengers in desperate need of quick if uncomfort-
able passage, but rarely mentioned the service in public timetables.
Jolted and vibrated in a day coach lurching at the end of a mail
train offered discomfort to be endured only in an emergency, but it
introduced a few business travelers to a transport velocity that as-
tonished riders of so-called express passenger trains that operated
swiftly and comfortably.

Most important, it suggested to some urban businessmen what
observant small-town residents knew. The Fast Mail and Express
had vague but powerful implications for business development far
from great cities. Its railway post offices and privately operated Railway Express Agency cars carried the potential for ribbons of industrial, commercial, and residential development.

One of the best-kept secrets in both the history of United States
industrialization and in the present reorientation of United States
real estate development, the smooth functioning of the Railway Mail
Service and Railway Express Agency remains obscured by a byzantine mass of maps, schedules, and directives. Almost all the records
of the Railway Express Agency, a continent-spanning company offering international service as well, vanished with its bankruptcy
in 1975. Teasing out the ordinary activity of the Railway Mail Service and the Railway Express Agency proves maddening, until one
applies computer software that integrates train movement, timing,
and routing with geographic information systems analysis. Then
from the detritus of government record keeping and fragments of

Express Agency records emerges what a number of interest groups understood, however vaguely, in the 1950s, as they lobbied Congress to emphasize highway- and airline-based mail and express shipment. In a way calculated to inflate urban and suburban real estate values and decrease the value of property in small cities, towns, and rural hamlets, special-interest groups championing what became the 1958 Transportation Act derailed the Fast Mail and Express.

Whatever its weaknesses, the century-old Railway Mail Service did much to equalize postal service across regions and stimulate economic development in and between large cities. Its activities grew more and more complex as public expectation of improvement increased. For as long as it moved mostly first-class and bulk mail, especially catalogs and newspapers, it worked extremely well. Only when Congress began nudging it to compete against privately owned express companies in the 1930s did it begin to falter. Railway Express moved even refrigerated packages with aplomb; the post office found moving packages slowed the movement of first-class mail. Parcel-post service led to other service delays, then crisis in the 1960s as the post office, operating its service at a loss, ruined the Railway Express Agency, whose cars helped subsidized the mail trains. Suddenly postal patrons demanded that the government provide package express service equivalent to the vanished Railway Express Agency standard. The post office failed.

Until the first years of the twentieth century, the post office required most rural and small-town residents to pick up mail at local post offices. Only in large cities did letter carriers bring mail to street addresses, a service expedited by Railway Mail Service clerks who sorted urban mail. Although the advent of rural free delivery slowly changed behavior nationwide after 1900, until then many Americans drifted toward downtown—or to a quiet crossroads—first thing in the morning, or soon after the mail train roared through. Businessmen checked their boxes daily, and even more frequently in towns served by several mail trains. Farm families and others living farther from town might check their post office boxes much less frequently, often only on Saturdays. Analyzing such behavior, one can understand how the mail train and post office collaborated to energize small towns. When people came to the hamlet or town or small-city center to check for letters and newspapers (the post office moved no packages), they also visited with each other, shopped, and transacted business in banks and elsewhere.

Railroad depots proved an important "elsewhere," since every depot housed an office of a private express company that handled parcels, crates, and almost any other object requiring time-sensitive shipping. Express companies, amalgamated in 1929 into the Railway Express Agency, offered pick-up and delivery services to street addresses and farms, but many Americans preferred to save local charges and visit the depots themselves. Even after 1912, when the post office launched its parcel-post service (which delivered small boxes along with envelope mail to businesses, homes, and farms), millions of Americans organized their personal and business activities around the schedule of the local Fast Mail and Express. Patterns of industrial, commercial, and office enterprise, including real estate investment, developed in the matrix of the ten thousand mail and express trains.

Federal favoritism ruined the symbiotic mail-express relationship immediately after World War II. As taxpayer dollars subsidized the carriage of parcels below the rates charged by the Railway Express Agency, and far below the actual cost to the post office, more and more shipments moved from express to mail cars. Between January 1949 and December 1950, Railway Express lost about eighty million shipments to the post office, which in 1949 admitted that parcel post operated at an annual deficit of $104 million and that the deficit grew worse each year. Post office employment burgeoned, absorbing many former GIs, but customers found themselves less and less able to ship large or odd-shaped packages, let alone livestock, canoes, and furniture. The post office limited the size and weight of parcels, but federal regulation required Railway Express to accept any item for shipment, even giraffes, as Klink Garrett, a former senior executive, details in *Ten Turtles to Tucumcari: A Personal History of the Railway Express Agency.* As Railway Express lost its most profitable items to the post office by the millions, its employees found themselves handling only objects—including explosive and flammable ones—the post office refused.

The Transportation Act of 1958 strangled the still-healthy long-distance business and real estate development channeled along the routes of mail and express trains. By pouring federal dollars, directly and via subsidy, into the airline and trucking industries, the act shifted taxpayer investment into the handful of metropolitan regions boasting large airports. Forcing the post office to fly more and more first-class mail along with premium air mail eroded the flow of mail via train, something that isolated millions of Americans—and especially businessmen—in what had been "well-connected" towns and small cities. Even into the 1950s, the Missouri Pacific (which operated many mail trains out of St. Louis) and other companies were investing heavily in new mail cars. Suddenly most of those cars sat idle, while the remaining ones moved mostly parcel post, so slowly that rural and small-town customers complained.

Intercity airliners did not stop or even slow down as they flew high above cities, towns, and hamlets withering along railroads. As railroad companies already struggling with diminishing income from Railway Express lost contracts to move railway post offices in dedicated trains and as components of passenger trains, they began eliminating trains in what became a headlong rush by the late 1960s. Around the year 1967 the matrix of railroad-routed high-speed mail and express shipment frayed just enough to precipitate a rapid collapse.

As the post office began moving mail by truck after 1958, and as trucking firms proliferated and competed with Railway Express, the movement of mail and package express, including frozen-food specialty items, began to slow, especially away from metropolitan regions. The Kennedy and Johnson administrations struggled with a worsening situation, but found no way to reverse it.

The Railway Express Agency filed for bankruptcy in 1975, just two years before the remaining United States Railway Mail post office made its last run between New York and Washington, D.C. Neither company nor government service benefited much from early computerization, perhaps because both seemed almost too complicated to computerize. But far younger competitors understood computer-generated scenario analysis from the beginning and quickly skewered a company and service seemingly frozen in the nineteenth century. Few in the 1970s glimpsed the latent power implicit in the Railway Express Agency and Railway Mail Service, or at least no evidence indicates what savvy investors discover decades later by carefully mining the rich ore of dusty schedules and processing the ore into gold.

Nowadays the public sees little United Parcel Service trucks scurrying everywhere in cities and suburbs, now and then dodging Federal Express and Airborne Express vans. Unlike United States Postal Service trucks, which follow regular routes, stopping at each green-painted urban mail storage box or at every rural free delivery box, UPS and other private-carrier express trucks have no daily routes, only patterns ordinarily discernible only to their owners. Most businesses and households receive first-class and advertising mail daily, but not every address hosts a UPS or FedEx truck every twenty-four hours. Legally known as express shipment carriers, the brown and gold or purple, orange, and white trucks seem anything but locally focused. But their heritage runs back to the local railroad depot, be it the immense Cleveland Union Terminal or a tiny wood-frame structure along a branch line.

Pickup trucks take their generic name from the flimsy vehicles farmers and storekeepers altered from Model T automobiles. Replacing the rear seat with a wood box enabled industrious businessmen to drive directly to railroad stations and pick up urgently needed shipments. In so doing they avoided delivery charges by large railroad-company-owned firms like Railway Express and by locally owned parcel delivery firms that operated in small towns and rural areas. A farmer wanted his shipment of newly hatched chicks or goslings as soon as possible, and storekeepers wanted perishable food and seasonal goods—especially at Christmas—immediately too. Picking up shipments at railroad stations spared them delivery charges, but it often meant shaving a few minutes or hours from a delivery process everyone knew as *expedited* or *express*.

First horse-drawn delivery wagons and trucks and then pickup trucks carried parcels, packages, and other express shipments to and from railroad depots. Rarely did they carry freight. Express shipment involved the dropping off, calling for, and pickup and delivery of goods as well as their expedited shipping. Freight involved merely the movement of products loaded directly by shippers and off-loaded by consignees. The distinction remains critical in any analysis of the wrenching spatial and cultural change just now emerging.

At a coal mine, employees of a mining company load a railroad hopper car with coal, and far away employees of a fuel dealer or electric utility unload the car into bunkers. The railroad company merely provides the car and its transportation once full, then removes it once empty. Freight rates reflect the simplicity of railroad company obligation, as does speed: many shippers trade very low rates for slow if certain delivery, especially of bulk commodities. But the storekeeper ordering a second shipment of popular Christmas tree ornaments telephones his order long distance and sets in motion a process different from freight. The ornaments arrive via Federal Express perhaps, not by freight train or 18-wheeler, pretty much as they did in 1935.

In the Depression the ornament manufacturer boxed the order while telephoning Railway Express, which routed a truck to the factory and collected the box. Moved by truck to the local express office inside a railroad station, the box began its journey by rail, often moving from one dedicated express car to another at junctions, until it arrived at the station nearest the storekeeper. From there, another truck delivered the box as one stop in a series of daily runs looping outward from the local railroad station with the arrival of each train. In rush situations, the delivery truck might go directly from depot to customer, and some shippers and consignees requested a telephone call to alert recipients to prepare for arrival of the shipment.

In the minds of individuals and families who traveled often, express shipment merged willy-nilly with baggage shipment, until by the 1930s many people scarcely distinguished between express and baggage services. The day before someone started a long railroad trip, a telephone call to Railway Express brought a man to the door to remove the trunk filled with clothes. When the traveler reached his destination, he found the trunk had been delivered the day previously. In 1900 all but the poorest American travelers expected to manage only hand luggage themselves, and red-capped baggage helpers at urban stations and Pullman porters everywhere assisted with that task. Steamer trunks and railroad trunks flowed into the hands of express companies and traveled as quasi-express shipments, but passengers persisted in calling them "baggage."

In the minds of customers, baggage might be refrigerators. Housewives knew that early electric refrigerators quickly disassembled into three components, the cylindrical coil at the top, the boxlike chest, and the metal, legged base. Manufacturers produced such refrigerators so families could ask Railway Express employees to disassemble them, transport them a day ahead to summer homes, and assemble them (and plug them in) the day before families arrived. At the end of summer, housewives reversed the process. The trunk of summer clothes and the refrigerator left together, along with a canoe or rowboat or bicycles, and arrived together. Not surprisingly, most Americans understood *express* and *baggage* to mean about the same thing, since Railway Express Agency employees moved both. Whatever their legal definitions, express and baggage traveled in passenger trains, in special cars behind the locomotive, but some hand luggage not necessary on the overnight train moved in the baggage car too. Passengers aboard luxury trains expected Pullman porters to carry overnight cases to bedrooms and expected to find their hand luggage placed aboard waiting taxicabs at destinations. Women especially did not move baggage, luggage, or anything other than handbags. They no more thought about moving their own baggage than they did about moving coffins.

Corpses, or what railroad companies called *remains,* moved as express. But coffins usually moved by hearse to railroad stations, and undertakers helped express car employees load them, and unload them when they arrived at destinations. Nowadays few railroad museum visitors realize that the so-called baggage wagons that depot masters once pulled alongside baggage express cars stretch just long enough to carry coffins. Lugubrious ballads about widows and widowers traveling in trains carrying the remains of departed loved ones make clear the legal nuances of coffins en route. Like trunks with handles, coffins are clearly baggage, but they are boxes too, temporarily guarded by express messengers. Never are they mail, not even parcel post.

For decades, small and large shipments moved hurriedly via express, chiefly the Railway Express Agency, formed by a consortium of railroads in 1929 from a loose-knit group of competing express companies, including the famed Wells Fargo Company. In a symbiosis whose significance would be difficult to overestimate, the Railway Express Agency and the Western Union Company dominated most of the package and electronic message sending and delivery, their agents working out of most railroad stations, urban and rural. For decades, only Railway Express sold American Express money orders (in the Depression a hundred-dollar money order cost only twenty-four cents) and travelers' checks, causing many customers to cheerfully confuse the two firms. Into the 1950s manned Railway Express cars operated in ten thousand trains covering some 190,000 miles every day. As Garrett explains in *Ten Turtles to Tucumcari*, the local agents and the onboard express car messenger specialized in pets, flowers, and highly flammable nitrate motion-picture film, but they moved just about anything else shipped in haste: vegetables, human remains, dynamite, fresh oysters, automobiles, dishwashing detergent, and animals sent from one zoo to another.

Long before the amalgamation of regional express companies like Wells Fargo, Adams, Southern, and Pacific into Railway Express, the post office had not bothered with shipping packages. It could not compete with private-sector excellence. It carried letters, magazines, and newspapers, and until New Year's Day 1913 nothing much else: on that day it inaugurated parcel post, but for decades the service remained a political boondoggle. Stretched by funding rural free delivery, which it began experimentally in 1897 to bring mail to farm families six days a week, the post office viewed package shipping with suspicion. The express companies had made Sears and Roebuck, Montgomery Ward, and especially J. C. Penney successful beyond imagination. A farm family mailed a letter, often enclosing an express company money order, via the post office, but knew that the great retailers would ship goods via express. Railway Express frightened the post office simply by guaranteeing that any shipment would arrive anywhere in five days. Not surprisingly, almost all long-distance shopping meant mailing or telephoning an order and then either visiting the railroad depot express office or having the local Railway Express agent deliver the package.

Packages ranged from golf clubs (if not in boxes, then with all clubs tied securely) to live bees (shipped in special crates in which queen and bees drank sugary syrup); from live hogs (in special crates that enabled the hogs to lie down) to butter, cream, and dressed meat (carried in refrigerated lockers), and human ashes (moved in safes that carried cash, and treated as shipments of cash); from explosives to whiskey to guns to gold nuggets. Larger packages included prize racehorses, and special shipments ranged from a collection of half a million butterflies to the Smithsonian from Decatur, Illinois, to a meteorite from Paragould, Arkansas, to McPherson, Kansas. All animals moved in cages fitted to provide food and water, and dogs often moved with their leashes so that express messengers could exercise them, and express messengers and agents summoned veterinarians when they noticed animals ill. Ordinary live fish moved in water changed every three hours, but live tropical fish received far more delicate treatment, since the agency had to maintain water temperature according to shipper instructions.

Express company bulletins and other ephemera clarify how shipper instructions dovetailed into company practice. Moving racehorses meant bringing 175 horses from Kentucky to a race in Juárez, Mexico, in 1915. Moving seafood involved constant icing and extremely rapid handling, and moving flowers meant thousands of special movements for special occasions. When a new furniture store opened in Flint, Michigan, in August 1925, the American Express Company delivered twenty thousand roses for the occasion. Moving caged pet parrots required separation from caged shipped cats, whose presence annoyed the birds. For perhaps fifteen years after 1915 (most records are lost), Wells Fargo moved automobiles as both express shipments to auto dealers and as baggage for luxury train passengers who wanted to find their own cars waiting for them at distant destinations. Just as the Eastman Kodak Company located its film-processing facilities on high-speed mail and express routes (before it invented easily removable spool film, Kodak had camera users ship whole cameras for reloading), so other companies discovered how the matrix of mail and express routes made cities like Lynchburg in Virginia spectacular places in which to do business.

Perhaps J. C. Penney understood the relationship of the post office, express companies, and Western Union best. In ways that anticipated experiments by his competitors, he juggled catalog sales and retail stores. Fairmount, Minnesota, proved a superb location for a new J. C. Penney store in 1925, in part because catalog customers who received Penney merchandise extremely quickly guaranteed product loyalty from opening day, something American Express pointed out in its November company bulletin, the *Express Messenger*.

In a way vaguely resembling contemporary disputes about the impact of Wal-Mart on small-town Main Street stores, between about 1890 and 1950 the express system sometimes focused public attention on competition and choice. A farm family or small-town resident might buy locally, but almost all might choose to "mail order" from the great urban catalog merchants or from advertisers in national magazines. Small-town retailers emphasized personal service against the range of items and sometimes lower cost of the catalog companies, but thoughtful Americans understood the personal service provided by the local Railway Express Agency agent too. Almost always one of the most respected businessmen in any small town or suburb, part of an extremely sophisticated company of national and international reach, he spent decades not only receiving and shipping packages but building demand for a service that often functioned better than a well-oiled machine—simply because the agent often anticipated client needs. A good agent not only moved money for bankers, dogs for hunters, and specialty paper and cardboard for printers in a desperate hurry, but constantly visited business owners to solicit business by understanding special needs. As he learned the needs of his customers, the customers often found themselves pleasantly surprised, as when the agent made a special, no-extra-charge delivery to a distraught farmer needing a part for a broken tractor in plowing season.

By the 1940s, however, the post office increasingly dominated the moving of ordinary small packages, leaving Railway Express to move the trunks of summer campers and Scouts heading to jamborees, the surge of Christmastime boxes, and seasonal rushes, especially of fresh fruit sent as gifts, along with all the difficult shipments, especially fresh seafood. Despite successfully entering the airline express market in the 1960s, by 1972 the company, by then renamed REA Express, had watched its overall shipments drop to half of what it moved in 1965. In 1925 so many American Express Company cars moved daily between Washington, D.C., and Cincinnati that the Chesapeake & Ohio Railway dedicated an entire train, No. 101, to fourteen of them. By 1965 the Railway Express Agency moved so little express that its cars scarcely subsidized the passengers in the coaches and sleepers behind. The agency crashed into a series of corporate scandals, deficits, and intense competition from United Parcel Service, Federal Express, and Emery Worldwide, and most railroad companies dumped their remaining passenger trains into the new Amtrak. Only two years after its founding in 1973, Federal Express found itself competing against a bankrupt Railway Express Agency. A firm that once prided itself on its on-time performance and sparkling clean railroad cars, offices, and trucks vanished completely a few months later, and even its records disappeared. In Alvin Toffler's *Future Shock* terms, the nation reacted with amazement or indifference and sometimes annoyance: no longer could it easily ship pets, pianos, canoes, and hundreds of other awkward items. Klink Garrett, who finished his career in upper management at Railway Express, observes that Federal Express prospered by focusing on the on-time performance and personal service that Railway Express once championed, while moving only envelopes and small boxes. UPS, from its beginning in the 1960s, prospered by moving slightly larger boxes. No upstart company moved racehorses or antique tables bequeathed by distant great aunts, let alone items nowadays almost impossible for individuals to ship—windsurfers, surfboards, and personal watercraft, for example. Federal Express and UPS avoided rail transport totally, and moved almost effortlessly into airborne shipping.

Understanding the flow of mail and express via train nowadays means assembling several classifications of data, almost none available in libraries and archives. Much of the government information is virtually unobtainable because officials considered it so ephemeral that they regularly pulped it. A fierce interest in efficiency, combined with efforts at preventing mistakes, forced employees of both the Railway Mail Service and the Railway Express Agency to destroy tariffs, general directions, and schedules the moment they became outdated. But something more than antiquarian or hobby interest explains the surprisingly vigorous acquisition of such documents on eBay and other Internet auction sites, and by secondhand booksellers acting as agents. Assembled, oriented, and analyzed by software focused on mobility across vast regions, the data provide a reasonable sketch not only of a long-gone national landscape and an economy still not accurately understood but also of possible prototypes for the futures currently in the design stage.

Today, regular mail is growing less and less important, although Netflix and other companies demonstrate that locating warehouses near regional post offices means next-day delivery at first-class rates. Faxes and e-mail devastated the overnight document-delivery express business in the early 1990s, but the volume of package shipments continues to grow, driven in part by Internet-based online ordering. Detailed analysis of how objects once moved in a specific region consequently suggests scenarios involving a future beyond Wal-Mart, Netflix, and contemporary express delivery services.

In 1935 some forty-six mail trains arrived and departed Kansas City, Missouri, six days a week; many operated on Sundays too. Analyzing the operation of only a few means finding arcane, ephemeral books, the most important of which are two published by the United States Post Office Department, *General Scheme of Kansas, 1935* and *General Scheme of Texas, 1935*. These now-rare volumes lack much value until collated against two other, even rarer books printed in 1935 by the General Superintendent of the Railway Mail Service: *Schedule of Mail Routes No. 513, Seventh Division, Kansas and Missouri* and *Schedule of Mail Routes No. 294, Eleventh Division, Arkansas, New Mexico, Oklahoma, and Texas.* All are public documents, but only the former originated in the Government Printing Office; private printing companies in Fort Worth and St. Louis produced the latter. None is much use without a copy of *The Official Guide of the Railways* for 1935—a privately produced, ephemeral tome printed on high-acid paper that self-destructs—or without detailed period maps identifying railroads by name. Since some mail trains carried no passengers, the *Official Guide* makes no mention of them. Any inquirer hoping for completeness must also obtain 1935 employee timetables for the several railroads over which certain all-mail-and-express trains operated. Finding the raw material of historical analysis proves almost mind-numbing, since all the documents changed at least yearly, and sometimes more frequently, and employees tended to follow orders and discard them. But the documents enable the sketching of a long-forgotten but extremely efficient mail and express system.

Railway Mail Service route numbers rarely corresponded to train numbers issued by individual railroads. Without employee timetables, contemporary researchers have difficulty learning when mail trains blasted past small depots, depositing and collecting mail on the fly. The Railway Mail Service focused on speed and precise rendezvousing at junctions, where trains met to switch entire carloads of through mail or to exchange one or more pouches. The Railway Mail Service expected promptness at waypoints too, but announced such times to local postmasters and Star Route Rural Free Delivery carriers, assumed railway mail clerks knew the sequence of drop-off/pickup points and whether or not their train was on time or late, and knew that railroads forbade trains to pass waypoints ahead of schedule. What the post office designated the *general scheme* of mail routing, pickup, and delivery in any of its geographical districts originated around and depended on railroad routes and schedules. But this scheme evolved into a complex matrix managed wholly without computers and completely understood by no one, including the postmaster general and the CEO of Railway Express. Nowadays discernible only in documents like the 1938 post office publication *Instructions and Rulings with Reference to Transportation of Mails by Railroads,* the complexity involved minutiae such as the problem of balancing the flow of railway post offices in holiday seasons and the importance of junction cities.

More or less by happenstance, the complexity made Kansas City and other cities surprisingly important, especially in the first half of the twentieth century. Just as Lynchburg proved an exceptionally busy passenger train junction, so Kansas City served not only a broad range of passenger trains but also a swarm of mail and express trains, all of which "worked" some mail in addition to carrying pouches of through letters, sometimes enough to fill entire storage cars. Working the mail meant that clerks sorted letters as the trains moved, "setting up" mail for waypoints (most of them too small to require stopping the train) as well as for points beyond the Seventh Division (Kansas and Missouri). Aboard some trains, clerks sorted mail by street so that city-based mail handlers could move it directly into the hands of individual letter carriers. In a way, the mail and express trains not only made Kansas City important but became the tentacles of something that might be called "Greater Kansas City." Instead of sprawling spatially across rich farm country, Kansas City spread its influence via mail and express trains.

Some trains left Kansas City westbound for a run that the post office designated the Kansas City & Albuquerque Railway Post Office (RPO). Most of those trains operated as segments of Chicago–Los Angeles runs that originated and terminated in Railway Mail Service divisions beyond the Seventh. RPO 7 left Kansas City at 10:00 in the morning along the main line of the Atchison, Topeka & Santa Fe Railroad; it worked mail for Colorado, Kansas, New Mexico, Oklahoma, Texas, Arizona, and California, and as it streaked across the plains its clerks worked local mail via street address for the city of Albuquerque too. At 5:35 it arrived in Dodge City, Kansas, where it paused to load and unload mail, some of it for Bucklin, twenty-seven miles southeast on a branch of the Chicago, Rock Island & Pacific. But Bucklin, a very small town indeed, also lay on the main line of the Rock Island Road, which carried other mail trains focused on Kansas City, mostly ones operating beyond Tucumcari over the Southern Pacific to El Paso. RPO 3 departed Kansas City twenty minutes before RPO 7 and ran roughly parallel west-southwest, giving Bucklin direct access to a national mail train route and tangential access to another extending northwest to Dodge City and from there directly to Chicago and Los Angeles. At 8:32 every weekday morning and at 6:03 every weekday evening, westbound RPOs paused at Bucklin; eastbound service halted at 11:59 and 7:30. But Bucklin also received and sent mail via Dodge City in the north.

Today Bucklin is home to 725 people living in 338 houses. The town covers about half a square mile and is slowly growing: contractors build about one new house each year. The median age of the residents is about thirty-nine years, and the median income $51,400, with a range of less than $10,000 to greater than $200,000. The average house value is approximately $50,000, slightly less than the median income. Bucklin is not exactly easily accessible, but State Highway 54 is certainly well paved and well maintained, as is State Highway 154, which links Bucklin to Dodge City. While a first-class stamp costs the same in Bucklin as anywhere else, real estate is inexpensive; many inhabitants of Bucklin own houses that cost approximately one year's income to purchase. But mailing a letter or package from the village is not exactly simple, although Bucklin boasts a pleasant post office on South Main Street. Mail is carried by truck nowadays, not by mail train.

If mail still moved by train, Bucklin might be remarkably well connected, for the Union Pacific Railroad bought much of the bankrupt Rock Island. Today the main line on the northern edge of the town is still a major Kansas City–El Paso route, and the branch line to Dodge continues to run too, as the Buckhill & Western, a freight-only short line. As in so many small towns in the center of the continent, the post office, stores, and houses of Bucklin abut a highway that parallels a railroad track. Across the Union Pacific main line is only Highway 34 meandering northwest through farm country to Dodge, itself paralleling another railroad, the Buckhill & Western. Bucklin is not on the main road to anywhere, but it is likely to be on the main track to a future already emergent in northern New Jersey, around Houston and Galveston and, especially, near the Port of Los Angeles, where imported goods jam wharves and warehouses.

Manufactured items need to be delivered from factories and from ports of entry. Items manufactured outside the United States arrive at only a few ports and must be distributed from them. The gridlocked confusion of northern New Jersey, apparent to any motorist on I-95 approaching the George Washington Bridge from the south, resembles that of other ports that will be analyzed in a subsequent chapter. But the port concentration that strangles adjacent highways energizes inquiry into distribution networks that once reached everywhere in the United States.

United Parcel Service embraced a new realization two years ago. It increased the upper weight limit of any single parcel to 150 pounds. Interested parties focused on the competition Amazon. com offers to independent bookstores have observed that UPS is a major player in shipping books from regional warehouses and widely scattered secondhand booksellers. But the chief opportunity opening to investors lies not in moving small parcels such as books but in shipping larger and heavier cargo, say household refrigerators.

Often consumers purchase new refrigerators in a hurry, perhaps in the wake of some domestic disaster, as steak and ice cream thaw. Newlyweds tend to accept whatever refrigerator the landlord provides, and buyers of houses often buy refrigerators in situ or have time to pick out specific ones. Redecorating sometimes influences refrigerator purchase. But usually it is refrigerator failure that sends homeowners scurrying to the nearest appliance store. The Web might offer a broad choice in refrigerators someday, but only if on-line ordering means ultrafast delivery.

Refrigerators, washing machines, and other "white goods" move in special boxcars. Hy-Cube cars are taller than most boxcars because appliances are not particularly heavy and most stack reasonably well, if crews follow this-end-up directions accurately. A fifty-foot Hy-Cube boxcar towers over a line of ordinary boxcars by four feet or so of extra height. Just as the height of the typical dishwasher now governs the height of the typical kitchen counter everywhere in the United States, the height of appliances governs the shape of the boxcars designed to transport them. But white goods move as freight, in bulk, in trains rumbling along at forty-five miles an hour. Appliance wholesalers want on-time delivery, but are in no particular hurry.

Stalking United States appliance manufacturers is the specter of Asian competition. Already pioneering in low-voltage appliances for yachts, gigantic recreational vehicles, and wilderness hunting cabins, Asian manufacturers experiment with appliances that might operate off solar-charged batteries, windmills, or other environmentally friendly technologies. But true competition lies in Asian expansion from television and computer manufacturing into mainstream 110-volt appliances. Comfort-zone air-conditioning units (which supplement window and central-air units) may be the beachhead of invasion, but perhaps the great thrust will involve electric stoves. Today Asian-built appliances must move through existing appliance distribution networks, but tomorrow they might not.

Suppose a customer in Bucklin ordered a new refrigerator from a retailer in Kansas City. In 1935 the night mail and express train left Kansas City at 11:55 PM and arrived in Bucklin at 8:32 the following morning. Today, given a similar train operating on the same schedule, a customer might order via the Internet until about 10:00 in the evening. The retailer would move the perfect refrigerator to the express company's loading dock at the Kansas City station, and the following morning an express agent would off-load the unit, deliver it, and set it in place, removing the failed refrigerator and consigning it for recycling. Nothing much futuristic shapes this scenario. Railway Express agents routinely delivered and installed refrigerators; for that matter, they installed the monthly refill bottles of fancy urban dishwashing liquid 1930s small-town housewives enjoyed.

Tweaking the scenario produces an assortment of potential variations on the theme. The local agent might be someone holding a franchise, not a Railway Express employee; after all, the 725 people of Bucklin might not justify a full-time agent. The refrigerator might begin its journey somewhere other than in Kansas City without adverse consequences; if the customer ordered before noon, it might arrive from El Paso by 7:30 the same day. Or maybe private investors will buy the already quasi-privatized United States Postal Service and merge it into some overarching express company. In 1929 the railroad industry created the Railway Express Agency from a half-dozen successful express companies: why not combine UPS, FedEx, and the USPS?

Only at first glance does such a scenario appear outlandish. Few would argue nowadays that moving the mail, especially first-class letters, remains so critical to a free and independent republic that only the federal government can undertake the task. For most Americans and corporate entities, Federal Express provides the security and privacy required for urgent mail delivery. The quasi-public Postal Service has moved with much success away from 1960s difficulties similar to those that destroyed the Railway Express Agency, and now often strikes customers as a private company. Yet despite its accomplishments and tremendous power, its 800,000 employees labor in a workplace shaped by the 1960s restrictions that empowered Federal Express, UPS, and other contemporary competitors. Just as Congress slapped a seventy-nine-miles-per-hour speed limit on passenger trains after World War II, so it hampered post office innovation with the Transport Act of 1958.

As Comarow demonstrates convincingly in *The Demise of the Postal Service?* in the 1960s the post office was more ineffectual than the Hudson & Manhattan tunnel railroad. Political patronage and archaic regulations had almost strangled the department even as it faced stiff private-sector competition. Reform proved partial, leaving control of wages and—ominously—health insurance and retirement benefits in the hands of politicians. Just as 1995–98 changes to the Internal Revenue Service resulted in a precipitous drop in corporate and upper-income audits, so-called reforms still pull Postal Service employees, especially managers, in two ways, forcing them to be both entrepreneurial and bureaucratic. Nowhere is this split more clearly revealed than in the way urban and regional planners think about post offices themselves.

Party-line followers across the design professions champion the location of post offices downtown, on small-town main streets, anywhere they might revitalize business or invigorate "smart growth" efforts. The United States Postal Service, in the eyes of designers, planners, and real estate developers, exists first as a government force that maintains or raises real estate values in "traditional" settings. Never mind that downtown post offices prove poorly accessible by trucks, lack expansion room for automatic devices, and, at least sometimes, lack room for additional employees to accommodate growing business. No one says much about the location of regional distribution hubs by Federal Express, UPS, and competing firms, which choose sites based on accessibility, land cost, and potential for growth. Increasing efficiency in the Postal Service often takes second place to a plethora of half-stated, vague, and sometimes secretive goals of private parties anxious to manipulate public goods for private ends by insisting that post offices be sited according to 1930s memories of Main Street and mail trains.

The Postal Service maintains offices in most municipalities, and in rural areas operates so-called Star Routes along which farmers and other customers can buy stamps, money orders, and so on from rural free delivery carriers. The RFD box mounted atop a post remains an American icon, but it receives little scrutiny from a public that expects to pay extra for Federal Express to pick up an envelope. The Postal Service carrier stops whenever the box-owner raises a red flag, and a Star Route carrier charges nothing extra for picking up a box, bringing it to a rural post office for weighing and postage, then bringing a bill the next day for payment the day after. Federal Express and UPS charge for pickup services, and expect on-the-spot payment from private citizens; neither firms extends credit to individuals in the time-honored way of RFD Star Route service. Rural Americans sometimes marvel at city-only USPS services like special delivery, and urban Americans marvel even more at farm families putting out unstamped letters for pickup. The Postal Service practices widespread spatial discrimination under a pall of so-called universal service; most of the discrimination dates to the mail-train era and its immediate aftermath. As Comarow suggests, only lately do private investors think about picking the profitable parts of the system and leaving the taxpayer responsible for unprofitable rural and wilderness service.

Imagining postal service as it worked in 1895, when private express companies carried all packages and the bulk of expedited mail, and when small-town and rural residents expected to pick up mail at post offices, offers a ready-made scenario for a privatized Postal Service.

If the Postal Service sold stamps only from vending machines as strategically placed as those selling Coca-Cola, and contracted the shipping of packages to strip-mall stores like Mail Boxes Etc. or even Dollar General, it might lay off many employees and pass savings along to customers. Shopping carts fitted with scanners that record the price of each item enable supermarket customers to avoid lines at cashier-staffed and self-checkout registers; grocery store innovation may shape postal operations. Senders might pay lower postage for items delivered to boxes rather than street addresses; recipients might pay less postage on items mailed from gas stations, conve-

nience grocery stores, or other businesses willing to subsidize postage costs in return for increasing customer flow. Whatever Postal
Service unions think of such scenarios, no one doubts that a soft-
drink-like vending machine might have a slot in which a customer
could place a heavy envelope, drop in some change according to an
electronically displayed message, and hear the machine whine or
click as it postmarks the letter. The technology seems available. But
in the end, moving mail proves far more complicated than it looks,
in large part because of hidden subsidies to airline companies. Magazine publishers ship issues from the United States to Canada by international air mail rather than by surface mail, simply because air
shipment is cheaper. Changing almost anything about the system
produces serious anger, and not just from employees fearing closed
post offices. Raising stamp prices, ending Saturday delivery of mail,
even removing less-used urban mailboxes prompts customer protest, and direct-mail advertisers protest most loudly of all.

Some nine million Americans work in the so-called mailing industry. Advertising mail, often dismissed as "junk mail," produces
a huge chunk of Postal Service revenue while prompting some recipients to buy products, sometimes shipped by mail. Essentially,
the USPS subsidizes mailings by nonprofit organizations, most
of which pay only about 60 percent of the rates charged to for-
profit firms. College alumni magazines, hospital fund-raising bulletins, hobby-group newsletters, and much other material travels
extremely inexpensively. Indeed some analysts argue that bulk mail
both subsidizes first-class postage rates and keeps many post offices
from incurring losses that now trouble sixteen thousand small-
town post offices. In the end, junk mail postage is priced according
to decades-old political agreements, and as the nation shifts toward
e-mail communication the Postal Service faces a serious dilemma:
whether or not to continue universal service.

Already many Americans accept rural free delivery and short-
ened post office hours even though they are aware that big-city post
offices stay open later. A first-class stamp buys more or less service
and convenience according to location, and even now express mail
does not serve every post office. Special delivery remains an urban
amenity. But at some point Postal Service losses mean the market

pricing of all postage and the loss of some or all service to certain localities. Does the population of Bucklin, Kansas (725 people), justify a full-time post office, let alone door-to-door mail delivery?

Exploring the symbiotic relationships among a railroad station agent, a Western Union operator, and a Railway Express agent circa 1935 may prove suggestive. Do citizens really need daily delivery of mail? How much will they pay for it in the near future? Could other options—say weekly delivery—prove more efficient? Imagining a transformed Postal Service may involve imagining corollary changes that increase the value of small-town centers, hamlets along railroads, and nascent logistics technologies such as those transforming supermarket shopping.

Throughout the 1990s strange silver boxcars trailed many Amtrak passenger cars. So-called merchandise cars offered a long shot at additional revenue: Amtrak trains would move packages, newspapers, and other time-sensitive lightweight goods under regular contract. The service originated in early Amtrak efforts to duplicate older Railway Express Agency successes, and throughout the 1980s wavered between success and failure. On-time performance problems routinely crippled attempts, and Amtrak ran over too few routes anyway. Its present matrix is less dense than the 1965 passenger train version that proved too thin to maintain Railway Mail and Railway Express Agency service. Beyond that, when the service did succeed, Amtrak faced a problem it only half expected: more express cars meant heavier trains, and thus the necessity for more locomotives. But it is the merchandise cars that deserve the closest scrutiny.

They evolved not so much from old Railway Express Agency cars but from innovative boxcars that appeared in freight trains as early as 1979. Formed as a subsidiary to the Trailer Train Corporation in 1974, the American Rail Box Car Company at first produced fifty-foot-long boxcars fitted with ten-foot-wide doors, one on each side. As more and more shippers used forklift trucks and other mechanized devices to load the cars, materials handling experts realized that as employees filled cars with cargo the loading devices had less and less room to maneuver. In order to speed loading, American Rail Box Car began adding a six-foot-wide door to the left of the larger one, making a sixteen-foot-wide opening for loading equipment. Such innovation not only made boxcar loading far more efficient than the loading of 18-wheeler trailers but made investors think. Clearly such a car might carry express and containerized mail in passenger trains, for machines might load and unload parts of its cargo in a minute or two at any passenger station.

Amtrak and its shippers saw the first merchandise cars as potential alternatives to trucks. In at least some small towns, the one train each way attracted just a bit more than passing notice day after day. Obviously, passengers rode in the coaches, in the dining cars, in the sleeping cars; even children saw them. But the silver boxcars rolled in mystery, and at least some people in the for-profit realm grew thoughtful about the shipping of packages, larger items, even mail. If mail arrived in the silver cars, the post office might remain downtown, albeit perhaps near the abandoned or geriatric railroad depot. Here and there a city councillor or business-boosting activist considered the innovation and envisioned a future quickly discovered to be grounded in the past. Elsewhere, not only in small towns but in large cities that were once hubs of rail passenger service, experts in materials handling, automated warehousing, and time-sequenced delivery glimpsed in the silver cars a potential.

Always the investigation slows at the byzantine sophistication of the old mail and express train matrix. Computer-assisted analysis demonstrates repeatedly that if the matrix existed today, the Internet would make possible extraordinary changes in shipping time-sensitive items. As more people rely on e-mail, even to pay bills, the Postal Service more clearly understands the looming crisis involving flying first-class mail. The volume of first-class mail shrinks and drives up the cost of a first-class stamp in order to pay airline charges, pension contributions, and other costs. Immediately ahead lies a break moment remarkably similar to that created by Congress in the 1958 Transport Act. Just as Congress wrecked the for-profit, taxpaying Railway Express Agency with parcel-post service, then pulled first-class mail from railway post offices, then finally ended domestic air mail, so the Postal Service realizes that flying first-class mail will soon become prohibitively expensive. Utility companies and other firms will respond by charging customers more to receive paper bills delivered by mail, and soon companies will surcharge customers paying by check. Most banks no longer mail canceled checks to customers, and many Americans grudgingly accept it. But all such effort merely postpones imminent catastrophic change that begins to interest long-range investors wondering whether the United States Postal Service might be privatized, perhaps along railroad routes offering services in need of private subsidy.

A matrix of mail and express trains offers an alternative to a retail market dominated by Wal-Mart, shopping malls, high-end urban stores, and Internet sites. If Kansas City and other cities extended their spheres of influence, but not their physical fabric, then living in Bucklin and many other small towns might become highly desirable. People might move to places situated along flows of information and goods alike. Real estate investors examine places like Bucklin now not for what they are but for what they will be—based on what they were decades ago, and on plans made long ago but never realized.

In 1930 the Pennsylvania Railroad, already determined to compete with the fledgling airline industry, began surveying its main line between Harrisburg and Pittsburgh as the first step toward electrifying service. Despite the curving grades that carried track over the Appalachians and steam locomotives pulling trains west of Pittsburgh, the company believed that electrification might produce twelve-hour service between New York and Chicago. The Pennsylvania Railroad undoubtedly thought of its Broadway Limited and other luxury trains in beginning its pre-Depression research. But the company must have realized how well train No. 11, the Fast Mail, might compete with airliners unable to deliver and pick up mail at intermediate cities, or to sort mail en route. A two-cent stamp on a letter mailed in New York before 5:00 on any business day would buy next-day delivery in Chicago, and in Salem, Canton, Massillon, Orrville, Crestline, Bucyrus, Lima, and Fort Wayne too. In 1930 neither the Post Office Department nor the airline industry knew how to deliver air mail, let alone first-class mail, that promptly. But the brand-new Railway Express Agency, amalgamated from a collection of smaller express firms, understood the implications for *next-day* delivery of packages ordered from New York department stores. Mail and express movement, not the transport of passengers, focused railroad executive attention to innovation as late as 1960, and it focused shipper attention forever after that.

The whistle of the Fast Mail echoes now in the minds of readers of a plethora of magazines deserving wider notice: *Parcel Shipping and Distribution, International Railway Journal, Materials Handling Management, Logistics Management, Warehousing Management*, and *Industrial Distribution*. For the historian, the whistle recalls mail and express delivery in a time before metropolitan sprawl and traffic jams, especially those caused by long-haul large trucks. For the investor, especially the venture capitalist scrutinizing high-speed freight trains carrying only UPS trailers between great cities, it produces ideas. It might be possible to bypass local liquor stores, provide prescription medicine or organic produce in exurban or rural areas, supply small manufacturing plants, deliver automobiles, and compete with Wal-Mart Supercenters in ways that reinvigorate downtowns and boost the value of undervalued real estate, especially that away from highways. After all, they have the example of the UPS train before them.

SOURCES: Canton, "Fight for Survival"; Comarow, *The Demise of the Postal Service?*; Garrett, *Ten Turtles to Tucumcari;* Hediger, "New Railbox ABOX Boxcar"; Lamson, "Catching and Throwing the Mail"; Long and Dennis, *Mail by Rail;* Railway Mail Service, *Schedule of Mail Routes No. 513,* and *Schedule of Mail Routes No. 294;* United States Post Office Department, *General Scheme of Kansas, 1935; General Scheme of Texas, 1935;* and *Instructions and Rulings.*

Ordinary freight trains roll along routes still emblazoned with long-gone corporate names; such routes often carried passenger trains on timetables freight trains will soon duplicate.

FAST FREIGHT

Cabooses disappeared in the 1970s, a few years after mail trains rolled into oblivion. Freight trains rumbled on, but older Americans saw them as sentences without periods. For generations, the little box-like cars, most surmounted with cupolas and painted red, punctuated the rear end of freight trains. For parents stuck at railroad crossings teaching young children to count freight cars, cabooses marked the end of the arithmetical exercise. A stubby red or yellow caboose rolled past the crossing signals, a denim-clad man waved an apology for the delay from the cupola window, and the train was gone. In daytime a pair of red flags whipped from the ends of the caboose. At night a pair of red lanterns glimmered in the dark.

Today an electromechanical device replaces most cabooses. The Federal Rear End Device, christened "Fred" by railroaders, rides atop the coupler of the last car, constantly monitoring air-brake pressure and transmitting data to the locomotive engineer. Its blinking red light warns following trains that ahead of it rolls a freight train. But Americans in their forties and older see the modern freight train as somehow incomplete without its trailing caboose. In the past it housed brakemen sleeping in bunks, conductors cooking breakfast over potbellied, coal-burning stoves, men swinging down from platform steps, lanterns slung from elbow crooks. Fred replaced cabooses as United States heavy industry changed forever in ways that disconcert middle-aged people.

Engineering experts in the 1970s envisioned trains that needed no humans at all. Unionized employees shook their heads, but research rolled on. Fred had climbed aboard like a hobo in the dark, and had somehow hired on for good; a high-tech revolution had begun to transform transportation, but almost no one noticed anything other than cabooseless trains.

Children don't miss cabooses, for they rarely see one anywhere. What people do notice, often while sitting in traffic, is that freight trains roll faster than highway vehicles and carry 18-wheel truck trailers. By the middle 1990s politicians in many states had begun to consider whether truck traffic ought to be diverted onto railroads in order to ease traffic congestion. As Richard Saunders reports in *Main Lines: Rebirth of the North American Railroads, 1970–2002*, using computer-generated scenarios, railroad management looked ahead and discerned to their consternation that train movement already approached track capacity and, depending on short-term economic ups and downs, would choke sometime before 2010. Converting from double-track to single-track main lines, ripping up sidetracks, eliminating steeply banked, high-speed curves, and abandoning secondary routes to nature trails had produced a situation unknown to most Americans, even to stockholders and shippers. The 2003 nationwide shortage of train crews attracted little media attention, but it confirmed management's understanding and strengthened the hand of those railroad executives who saw the situation as pregnant with opportunity. Railroad companies now move according to a new vision grounded in hard-fact reality, and they intend to prosper, not by bringing back the caboose, but by playing piggyback.

Company public-relations officers use *intermodal freight* to designate rail carriage of truck trailers and international shipping containers. Railroad employees call such carriage *piggybacking,* and freight trains dedicated to such service *pig trains.* Often rolling faster than Amtrak—and far faster than 18-wheel trucks on interstate highways—many pig trains carry not just freight but mail and express. West of the Mississippi, young children on coast-to-coast auto trips might ask parents about the freight trains that parallel the interstate but run at speeds above eighty-five miles per hour. The creaking, swaying freight train of 1980 now outpaces the family minivan.

South of Kansas City long-haul trucks throng I-35. As Larry McMurty eloquently points out in *Roads: Driving America's Great Highways,* the trucks diverge from east–west I-70 for the run south to the Mexican border at Laredo. More than the North American Free Trade Agreement sparked the staggering truck traffic on I-35. NAFTA merely codified a fact known to industrial analysts since the 1980s: Mexico had become a great industrial power, in part by avoiding many of the antipollution, workplace safety, and wage-guarantee laws enacted north of its border. A vast flow of manufactured goods moves into the United States not only through Atlantic, Gulf, and Pacific ports but from Mexico, and while much of the flow bifurcates at Kansas City to the east and the west, much of it continues north into Canada. The highway impact of Mexican and Canadian industrial and population growth is blatant and grim. I-35 south of Kansas City carries a stream of heavy trucks that unnerves automobile drivers and annoys residents, chambers of commerce, and especially tourist bureaus. But the stream threatens the financial health of the trucking industry, too. On I-35, as on I-90 in northern Ohio, I-95 between Connecticut and Maryland, I-40 in east Tennessee, and the interstate highways merging in coastal California south of San Francisco as far as Bakersfield, trucks run into jams that destroy schedules.

Modern fast freight trains, especially pig trains, seem fast streaming across the High Plains, but they madden urban motorists stuck in traffic jams. Silver commuter trains flashing to and from great cities inhabit a perceptual otherworld psychologists study too infrequently. Motorists, even those stopped in traffic, somehow fail to realize the speed and implied convenience of the trains they might board. But they seem to notice speeding freight trains.

Reaching south from Kansas City runs a powerful railroad. The Kansas City Southern (KCS) terminates in Port Arthur, Texas, on the Gulf coast, but in Shreveport, Louisiana, its main lines branch east to Jackson, Mississippi, and Mobile, Alabama, and west to Dallas. Marketing agreements with the Burlington Northern Santa Fe (BNSF) and the Canadian National–Illinois Central extend KCS's reach across the whole of the United States west of the Mississippi, and north from New Orleans to Chicago, and from Chicago north across the whole of Canada. But what fuels KCS's growth lies south: the Grupo Transportación Ferroviaria Mexicana, a large chunk of which the KCS owns, and whose operations integrate with those of the KCS. The TFM rail routes reach south from Laredo and Brownsville and converge at Monterey in Nuevo León to run south to Mexico City via San Luis Potosi and Querétaro. Branch main lines extend to Tampico and Veracruz on the Gulf and Lazaro Cárdenas on the Pacific. The TFM connects with another KCS affiliate, the

Tex-Mex Railroad operating between Corpus Christi and Laredo, just north of the international border. In the near future, KCS may merge all three railroads into a new firm tentatively called NAFTA Rail—a railroad with the potential to reshape the commercial landscape of the middle United States.

From 1998 through the end of 2001, KCS-TFM cross-border traffic grew at an average of 9 percent annually, but in 2002 that growth rate doubled to 18 percent, and in 2003 it grew to 25 percent. Despite the intricacies of accounting in two currencies (the Mexican peso devalued in 2002), cross-border traffic produced a 44 percent growth in revenues in 2003. The rise of Mexico into a global industrial power shipping a massive volume of product to the United States—and through the United States to Canada—is transforming the KCS, but in part because the KCS passed through the 1960 to 1990 period as a most conservatively run railroad. Unlike so many competitors, it invested heavily in track and locomotive maintenance, and so found itself superbly positioned for radical economic change.

The KCS is scarcely backward. It leads its industry not only in safety but in technological innovation that betters its positions with connecting railroads. Its Meridian, Mississippi-to-Dallas main line, recently termed "The Speedway" in company advertising, now boasts more remote-controlled power switches (with more being added) and alignment reconfigurations such as the one at Vicksburg, where the company broadened a tight curve to permit higher speeds. The Meridian–Dallas route moves time-sensitive intermodal freight between the eastern seaboard region served by the Norfolk Southern and the immense western region—including the Pacific Coast—served by the BNSF. The KCS route enables its two partners to avoid the delay-prone rail hubs in Memphis and New Orleans. For KCS stockholders, the Speedway demonstrates how efficiently a well-maintained main line can be upgraded quickly and economically to a higher-speed one that attracts traffic; then further upgraded to one permitting much higher speeds that attract even more traffic, especially that formerly moving via truck. For state, regional, and city planners and for economic development agencies, the Speedway slams home the lesson that a rail connection can emerge from relative obscurity almost overnight and put Meridian, Mississippi, on a high-speed corridor with international connections and implications. The KCS Speedway exists wholly to move intermodal cargo units off Interstate Highway 20. Its pig trains compete directly with trucks. And they win.

Understanding the KCS Speedway in the context of its Mexican connections leads the inquirer to the discovery that the KCS is converting a redundant Kansas City air base into a United States Customs preclearance facility. The KCS intends to use the new facility to expedite the movement of intermodal shipments from Mexico, Latin America, and the Caribbean, and to merge its shipments of new automobiles and light trucks with its intermodal operations. Already the KCS ships Mazda automobiles and Ford pickups built in Kansas City, but its management also realizes how many finished vehicles move north from Mexico, built with parts the KCS rolls south from the upper Midwest. Several trucking firms already contract with KCS to move trailers along the Speedway. Thus brand-new Mazdas and Fords whiz parallel to I-20 faster than speed limits permit motorists to drive the vehicles after purchase.

Watching a KCS Speedway train or examining a map of its route leads one to wonder about the long-term impact on communities and businesses centered on, for example, Memphis and New Orleans. At 10:15 every evening in 1935, the KCS swept Railway Post Office 15 south from Kansas City on its 822-mile run to Port Arthur. At Shreveport, the train halted to move mail to connecting trains on the east–west main line now operating as the Speedway. The brief pause at Shreveport remains a footnote in the history of postal service until some real estate developer—perhaps a warehouse or factory locator—happens to consider the significance of the transfer for municipalities like Poteau or Howe in Oklahoma, Vicksburg in Mississippi, Monroe or Ruston in Louisiana, or Marshall or Longview in Texas. Those places are served by I-20, so perhaps any change might be gradual. But no interstate highway reaches southwest from Shreveport to Lufkin, Texas, for example, although the Union Pacific serves that city. Like Lynchburg, Virginia, Lufkin sits far from congested interstate highways, but on a main line that might make the Speedway not just a fast route but a shortcut of significant implications.

Railroads compete with each other as fiercely as they compete with the trucking and barge industries, but for decades that competition scarcely focused long-range rural, metropolitan, or even urban planning. The KCS Speedway links the Norfolk Southern and the BNSF, to the disadvantage of the Union Pacific. If the Union Pacific acquired the KCS in a merger, Lufkin might be transformed as rapidly as Meridian is transformed today. Too many intellectuals still conceive of trains in terms of boxcars, not "double-stack pigs" outpacing trucks on I-20 and other highways. The boxcar era is gone, although specialized Railbox, Hy-Cube, and other boxcars still move important, high-value freight. Intermodal freight boxes carry much of the present, and will move most of the future.

A year after Southern Railway No. 8 rolled out of Lynchburg as a one-coach train departing a platform built for multiunit locomotives hauling fifteen-car long-distance streamliners, F. C. Margetts, a British transportation expert deeply involved in creating the European piggyback system, warned that piggybacking would either transform North American railroading or that freight trains would almost disappear.

As early as 1961, experts knew the United Kingdom rail network faced calamity, but not until the British Railways Board released *Reshaping British Rail* in 1963 did investors and railroad executives begin to consider rail transport as an alternative to highway building. At first glance the nationalized British rail system scarcely seemed a role model for anything: one-third of its tracks carried only 1 percent of the total ton-miles of freight, nearly half of its freight stations produced only 4 percent of the freight traffic, and most of the rolling stock creaked along in decrepitude. The short runs of most British freight trains had produced a situation in which most of the 450,000 freight cars moved an average of sixty miles a week. A nation roughly the size of the state of New York demonstrated beyond argument that highway freight movement outperformed rail service, especially over short distances. Tractor-trailer trucks, what the British call "articulated lorries," competed in ways that presaged their success in the United States.

But British trucks jammed British roads, especially in cities, and choked ferry ports opening on the Netherlands, Ireland, and France.

As Britain prospered from increased trade with the Continent and with Ireland, its roads and ports began to jam in ways that predictably infuriated motorists and shippers.

Presciently, the British Railways Board realized the potential implicit in intermodal container shipping. Since 1926 British railroads had experimented with containers, and by the 1950s Europeans saw British Rail containers on trains as far east as Italy and Sweden. In 1933 the International Container Bureau began standardizing rail containers, something the postwar International Standards Organization (ISO) accelerated. Despite wartime destruction and postwar problems with shipping to Communist countries behind the Iron Curtain, container traffic increased slowly, and the nationalization of British railroads in 1948 did little to bolster innovation. By 1960 management realized that the containers were too small, that they often merely replaced boxcars in the minds of shippers and railroad executives alike, and that the total volume of shipping meant that containers traveled on flatcars hauled in ordinary, slow-moving freight trains. In order to save itself from oblivion, British Rail focused on intermodal shipping as the best chance to increase revenue. Its directors believed that in so doing they would ameliorate the growing congestion of highways, especially in urban and rural areas attractive to tourists.

By 1965 British Rail had begun to experiment with a new concept in freight trains called "Liner Trains," a name soon changed to "Freightliner." Linking Glasgow and London, the trains operated as semipermanently coupled strings of flatcars on which British Rail loaded the eight-by-twenty- or eight-by-thirty-foot containers it or its shippers owned. Bypassing railroad yards and operating on strict schedules, the trains carried containers as passenger trains carried people. A shipper reserved a space on a given train, brought his container (as a box sitting atop a flat articulated lorry trailer) to either terminal, and a crane swung it aboard a train guaranteed to leave and arrive at specific times. In 1966 the trains carried 27,000 containers; two years later they moved 281,000 and by 1973, 634,500. When the energy crisis spiked the price of highway fuels in 1974, volume shot up to 711,400, and by 1975 the Freightliner trains, operating between twenty-nine terminals linked by seventy-five routes (including ports for Irish and European ferries), had proven a success. ISO-compliant shipping containers and scheduled trains open to any shipper had created an integrated system in Britain, and prompted Spain to establish a nearly identical system.

Eleven years after British Railways inaugurated Freightliner service, Margetts, a former director, envisioned standardized containers moving swiftly across all of Europe. The technology would transcend political division: by 1976 East Germany, Czechoslovakia, and other Soviet-bloc countries had expressed interest in the intermodal revolution. But Margetts saw far further around the curve of time. The Soviet Union moved 80 percent of its freight by rail, much of it over electrified routes; it offered a magnificent opportunity for containerized service itself. But as a land bridge to Asia, its Trans-Siberian Railway opened directly on the manufacturing enterprise of South Korea and China and, via the port of Nakhodka, Japan. Given improved political situations, manufactured goods might move swiftly from Asia across the Soviet Union to western Europe, Britain, and Ireland, and perhaps from the British Isles to Halifax in Nova Scotia.

More than many observers suspect, Freightliner service did much to stimulate the development of the European Union. It focused capital on tunneling beneath the English Channel, and it transformed ferry service across the Baltic and the Irish Sea.

The fragmentation of the Soviet Union and the continued intransigence of North Korea still partially offset the vast manufacturing capability of China. Routing containers from Japan via Nakhodka still competes unfavorably with sending them via container ship. But the extraordinary railroad revolution that began about 1960 in Great Britain continues to shape both private and public policy there and across Europe to South Korea. Operating freight trains as scheduled vehicles onto which any shipper may load a built-to-standards container has not only proved profitable for shippers and railroad companies but also enabled governments to embark on social improvements. In 2005 Britain determined to reduce truck traffic by one billion lorry trips per year. Such decisions depend on an efficient rail system that can easily absorb increased traffic.

Since 1960 many Americans have become familiar with British

and European train service as users of tourist rail passes. College students, vacationers, and senior citizens discover what business travelers find: passenger trains run on time and usually frequently. Without such rail lines and their once- or twice-a-day trains of intermodal containers, remote regions dependent on tourism would be marred by truck traffic. The quaint English or Scottish village, the remote Danish inn, or the river valley German town in which tourists relax, visit historic sites, and shop benefits from both passenger train service and a freight train that passes at the same time each day. A bit of noise, a bit of blur, and the train is gone. The tourist haven becomes quiet, and perhaps the occasional American tourist realizes what is missing: trucks.

By the late 1970s a British firm had perfected a truck trailer equipped with a pair of small lifts that enabled a lone lorry driver to park parallel with a railroad flatcar and slide an ISO container box between vehicles. Blatchford Stack Cranes moved both forty- and twenty-foot-long containers with ease, adjusting for uneven heights between parking lots and railroad sidings. Stack cranes freed shippers from using transfer terminals. In particular, they enabled rural and wilderness shippers to make full use of intermodal cars in low-traffic locations that failed to justify the installation of permanent transfer equipment. Blatchford Stack Cranes offered remote regions in Britain and Europe intermodal shipping and freedom from long-distance truck traffic. One local trucker owning a flatbed truck equipped with such units might move dozens of containers to and from flatcars stopped on an ordinary railroad siding, but the truck itself would never venture far from its home neighborhood.

American railroads began experiments earlier than their British counterparts, but for decades their efforts floundered. In the first years of the twentieth century, the Long Island Rail Road tried moving loaded farm wagons directly into New York City: horses traveled in special boxcars, and once in the city farmers hitched the horses to wagons and proceeded to hawk vegetables on residential streets. Not until 1926 did the Chicago, North Shore & Milwaukee experiment with moving loaded truck trailers aboard flatcars in a manner based on circus train experience. However cumbersome—tractor-trailer drivers had to back up ramps and then along the tops of a line of flatcars, unhitch tractors and drive forward, freeing a path for the next driver in line, a process repeated in reverse at the delivery point—by 1956 truck trailers had begun to move coast-to-coast aboard American freight trains. From the beginning, rail experiments clashed with efforts to move truck trailers on barges and riverboats, an effort begun by Seatrain Lines, Inc., in 1929. The opening of the St. Lawrence Seaway in 1959 profoundly altered the mindset of manufacturers and shippers, who suddenly discovered Cleveland and other Great Lakes cities to be international seaports. For twenty years after 1959, most American transportation experts assumed that entire truck trailers would be transported by rail, river, and sea pretty much as they moved over the road. They would "roll on/roll off" railroad cars, barges, and ships, and perhaps even airplanes, a concept backed by a military anxious to move matériel as rapidly as it did motorized equipment.

Roll on/roll off, quickly designated RORO by its advocates, proved far more time-consuming that anyone first guessed. Loading twenty trailers from the end of the last flatcar in a string meant the first trailer might back three-fourths of a mile along the flatcars, a tricky, slow operation. Then each truck trailer had to be chained down, again a slow and labor-intensive task. When the train arrived at its destination it had to be oriented to permit truck tractors to back up a ramp and remove the trailers one by one. Despite some innovations, especially a hydraulic hitch that moved upward from the floor of the flatcar and securely grabbed the truck trailer, and clawlike devices that picked up entire truck trailers and moved them to and from flatcars, railroad company enthusiasm for moving truck trailers atop flatcars fluctuated.

In the 1950s the New York Central developed its Flexi-Van system, apparently because the low tunnels and bridges east of Buffalo precluded moving truck trailers towering atop flatcars. Essentially a hydraulic-powered swiveling flatbed trailer that shoved containers to and from specially equipped flatcars, Flexi-Van proved an efficient innovation. One truck driver would back his rig at right angles to a flatcar, and in less that two minutes transfer and secure the box. Sending the box alone, minus frame and wheels, offered many advantages. Lowering the center of gravity increased safety and permitted higher speeds, and reducing the profile of the loaded car decreased wind resistance, especially by eliminating air eddying beneath trailers. Shipping only the box meant sparing the bearings on the truck wheels left behind: stationery truck trailers bounced on their springs aboard moving flatcars, ruining wheel bearings designed to bear weight while rolling. Finally, eliminating wheels, rear bumper, and other impedimenta reduced weight and so lowered cost. A handful of Flexi-Vans moved onto Santa Fe, Milwaukee, and Illinois Central rails, but the boxes were useless without the custom-designed truck trailers and flatcars.

Inquiry into United States and Canadian efforts to improve piggybacking after 1955 reveals strenuous if extremely competitive and counterproductive effort. The Pennsylvania and Southern Pacific focused on long-distance trailer-on-flatcar (TOFC) movement, while the Canadian Pacific experimented with a container-on-flatcar (COFC) service it called Portager. TOFC required heavy, specially built flatcars eighty-seven feet long that carried two forty-foot-long trailers. COFC efforts proceeded in fits and starts, especially since Canadian advocates experimented with lightweight, four-wheel (instead of the standard eight-wheel) flatcars. Despite the collapse of Canadian Pacific efforts in the early 1960s, that railroad envisioned matters far more clearly than did most United States firms. From the beginning, it embraced a vision of passenger trains that included a few lightweight flatcars from which standardized containers could be transshipped in two- or three-minute station stops. Small towns and isolated depots in Manitoba, Alberta, and other sparsely populated provinces seemed ideal candidates for transshipping containers in very simple, quick ways, perhaps by using old school buses shorn of their bodies. The Canadian Pacific was familiar with the latest thinking in Great Britain, too. In 1961 it shipped a Portager container loaded with peanuts from Montreal to Liverpool, and brought it home filled with auto parts that then moved by rail to a factory in Ontario. But in the same year the limited-access highway between Montreal and Toronto opened, and trucking firms focused on driving rather than shipping trucks. The reluctance of United States shippers, transportation firms, and government regulators to accept ISO-mandated containers undoubtedly contributed to the slow growth of intermodal shipping of all sorts into the 1980s, but even the Canadians confronted difficulties of scale and integration.

Always the military focus on RORO technology stymied advocates of other systems, especially COFC ones. As late as 1977 one industry expert lamented that United States shippers often insisted on putting truck wheels beneath containers sent by rail, simply because rates proved lower that way. As Seatrain Lines and other freight-forwarding companies experimented with dedicated trains modeled on British Freightliners—Seatrain Lines operated COFC trains from Weehawken, New Jersey, that linked United Kingdom shippers with California destinations—politicians discovered the pain of change. Longshoremen unions, shipping companies, and warehouse firms in New Orleans complained to the Federal Maritime Commission that the dedicated trains had diverted ships from that port to Weehawken. Suddenly a modest experiment—Seatrain Lines chartered one train a week—produced major dislocation in New Orleans and other ports, just as other experiments in moving containers from Long Beach in California galvanized groups elsewhere along the Pacific seaboard. Retrospect suggests that military thinking underlay much railroad industry confusion. A major TOFC company, North American Car Corporation, moved with dispatch toward nationwide RORO service. Its CEO, a general formerly in charge of the United States Army Corps of Transportation, understood the powerful attraction of a truck trailer delivered ready for the road—by rail.

As early as the 1950s a compromise vehicle emerged, a truck trailer fitted with both rubber tires and steel wheels. On the highway, it performed essentially as an ordinary trailer; on the rails, it coupled with identical trailers and, with an adaptor, to any locomotive or freight or passenger car, although its builders preferred that the cars operate in homogenous trains. Invented by the Chesapeake & Ohio Railway as a way of moving time-sensitive freight in passenger trains, so-called Railvans had almost vanished by the 1960s. Not until the 1980s did they reemerge, chiefly as experiments, and by 2000 they had begun operating in once-a-day dedicated trains between San Bernardino, California, and Chicago, with connections there for New Jersey. The Railvan itself morphed into the contemporary RoadRailer; no longer must it carry its steel wheels when it moves over the road. Triple Crown, a private company equally expert in trucking and railroading, operates the fleet that moves over certain routes the company calls "lanes." The BNSF Railroad discovered in its Ice Cold Express service between Southern California and Chicago that refrigerated, air-ride suspension RoadRailers rarely damaged vegetables and fruits. In 1982 the Illinois Central Gulf learned that the close-coupled, air-suspended sinuous trains operated over the curvy, hilly track between Louisville and Memphis at higher speeds than TOFC trains managed. For very time-sensitive, delicate products, and for paper and other tougher shipments, Road-Railer offers an alternative competitive with long-distance trucking. No longer does the railroad company need a special flatcar and terminal: the container uses steel wheels, and drops them when it connects to the eight rubber-tired ones that convert it into a truck trailer. A truck driver need only back his trailer onto steel rails embedded in asphalt to convert it into a railcar. RoadRailer is RORO technology with a twist, and the twist makes it competitive with newer COFC technology.

Over long distances, stacking ISO forty- and forty-five-foot-long containers one atop another proves extremely efficient. Although the Southern Pacific Railroad bought the first double-stack cars in 1981, it was a steamship company, American President Lines, that sparked a revolution by buying its own cars and asking railroads to bid on their operation between Los Angeles, Seattle, and New York via Chicago. By ordering train schedules around ship sailings, American President Lines produced a means of moving ISO standard containers at speeds comparable to those offered by trucking firms. Sea-Land, a global freight company, quickly copied the idea and launched dedicated trains from Tacoma in Washington to Chicago. It found the service so useful it purchased its own rail terminal for New York service, at Little Ferry, New Jersey. As double-stack service spread to other port cities, especially older ones like Boston, Philadelphia, and Baltimore, railroad companies again confronted the low bridge–low tunnel problems the New York Central faced in the 1950s. But by the late 1980s railroad companies foresaw serious

profit, and began raising bridges and tunnels—or depressing tracks
to accomplish the same gain in height. In some instances, government agencies such as the Port of Seattle, mindful of business lost a
decade earlier when ports were bypassed by Seatrain Lines experiments, encouraged railroads to begin double-stack service. By 1986
Burlington Northern operated six trains of double-stack cars between Seattle and Chicago. Today anyone who glances at a mainline
track sees double-stack cars, usually in special, fast-moving trains.

Just over a mile long, carrying two hundred containers (each
about forty-five feet long), and able to move easily at seventy miles
per hour or much faster, double-stack trains offer a special advantage to railroads: they halve the number of trains or lengths of
trains. Their chief efficiency lies in fitting two hundred containers
on a sidetrack that otherwise holds a train of one hundred. Whatever the other advantages of double-stack technology, limiting the
need for more passing sidetracks is perhaps the greatest, although
halving train crews cuts costs as well. As traffic booms, no train
crews are laid off: others must be hired and trained. Almost certainly the heavy machinery needed to unload the double-stack cars
remains the chief disadvantage. At urban terminals the machinery
moves with impressive quickness, but no one dreams of unloading
a double-stack car at a rural depot. Double-stack containers are not
express, even if they move fast.

Consequently, the Amtrak experiment in moving RoadRailers as
components of passenger trains intrigued many rail industry watchers, as Cody Grivno reported in a 2003 article describing the units
and their use. In 1986 Amtrak formed a subsidiary, Amtrak Express,
to improve its movement of express and mail. By 2002 the Amtrak
rail yard at Lumber Street in Chicago had three tracks embedded in
asphalt for the making up and breaking down of RoadRailer trains
to be attached to Amtrak passenger cars. Yet at the same time, Amtrak had moved away from carrying mail and packages in special
boxcars. The difficulty Amtrak faces is simple: its trains run too infrequently. Just as a once-a-day passenger train invites few riders, so
the same train lures few shippers to desert trucking companies. And
Amtrak almost certainly runs its trains too slowly, something that
railroad companies discovered in the 1990s when UPS and other

time-sensitive shippers suggested innovation beyond anything Amtrak accomplished. Amtrak struggled to make its RoadRailer service profitable and even changed train schedules to suit shippers, in ways that angered passengers and eventually prompted them to avoid trains.

Frequent, reliable, very fast TOFC or COFC service intrigues UPS simply because it intrigues other firms. Slicing a full day from coast-to-coast shipping schedules might give UPS a powerful edge over its many competitors. Railroads consequently experiment when asked, and trial runs of so-called bullet trains demonstrate the feasibility of four-day transcontinental movement of truck trailers and other containers by rail—in freight trains.

In 2003 Fred W. Frailey, editor of *Kiplinger's Personal Finance*, published an hour-by-hour account of one experimental run. His detailed story in *Trains* focuses on four days following the 4:30 AM departure of a test train on March 5, 2002, along the main lines of the BNSF and CSX from Los Angeles via Chicago to Little Ferry, New Jersey, just outside New York City. The readership of *Trains* is chiefly a mix of professional railroaders of all ranks and amateurs deeply interested in contemporary railroading. But it includes another component: investors who read the magazine to help make sense of what they find in company annual reports and other industry documents and what they glimpse in the larger landscape.

Glimpsing the test train meant not blinking. While never running above seventy miles per hour, the train slowed only in a few places, and then not for long. Its owners expected it to operate 3,154 miles in sixty-five hours, with part of it splitting off just south of Albany to run to the UPS central New England sorting facility in Worcester, Massachusetts. It succeeded. But its dash across the continent, along with other experimental high-speed dashes by other trains, produced more proof that existing equipment and track can move freight easily as fast as 18-wheel trucks operated by two-person crews in sleeper-equipped cabs, and with a bit of improvement, far faster.

Overtaking slower trains proved a major difficulty. Even on double-track stretches fitted with switches operated remotely, some other fast freights had to slow in order for the very fast train to pass. Chicago-area track work slowed the train, simply because in fifty-six miles it rolled over eleven crossings of other railroads and through six junctions, and a one-mile section of track limited to ten miles per hour. For a few miles it operated over the Indiana Harbor Belt Railroad (a line that exists chiefly to move strings of cars from one railroad yard to another), which cooperated fully in getting the train to Blue Island Junction, where CSX tracks begin. From Los Angeles to New York, however, the problem of overtaking trains vexed dispatchers. Trains moved west on parallel tracks, and only rarely did the fast train affect them as dispatchers now and then shifted it onto west-bound main lines in order for it to pass slower east-bound trains in a tightly controlled game of dodgems. Frailey articulated the crucial difficulty: no longer did the railroads operate high-speed passenger and mail-express trains that long ago intertwined among the freights. Employees had the skills to manage the movement of a very fast train, but they no longer had the extra passing tracks from the streamliner era.

After the 1970s, eliminating cabooses meant that on long sections of single track not controlled remotely, pulling a mile-long freight train into a passing siding involved someone having to climb down from a stopped locomotive and open the track switch, then wait until the train rolled into the siding before closing the switch and *walking a mile back to the locomotive.* After another train had passed on the main track, the same employee then opened the switch ahead of the locomotive, waited while the engineer pulled the entire train onto the main track, then closed the switch and *walked another mile forward to the stopped locomotive.* What had been accomplished in 1920 with whistle signals, arm waving, and—at night—swinging kerosene lanterns between locomotive and caboose had by 1990 become so cumbersome that railroad companies tried to avoid it. As traffic picked up, railroad executives bemoaned the loss of the double-track mileage reduced to single track following the demise of most passenger train service. BNSF officials determined that the fast freight overtook forty-two other eastbound freights, including several fast freights loaded mostly with UPS trailers. Without cabooses, only the most up-to-date remote control of track switches permitted such overtaking.

Something more important to real estate developers was the fact that freight trains no longer curved around great urban terminals. At Kansas City, Buffalo, and elsewhere, the fast freight rolled directly through cities, usually on elevated or depressed tracks, often past the locations of long-gone passenger stations. Through Utica, New York, a city of 270,000 people, the train scarcely slowed; nor did it slow for Syracuse (732,000) or Rochester (1,100,000). In almost no city east of Los Angeles did the experimental fast freight slow, except for regular thousand-mile safety inspections, refueling, and crew changes, usually in tiny towns. Only the suburbs of Chicago slowed the train.

A consideration of geography will reveal why the CSX was so interested in pleasing UPS. The train moved northeast across the continent, snaked through Chicago, and then rolled east to Albany before rushing south along the Hudson River. A CSX competitor, Norfolk Southern, pursued a more direct west-to-east route from St. Louis to the New York metropolitan region, and offered to move UPS cars free from New York to Worcester for the privilege. A shorter route, probably via Pittsburgh, might prove faster, despite the added cost of moving trains over the Alleghenies rather than along the old "water-level route" following the Great Lakes, Erie Canal, and Hudson River. The fate of very fast freight trains remains in the hands of shippers, especially UPS, which has yet to commit to the sixty truck trailers per train per day on which the BNSF and CSX are willing to set a price. But as the *Wall Street Journal* reported in a front-page story on July 25, 2003, UPS has already achieved one goal: CSX and Union Pacific have combined to operate dedicated trains on a sixty-three-hour schedule.

Two economic factors will determine how many faster freights operate in the immediate future. One is simple: the price of diesel fuel will make high-speed transcontinental truck haulage less than competitive with rail service. The other is complex: Freight trains operate optimally at speeds between sixty and seventy miles per hour; speeds above that produce expensive wear-and-tear on track and schedules. Equipment like RoadRailer might well reduce the maintenance costs, but the scheduling problems may prove intractable. Many parallel lines of long-ago competing railroads have been ripped up or converted to local-service mileage, and even double tracking single-track stretches does little to improve the flow of very fast freights among other such trains, like unit trains carrying coal or grain. Where rails did not become hiking trails, companies began operating some lines as one-way routes, using nearby parallel lines, usually acquired from old competitors in mergers, in ways suddenly profitable. In the late 1990s the Union Pacific converted the old Cotton Belt Route between St. Louis and Texas into a one-way southbound route via Pine Bluff, Arkansas, and used the old Missouri Pacific main line as a one-way northbound route through Little Rock. In *Main Lines*, Saunders explains what tourists discover in the Old Southwest. The former Southern Pacific main line west from New Orleans to Houston is one-way westbound, and the old Missouri Pacific line between the two cities is entirely eastbound. Across east Texas, Louisiana, and Arkansas, increasingly heavy traffic and especially high-speed, critical-schedule container trains flow smoothly—most of the time—in a validation of Union Pacific innovation. Observers may occasionally note that all the trains in a particular region operate only in one direction. Canny investors think about developing real estate along such high-speed rail routes. But railroad management wonders what happens when the one-way routes themselves can no longer accommodate more trains. Double tracking is the only viable answer.

Across most of the middle third of the United States, railroad companies work tirelessly to add automated passing sidings, extend miles of double track, and even lay third tracks alongside heavily used double-track mains. Double stacking ISO containers bought many railroads a grace period of five or so years; now most need double track. But as oil drives up the cost of diesel fuel, another solution shimmers on the horizon.

When the Pennsylvania Railroad studied electrifying its main line over the mountains between Harrisburg and Pittsburgh in 1930, it determined that electrification would shave four hours from the sixteen-hour schedule of its New York–Chicago luxury train service operating over state-of-the-art double track. Depression and war stymied Pennsylvania management, but the findings remain potent: the twelve-hour passenger service would eliminate airline competition between many intermediate stops, if not between New York and Chicago. In 1955, long after diesel-electric locomotives replaced steam for its very fast trains, the company commissioned another study focused on electrifying its route west of Harrisburg. As Michael Bezilla noted in a seminal 1978 article, "The Electrification That Might Have Been—and Might Still Be," some farsighted managers and investors mindful of British piggyback innovations knew the route had approached fast freight capacity. Old electrification studies now offer valuable information for shippers interested in moving freight fast, and for advocates of nuclear-generated electricity as well. Electrification may obviate the need for some double track, but it will succeed best in places lacking space for double or triple track, especially in cities and densely built suburbs.

Venture capitalist interest may well drive the upward spiraling prices offered for what seems at first glance to be mere railroad industry memorabilia. Investors considering opportunities in Rust Belt cities might well profit from reading a scarce document, the New York Central Railroad's *Fast Freight Schedule, November, 1948*. Distributed during the postwar era only to favored shippers and would-be shippers thinking about high-speed freight service, the document has more than historical value today. It explains what a railroad accomplished half a century ago, and might reinstitute, given demand.

Twenty-three years before Frailey's high-speed experimental trip, another author detailed regular piggyback service on the Chicago & North Western (C&NW) west from Chicago to Fremont, Nebraska, a junction with the Union Pacific northwest of Omaha. F. K. Plous recounted the dedicated effort of a company threatened by the flood of freight moving onto the new Interstate 80 after 1969. What was to be done with a multitrack railroad built for high-speed express passenger trains? In 1970 the ten thousand employees of the company bought it from its shareholders, began abandoning rural lines across South Dakota, Minnesota, and other states, and started improving its main line west of Chicago. Nevertheless, the employee-owned railroad could not get past the mid-1960s calamity of converting so much of its double-track mileage into single track. In 1978 train No. 243, part of the C&NW Falcon piggyback service, carried a caboose, avoided the Omaha passenger station, and moved in the very dawn of innovations like coal-carrying unit trains, but it rolled over track no longer in shape for the passenger trains that had raced over it in the 1950s. Its crew had in hand the bits and pieces that so impressed Frailey years later, but even with energy-crisis fifty-five-miles-per-hour interstate highway speed limits, the time had not come. For No. 243—indeed for the entire C&NW Railroad—the gravitational pull of I-80 proved too powerful. Creston and Rochelle in Illinois, and De Witt, Stanwood, Cedar Rapids, Ames, Boone, Grand Junction, and Dunlap in Iowa no longer glistened as jewels along a high-speed rail route. C&NW business worsened. Eventually the mighty Union Pacific bought the company, improved the track, and began to compete head-to-head with I-80 truck traffic.

Nowadays railroad companies, UPS and other shippers, and real estate investors look at RoadRailers, double-stack cars, and fast freight trains with focused attention. The distribution of light-weight, time-sensitive items already begins to move from highways and even from airliners as railroads recall the bygone era of very fast freight trains rolling along track fitted for even faster passenger and mail-express trains. So much freight has recently moved from trucks that railroads have been forced to clear jammed yards and port terminals by hiring trucking firms to move containers over highways. Railroads still experience extreme difficulty competing with first-rate trucking firms for time-sensitive shipments, and it will be years before they will compete favorably for shipments over less than eight hundred miles.

As more and more truck trailers and intermodal containers move onto high-speed freight trains charging parallel to interstate highways, would-be warehouse owners, investors, and consultants hired by overseas companies examine property adjacent to main lines. Potential sites for the new sorts of facilities Roy L. Harmon describes in *Reinventing the Warehouse: World-Class Distribution Logistics* must have access to vehicles that move fast day after day, and long-haul trucking companies can no longer promise such service unless they ship trailers by rail. Congress recognizes a new situation developing: *Planes, Trains, and Intermodalism,* a 2003 report of the

Committee on Transportation and Infrastructure, omits the word *trucks* from its title.

In Rochester and Utica, in Lynchburg and so many other small cities, especially on the High Plains, businessmen are glancing thoughtfully at the fast freight trains knifing across the landscape, especially those carrying UPS and other trucking-company trailers. They know that several hours later the freight train will be someplace else, on time, in a way that invites thought about long-term local real estate, warehousing and distribution, and even manufacturing opportunities unimaginable without fast freight trains. Freight trains that never stop in towns and small cities are the focus of intense analysis nowadays. People who watch people who watch trains may find much food for thought in regions far removed from large cities. Even on open highways west of the Mississippi, 18-wheel trucks rarely roll at more than seventy-five miles per hour; no one imagines them moving much faster in the future. Often trucks irritate motorists as they change lanes to overtake each other or slow down going uphill. Freight trains now and then pass the trucks, and motorists wonder why truck cargoes cannot be shifted from highways, leaving the roads clear for automobiles. Away from the coasts, railroad company television commercials emphasize the highway-clearing impact of fast freight trains carrying truck trailers. The commercials say nothing about a reorientation of warehouse and other commercial activity.

SOURCES: Bezilla, "The Electrification That Might Have Been"; DeViers and Lenz, "Recentralization"; Frailey, "Blank Bullet"; H. R. Grant, "Piggyback Pioneer"; Grivno, "Amtrak's Mail and Express Fleet"; Harmon, *Reinventing the Warehouse;* Howard, "Piggyback and the Portager Dream"; Hubbard, "Will 'Piggyback' Make the Boxcar Obsolete?"; T. Johnson, "Rail Yard Infill"; Machalaba and Chipello, "New Track"; Margetts, "Trains for Tomorrow"; McMurty, *Roads;* New York Central Railroad, *Fast Freight Schedule, November, 1948;* Overbey, "Piggyback"; Plous, "The Flight of the Falcon"; Saunders, *Main Lines;* Sperandeo, "The Bi-Modal RoadRailer"; Stephens, "What to Do with RoadRailer?"; Unites States Congress, Committee on Transportation and Infrastructure, *Planes, Trains, and Intermodalism.*

In a West Virginia freight yard, multiple unit trains of coal await clearance to begin their trips to electric power plants.

8

BULK

Rumbling through the night, the drag freight rolls as it always has, moving slowly and steadily despite being sidetracked for fast freights and the occasional Amtrak passenger train. Nowadays almost certainly a unit train comprising identical cars carrying identical or similar loads and destined for one or two giant customers, the train of coal, grain, ethanol, chemicals, or corn syrup saves the national highway pavement from destruction and intersections from gridlock.

By the late 1970s interstate highway deterioration could be discerned as a cryptic by-product of the 1973 gasoline crisis. Despite higher fuel costs and fewer Americans driving long distances, interstate highways decayed practically overnight. In a 1978 exposé entitled "Our Crumbling Interstate: A National Dilemma," E. D. Fales advised *Popular Mechanics* readers that decrepit long-distance highways resulted largely from ever-heavier trucks moving at speeds well above the energy crisis limit of fifty-five miles per hour. Despite encounters with experts arguing that deterioration resulted from severe winters, deferred maintenance, and simple aging of highways built twenty years earlier, Fales reported that many thought heavier trucks destroyed pavement.

Fales drove eight thousand miles while researching his article, and discovered that explanations involving poor initial construction and deferred maintenance seemed suspect. I-76, the Pennsylvania Turnpike, appeared in far better shape than the much newer I-80, and U.S. 301 south of Richmond, Virginia, offered a smoother ride than the newer I-95. I-40 across the South produced reports of holes in bridges and very bumpy surfaces, and I-43 in the upper Midwest had a reputation for cracks and potholes. Truckers considered concrete-slab pavement like that on I-90 between Cleveland and Erie a failure. The slabs settled, especially after harsh winters, producing jarring rides that tired drivers and jolted cargo. If harsh winters explained decay, Fales asked, what explained the good roads of Maine, Minnesota, and Montana? Perhaps heat caused I-5 in California to ripple. Maybe I-65 and other new interstates made older ones seem worse by simple comparison, but photographs of shattered pavement on I-81 near Shenandoah, Pennsylvania, did not lie. Almost overnight, something had changed.

Between 1973 and 1981 the costs of interstate highway construction and maintenance doubled. In 1972 the Nixon administration had already capitulated to fiscal reality and begun diverting a small portion of the federal gasoline tax to urban mass-transit systems. The 1973 gasoline crisis subverted the effort still lauded by environmentalists and antiautomobile crusaders. The ensuing sharp rise in housing costs, gasoline prices, and domestic heating costs meant that politicians refused to raise gasoline taxes until after 1983. Far too little money flowed to fuel the Urbmobile or even a city bus, although some was allocated to subsidize rural airports. As Mark H. Rose reveals near the end of his *Interstate: Express Highway Politics, 1939–1989*, the number of all paved-surface road miles built annually dropped from 172,000 in 1970 to only 66,000 in 1979. Apparently computer-driven scenario analysis shaped at least some decision making. In 1982 the National Research Council estimated that between 1980 and 1995, federal, state, and local governments would have to spend $350 billion just to maintain paved highways at minimum levels. The governments planned on spending only $235 billion. By 1986, as potholed reality slowed delivery and damaged cargoes, the national trucking organizations lobbied vigorously for increased highway spending. The heyday of interstate highway building lay in the past, and visions of cruising at 120 miles per hour became pipe dreams or hopes betrayed. In the 1990s federal, state, county, and municipal authorities agonized over the escalating cost of highway maintenance.

Few scholars analyze the very recent past of highway politics, but after 1980 engineering researchers began analyzing the physical realities of road maintenance. In 1983 two Purdue University experts, Benjamin Colucci-Rios and Eldon J. Yoder, raised questions that still resonate in political debates. In *A Methodology for Evaluating the Increase in Pavement Maintenance Costs Resulting from Increased*

Truck Weights on a Statewide Basis, they pointed out that one heavy truck may actually damage a road surface less than two or more trucks carrying the total weight of the heavy vehicle. But about one issue they had "90% confidence": increasing the legal weight limit translated into increased maintenance costs. Older pavements might wear more rapidly than newer ones, but such nuance mattered little in the end. If trucks put more weight on any sort of surface, some government entity would be forced to repair the damage. More trucks meant more damage, but more heavy trucks augured massive damage, especially at the local level.

Across much of the United States, local government means the county, the entity that provides three important services: police, education, and road maintenance. The county sheriff often patrols sparsely populated precincts that enjoy very low crime rates. The officers work with volunteer fire and rescue associations to offer a standard of response time that may shock suburban visitors accustomed to help arriving within five minutes. Rural police and fire assistance may be a half hour or more from someone dialing 911, an eon that explains rural devotion to firearms, sophisticated fire extinguishers, and well-stocked medicine chests. Counties provide public schooling—sometimes in a single building that houses all grades from kindergarten through senior high school; more often in several elementary schools and a lone junior-senior high school. Still called "consolidated schools" from an era when large structures replaced one-room schoolhouses, the public education systems depend on school buses operating over long routes. Police cars, fire engines, and school buses traverse county roads, often gravel ones graded seasonally and repaired after heavy rains. On local roads depend the emergency services and educational operations that bind rural dwellers together.

During the Kennedy administration, as large tractors replaced smaller ones and one well-mechanized farm family did the work that formerly required three or four, vast reaches of rural America depopulated. Fewer families per square mile meant fewer customers for crossroads stores and small-town main street merchants, and many retail businesses failed long before Wal-Mart opened. This mattered little until the late 1970s, when it became clear that fewer families meant fewer taxpayers to maintain the same mileage of county roads.

No historic landscape feature more clearly demonstrates the power of spatial reality to affect local and national politics than the networks of county roads crisscrossing rural America. The roads date mostly from horse-and-buggy days. East of the Appalachians they are contorted, often following valleys rather than crossing hills: the handle of a pail is the same length lying on the rim of the pail as held up, the old farmers said, and since hills tire horses, the more expedient way is the flat one. West of the Appalachians, as airplane passengers may occasionally discern from aloft, the county roads run in a great grid that makes the landscape into a checkerboard of fields and farms. Winding or straight, the roads serve vastly fewer people than they did in 1935, but the people have higher road maintenance standards than ever. Rural dwellers want asphalt pavement, and frequently they believe federal tax dollars ought to pay for it. After all, they argue, the safety of the school bus is paramount, especially on dark rainy mornings when the bus must ford flooding creeks. Rural road maintenance from Maine to Arizona is a sort of public welfare operation, offering nonfarm jobs to county residents employed by contractors frequently active in politics and funding dump truck and heavy equipment dealers. Always the rural road offers at least the potential for profitable traffic, if only a truck laden with harvested grain or chicken feed.

Farmers buy aging 18-wheel trucks and put them out to pasture behind barns, using them mostly at harvest time. Away from the agricultural Midwest, and indeed away from most interstate highways, few Americans spend much time wondering about the paucity of old trailer trucks. But at harvest time, and throughout the year in regions where farmers own their own grain-storage silos, aging heavy trucks rumble along dirt roads, across lightly built bridges, and over thinly paved roads, often converging in small towns boasting one or more grain elevators paying a slightly higher price for grain than those located on railroad routes far closer to many farms.

Large-scale farming means large-scale returns from seemingly tiny cost differentials. A few cents difference in the per-bushel price of grain often prompts a farmer to buy an 18-wheel truck, despite the annual registration and insurance costs of the vehicle. Kansas charges about $1,750 a year to register an eighty-thousand-pound truck, but farmers willingly accept that cost, plus insurance premiums, because the truck offers access to elevators paying a slightly higher price per bushel.

Railroads unwittingly precipitated the surge in rural trucking. After the passage of the Staggers Act in 1980, railroad companies freed from traditional antitrust rate-setting rules began experimenting with efficient innovations initially prized by stockholders and environmentalists alike. Large railroads, called "Class I" companies by industry experts, created hundred-car unit trains to move grain. Loading at automated facilities spread along main lines, the trains provided low-cost transportation, especially to ocean ports. Grain-buying firms benefited from lower transport costs and passed savings along to nearby farmers. Farmers far distant from the new facilities grew jealous quickly, but took years to act decisively. Over twenty years many of them deserted local grain elevators served by short-line railroads, replaced their small trucks that made many short trips to the nearest elevator with old 18-wheelers, and began grinding down rural roads toward loading facilities serving unit trains.

Kansas offers an illuminating example of massive economic dislocation, and nowadays serves researchers as a laboratory. In *Transportation Quarterly* and similar journals, independent examiners confirm the detailed results compiled by Kansas Department of Transportation experts. The short lines spun off as scarcely profitable by Class I railroads at first did well using labor-saving techniques and older equipment, but now suffer from an inability to offer rates competitive with those of unit trains. In the past two years, *Kansas Grain Transportation,* published annually by the Kansas State Board of Agriculture, has reported that many elevators served by short-line railroads now ship grain by truck to Class I loading facilities. Between 1990 and 1999 the truck share of wheat shipped from elevators rose from 37 percent to 47 percent, corn went from 62 percent to 72 percent, and sorghum from 35 percent to 56 percent. Farmer ownership of 18-wheelers becomes only a part of a far larger problem confronting rural counties in Kansas and other agricultural states. Large trucks often operate to grain elevators, and other large trucks often operate from those elevators to state-of-the-art rail-side loading facilities, mills, and animal-feed blenders.

Almost all of the dramatically increased truck traffic originates in a price differential of two cents per bushel.

Buying an aged 18-wheel truck becomes a sensible investment for many young men a few years out of high school or college, although for others it becomes a money-gobbling nightmare. Licensing requirements involving a year's driving experience for the owner of a heavy truck become unimportant when fathers are owner-employers. Initial low purchase prices of used trucks—along with fuel, insurance, and excise-tax costs—strike many young men as reasonable given the seasonal use of the truck. After harvest, some owners surrender registrations for most of the year, while others seek work moving animal feed or fertilizer. Along with rigs bought by large-scale family farmers and the growing number of corporate-owned farms rumble equally heavy, if creaky, trucks owned by young men who rarely risk operating on interstate highways. Like most agricultural truckers, they drive over back roads, surprising tourists and vexing highway maintenance officials.

Computer scenario analysis focuses on the short- and long-term impact of short-line railroad abandonment. Between 1970 and 1979 railroads abandoned 415 miles of track in Kansas; in the next decade they abandoned 815 miles; in the next, 1,246. Railroads gave up 335 track miles in the year 2001 alone, and the future projected by analysts seems grim. After 1990 short-line companies accounted for well more than half the abandoned mileage. Gone is the hope that accompanied the 1980 Staggers Act.

Imagining the economic future of Kansas both with and without four short-line railroads—the Kansas & Oklahoma, Kyle Railroad, Cimarron Valley, and the Nebraska, Kansas & Colorado—has occupied the attention of economists and transportation experts equipped with massive amounts of hard data. Michael Babcock, Eugene Russell, and Curtis Mauler's "Study of the Impact of Rail Abandonment on Local Roads and Streets," a paper presented at the Sixth International Conference on Low Volume Roads (1995), offers a useful introduction to what troubles the Kansas State Board of Agriculture. On the one hand, scenario analysis demonstrates that total transportation costs would prove virtually identical if all four short lines abandoned business and all wheat moved by Class I railroads and trucks. Many farmers would still drive their wheat in small trucks twelve to fifteen miles to local elevators along abandoned tracks, and those elevators would ship it in large trucks to Class I loading facilities. Farmer- and trucking-company-owned 18-wheel trucks might easily operate another hundred miles each way to such facilities, or reach even farther to the great terminal elevators in Salina, Hutchinson, and Wichita loading unit trains routed to export elevators at Houston. On the other hand, farmers in some regions of the state would suffer increased expenses from doubled handling costs as local grain elevators transshipped wheat to main-line railroad loading facilities. In a matrix involving farms, elevators, railroads, and truck carriers, scenario analysis suggests very little adverse impact from short-line railroad abandonment for farmers and other grain shippers.

Only when the question of highway maintenance enters the picture does the analysis shift dramatically. Russell and other researchers using sophisticated models of highway infrastructure deterioration have concluded that abandoning the four short-line railroads would cost $57.8 million annually in increased road maintenance costs.

Because one railcar carries grain equivalent to four 18-wheel truckloads, scenario analysts may wonder about increased tax revenue from diesel fuel sales. Unfortunately, the vast increase in truck carriage of grain would produce only $288,531 in additional fuel tax revenue, half of 1 percent of the $57.8 million in pavement repair costs.

Rephrasing the analysis makes equally bitter reading. In Kansas, grain-hauling trucks owned by farmers, contract truckers, and grain elevator co-ops do about $7.15 per truck per mile damage to the roads they travel. Every mile of short-line railroad abandoned tomorrow would cost $34,000 annually today, and much more in the years ahead.

Of course, trucks move over some roads more frequently than others. A very heavy truck might pass over a dirt road serving a handful of farms only once every three hours in harvest seasons. But less and less often do such trucks move toward local grain elevators strung along short-line railroads. Instead they merge into heavy flows toward state-of-the-art loading facilities built at widely distant points along Class I railroad lines. While such facilities pay property taxes to the municipality or county in which they do business, the revenue fails to cover increased road maintenance costs within the tax district. It does nothing to alleviate road deterioration just beyond tax-district borders.

Kansas highway authorities expect a new paved road to last thirty years, having received substantial maintenance after ten and twenty years. The rise in heavy grain-hauling truck traffic means, first, a much faster rate of pavement deterioration and, second, a far greater cost for building heavy roads better fitted for truck traffic. Across Kansas the $7.15 per-truck-mile annual average cost increases to $8.08 near loading facilities. Abandoning the short lines alone produces a large cost to Kansas state and county government, but it produces a particularly high cost to counties and municipalities hosting a loading facility drawing thousands of truck trips. Truck haulage of grain produces a sort of spatial discrimination across the Midwest and High Plains that angers local, county, and state taxpayers. Experts assembling at the annual meetings of the Conference on Low Volume Roads realize that local roads designated as low volume become high-volume routes in harvest time. So dramatic is the rising social cost of railroad abandonment in the Midwest and High Plains that the Department of Agriculture has begun to analyze it as a national problem. In *Long-Term Trends in Railroad Service and Capacity for United States Agriculture,* Marvin Prater and Keith Klindworth, researchers in the Agricultural Market Service division, conclude that present malpractice bodes ill for the immediate future.

Class I railroads—the largest ones in the nation—charge higher rates during harvest or "bottleneck" periods, often prohibit co-loading of unit trains operated by competing railroads serving the new loading facilities, charge higher rates to destinations off main lines, and interrupt traditional reciprocal car-switching arrangements and joint line agreements with connecting railroads. Moreover, Class I railroads have introduced the so-called super jumbo covered hopper car weighing between 286,000 and 315,000 pounds fully loaded. Only about two-thirds of short-line trackage has rails heavy enough to carry such cars, but national car-interchange agreements require all railroads, Class I and short line alike, to accept standard cars routed from any one railroad. Super jumbo hoppers are extraordinarily economical to operate, and railroads pass along part of the savings to farmers shipping grain in them from modern loading facilities. But they cannot move over some short-line rails, or even over some branch lines owned by Class I railroads, and their very existence may doom much light-rail mileage to the oblivion so evident across much of rural Kansas and western Nebraska.

Trucking companies loathe the super jumbo hoppers, since they dwarf the largest 18-wheelers and increase railroad efficiency beyond anything over-the-road carriers can match. But the immense railroad cars do offer some trucking firms, including rural ones owned by lone men with one old truck, the chance to transport grain from farms to the distant loading facilities served by the new railcars. Trucking company profits drop, and lone operators work longer hours and perhaps defer vehicle maintenance, but as scenario analysts make clear, for a few years longer short-haul truckers will enjoy competitive equality with short-line railroads stymied by Class I railroad indifference.

After that period comes serious trouble, albeit trouble hard to define precisely. Highway maintenance, repair, and rebuilding costs will balloon, producing taxpayer anger and almost certainly greater taxation of trucks. Truck traffic at transshipment nodes already angers motorists, and perhaps will reduce retail property values in the most adversely affected places. Short-line railroads will abandon operation: the first to go will be those dependent largely on grain shipments that farmers can truck to distant Class I railroads, and the next will be those seventy or more miles from main-line railroad competition. Other impacts, particularly collisions between trucks and cars, prove harder to calculate. As trucks jam rural roads converging at grain transshipment nodes, they will move more slowly and produce higher per-trip costs, but perhaps have fewer or less damaging accidents. Scenario analysis focuses the attention of farmers, truckers, and railroad officials, but only recently has it begun to shape the attention of real estate developers and others in businesses seemingly remote from farming and grain haulage.

Short-line railroads and branches of Class I firms haul more than grain. Harvest is the boom period for many such railroads. Increased traffic covers costs and often produces modest profit, but year-long fluctuations in the price of grain cause both farmers owning self-storage silos and local elevator co-ops and firms to ship some carloads at high-price, nonharvest times, often to the great profit of farmers who remain loyal to local business. Across the Midwest and High Plains, trains move yearlong, although sometimes only once or twice a week on some routes. So long as the tracks remain in operation, locomotives serve other industries and can even attract more business.

Some analysts insist that the short-line railroads produce a potential socioeconomic good every day. So long as the railroads operate trains over their weed-grown routes, they serve industries that may expand; they also may attract industries new to their service area. Industries based in lumber products, paper, steel, chemicals, and food almost always choose locations served by rail, especially if they intend to grow. Such industries deal with bulk commodities, either as inbound shipments or as finished products, and often as both. Any inbound or outbound shipment moving more than a thousand miles almost always moves more cheaply by rail than by truck (especially if it starts and ends at a rail-siding business), and a quiet, efficient short line like the Cimarron Valley Railroad may well attract a new industry, especially a high-tech one dependent on bulk freight. A little factory churning out plastic lawn furniture may take delivery of covered hoppers filled with plastic pellets, a wholesale bakery will require covered hoppers of flour and tank cars of corn syrup, and—because ethanol corrodes pipelines and must move in custom railcars—a wood-chip or crop-based ethanol plant needs to receive bulk raw material and ship bulk product. In the databases scoured by scenario analysts, the factory is part of the chemicals-based category, the bakery and ethanol plant components of a food-based one. To the observer, each is only one of the many small manufacturing enterprises blossoming across the rural

United States, often adjacent to sources of supply. But without the railroad these factories might be elsewhere.

The covered hopper behind the new plastics factory looks remarkably like that loading wheat a few hundred yards down the track, or disgorging animal feed at the mill at the next spur five miles south. It looks almost identical to the car unloading fertilizer at a dealership adjacent to the local grain elevator and not very different from the cylindrical tank car offloading propane gas. It looks like the tank cars, put into service in 1978, that move in units of ten and are connected by pipes; one nozzle empties or fills all ten cars. Train enthusiasts and model railroaders notice freight cars spotted at small-town and crossroads rural places, but until recently such cars attracted little attention from investors. Now the latter send analysts, and sometimes arrive themselves, to study rural places undergoing unmentioned but massive change. Farmers in southern Illinois no longer raise many hogs, or almost any other variety of livestock. Instead, they focus on growing corn, which moves via railroad to Texas, to gigantic, high-tech hog-fattening facilities fenced off from prying eyes. In southern Illinois, unit trains operate frequently, suggesting to some investors that underemployed rural populations might readily gravitate to work in well-connected factories.

Only when a grain-hauling short-line railroad lies abandoned do farmers realize that the two cents per bushel they saved by trucking their harvest to a far-off elevator is nowhere near enough to cover the increased costs of truck-hauled fertilizer and propane gas. The railroad that moves bulk grain shipments away from farms moves inbound single-car shipments of fertilizer, propane, and animal feed all year long. Inbound shipments rarely come close to the value of grain, but fertilizer keeps trains moving in spring, and propane shipments pay railroad company bills in the dead of winter. Once the railroad lies derelict, farmers and other county residents confront more than increased costs for fertilizer, fuel, and other heavy items. As taxpayers, they confront the soaring costs of maintaining roads mangled by heavy trucks operating in sparsely settled regions. In the 1990s county commissioners focused on attracting industries to increase tax revenue and provide jobs, and thus learned that many companies prefer to locate along railroad lines.

Rural highway commissioners had begun to divert maintenance and repair funds to routes used by the trucks. While shifting funds from roads used by motorists and school buses provoked local disputes, the short- and long-term consequences of focusing rural road networks on grain-loading facilities meant that long-haul trucks often followed less-favored routes once off interstate highways. For decades the larger agricultural landscape had been laced by short-haul roads linking farms and local-rail-served grain elevators, and by other roads linking farms and small towns with interstate highways. For as long as the latter roads received the bulk of the funding, rural taxpayers, including businesses, enjoyed time-consuming but otherwise convenient access to the national highway system. Traffic flowed, and businesses located along the flow, often on the bypass circumventing crossroads towns. By 1995 diversion of funding had begun to make driving from some farms to grain-loading facilities smooth and fast, especially outside harvest time. Risk-taking entrepreneurs had begun locating retail businesses near the grain-loading nodes, rather than in hamlets along hitherto "main-traveled roads."

Without notice, rural businesses began locating away from interstate highway/local highway interchanges. Long-haul truckers delivering almost anything to rural regions discerned the subtle signs of highway maintenance favoritism. No longer did the best-surfaced highway necessarily lead away from an interstate exit toward a small town fifty or a hundred miles away. In many regions the best-paved, about-to-be-widened highways led from clusters of prosperous farms to new grain-loading facilities remote from towns and even from crossroads hamlets.

Some towns get lucky. Casselton in North Dakota, a few miles from the Minnesota line, sits astride I-94 and only eighteen miles from I-29, a main Canada–Mexico truck route. In 2004 three grain elevator companies combined to open a facility that loads 110-car unit trains on the Red River Valley & Western Railroad, a "short-line partner" of the Burlington Northern Santa Fe. About a half-hour drive from Fargo, Casselton is home to long-time natives and a few commuters enjoying a small-town living experience. Once a junction of railroads, it remains a convenient place for intermodal activity; after all, some truckloads of grain arrive at the new facility along I-94.

Other towns lose out. Crete in North Dakota is scarcely a town at all. Main Street runs parallel to two other very short streets crossed by two others. Not one of the roads is a state highway, and until recently the tiny community focused on Crete Grain, Inc., a century-old firm formerly served by the Burlington Northern Santa Fe. When the owners of Crete Grain attempted to expand their elevator to load 110-car unit trains, they found themselves stymied by abutting structures. They moved their operation to Oakes, about ten miles away and coincidentally conveniently located at the intersection of two local highways, 1 and 11. At Oakes they built a multi-million-dollar high-tech facility consisting of four cylindrical silos 52 feet in diameter and 150 feet tall, split by a slightly smaller central silo fitted with loading and unloading machinery. Trucks arrive, are weighed on an automatic scale, and discharge grain into the four large elevators, each of which holds a quarter-million bushels of wheat, or into the central silo, which holds only 135,000 bushels. Automatic machinery enables the facility to load and weigh a 110-car unit train in exactly eleven hours. Positioned at the intersection of two highways, Oakes is a perfect location—so perfect that a nearly identical grain-loading facility operates only a mile away.

Railroad tracks surround Oakes on three sides. The town of 1,850 people includes retired farm couples and local business people, but its main activity involves the storage and transfer of grain. It is easy to smile at Oakes, with its quiet lifestyle and 13.5-minute average commute time to work; equally easy to picture Oakes in 1929, with trains of the Chicago & North Western; Minneapolis, St. Paul & Sault Ste. Marie; and Northern Pacific companies pausing at its two stations three-quarters of a mile apart. But the trains of 1929 make any thoughtful observer of the new grain-loading facilities wonder about imminent futures involving private investment: the center of business activity and train movement has shifted away from downtown, and the destination of trains isolates Oakes.

The C&NW operated trains through Oakes on its line between Des Moines and Rapid City, between Omaha and Jamestown, North Dakota—the end of the line, a city midway between Fargo and Bismarck, and nowadays located on I-94—and between Chicago and Jamestown. About nine C&NW trains a day stopped in Oakes, none of them particularly fast, most stopping at many other small towns, and all covering vast distances across sparsely populated country. Train No. 50 departed Chicago at 6:05 PM and spent almost thirty-six hours covering the 794 miles to Oakes. No. 54 took some seventeen hours to operate over the 511 miles from Des Moines. The Minneapolis, St. Paul & Sault Ste. Marie Railway, known across its vast territory as "The Soo," ran only two passenger trains a day through Oakes, on its St. Paul and Pollock, South Dakota, route. The Northern Pacific operated two on its St. Paul and Streeter route, two on the Fergus Falls branch line that terminated in Oakes, and two between Jamestown in Minnesota and Oakes. None of the passenger trains in 1929 or today could be called an express, or even a luxury train, and many included nothing other than day coaches and the ubiquitous railway post office and Railway Express Agency cars. Oakes existed as a junction of secondary railroad routes; the Northern Pacific North Coast Limited between Chicago and Seattle passed far to the north.

In 1929 Crete enjoyed only the slow branch-line Northern Pacific trains between St. Paul and Oakes via Fergus Falls. No. 9 clattered out of Wadena, Minnesota, at 1:35 in the afternoon and paused at Crete at 7:56 in the evening, moving over the intervening 143 miles at approximately twenty-two miles per hour; twenty-four minutes and eight miles later, it terminated at Oakes. Presumably anyone in or near Crete wanting faster rail transportation to just about anywhere hitched a ride into Oakes and boarded a faster train.

But the Northern Pacific provided regular and reliable service to farmers using the Crete elevator. For decades, grain followed similar but not identical paths as passengers. Grain moved more slowly and more circuitously until 1980, when the Staggers Act released railroad companies from decades of onerous restriction.

Unit-train transit of grain becomes highly profitable when the train not only turns around quickly but moves rapidly between loading and unloading points. Rapidity results not from high speed but from slow but steady, almost stately progress across distances most people prefer to fly. Old passenger timetables attest to the fact that unit trains of super jumbo cars must move rapidly for owners to recover the high costs of equipment that operates empty one way and sometimes idles after the harvest rush. The more grain unit trains carry, the sooner railroads cover initial purchase costs and begin to make a profit. Class I railroads consequently focus on the export market, and prefer to serve ultramodern grain facilities loading trains that will move such long distances that truck transport becomes uneconomical.

What strikes a well-managed trucking company as marginally economical may strike a farmer or underemployed truck driver (especially one paying off his aging rig) as well worthwhile, especially in the face of little other available work. A farmer with nothing more lucrative to do, especially a farmer working a farm without livestock in a North Dakota winter, may decide to drive his own heavy truck eighty miles to a modern rail loading facility. Almost certainly, however, neither he nor any commercial trucker, even an underemployed one, will move a truckload of wheat from North Dakota to Houston, or even from North Dakota to Kansas. Diesel fuel costs far outstrip the income realized from moving a bulk commodity so far over highways.

The old railroad route maps and timetables suggest something else to government and railroad industry analysts. States unable to build new roads for grain-hauling trucks unwittingly make reactivating or improving a weedy railroad route economical. Grain alone may not cover improvement costs, however, so railroads seek other shipments owner-operator truckers cannot handle. People willing to accept corn or wheat rumbling along in an old truck shy away from propane, liquid natural gas, and chemicals, including fertilizer.

The 1920s train-travel patterns presage future growth patterns across the sparsely settled High Plains. Back then, population and business growth blossomed along main lines, especially at junctions. Growth begat growth. Nowadays analysts, investors, and canny observers see the pattern repeated. The first communities in which investors build high-tech facilities for loading grain into unit trains receive improved track maintenance and more frequent train service. These communities attract more grain shipments, and perhaps other businesses. But communities that fail to attract initial investment in high-tech loading facilities often find themselves locked into depopulation and a downward economic spiral. Even worse, they often must pay dearly for road damage caused by trucks operating nonstop toward distant rail-side loading facilities.

Even in the depressed years of the 1970s, railroads held on to much of their bulk traffic, especially coal. Almost from its beginning, the industry profited from "open-top" cargoes: coal, gravel, sand, and raw ore—loads that stood up to rough handling, slow movement, and exposure to foul weather. Early in the nineteenth century, trains captured much bulk traffic from canals traversed by horse-drawn barges. Earlier on than most people—even history buffs—might suspect, eastern railroads began operating long trains consisting solely of cars carrying one commodity.

Long trains, sometimes experimental but more often ordinary, assisted the rapid growth in United States coal production after about 1850. From 8.3 million tons in that year it rose to 40.4 million tons in 1870, and the total nearly doubled by the end of the subsequent decade. In the beginning, miners worked the anthracite coal of eastern Pennsylvania, but as early as 1843 the Baltimore & Ohio had begun moving soft coal from Maryland. Coal moved across the northeast by the 1870s, and everywhere across the nation by 1880, much of it mined in the bituminous region of West Virginia and Kentucky and thence exported. Cleaner-burning anthracite coal powered factories and heated houses and other buildings, and it fueled railroad locomotives as well. Railroads outside coal-mining areas transported it even further afield: in 1880 the New York Central moved 1.6 million tons. While local freights switched single cars of anthracite coal onto small-town coal-yard sidetracks and factory spurs, most coal moved in seemingly endless trains.

Anthracite coal rolled in dedicated slow trains, often made up of small four-wheel cars called jimmies. While other four-wheel freight cars had vanished by 1850, jimmies survived because they fit perfectly under coal-mine loading chutes. In the late 1830s, some railroads moved trains of twenty to thirty cars; by the late 1850s many operated trains of nearly sixty cars. But railroads had begun to experiment with far longer trains. In 1850 the Boston & Maine ran a sixty-one-car train over a seventy-four-mile route; three years later, the Michigan Central ran a train of a hundred and eighteen cars. The Philadelphia & Reading pioneered much long-train experimentation; when it opened in 1839, its very first train carried eighty cars.

A few months later Philadelphia & Reading moved 101 loaded jimmies behind a single locomotive, albeit one operating largely downhill. By 1845 the Reading operated coal trains averaging 703 tons, an accomplishment of industrial technology almost invariably ignored even by historians, who imagine pre–Civil War railroading in terms framed by Thoreau. In 1879 the Lehigh Valley operated a coal train of an astounding 593 cars with no recorded problems.

Such trial accomplishments did not always translate into ordinary operation. Moving long trains meant lengthening passing tracks and making other capital improvements that sometimes proved uneconomical. In 1891 Lehigh Valley's coal trains usually consisted of 225 jimmies moving coal toward New York for domestic consumption or export. But in 1879 the Lehigh Valley operated a train *one and a half miles long.*

Such experiments produced a frenzy of locomotive redesign, and by the 1880s coal-hauling railroads had dramatically increased the size of their engines. One locomotive now did the work of two. Trains did not immediately become longer, but companies saved the expense of a crew for the locomotive formerly coupled behind the first. As locomotives grew larger, greater tractive effort revealed itself in longer and longer trains, especially those laden with coal. From Pennsylvania and West Virginia to Kentucky, and subsequently in the coal regions of Utah and other western states, long coal trains moved ponderously toward the blast furnaces of Pittsburgh, Birmingham, Gary, and Provo; to export facilities at Norfolk and elsewhere; and to New York and other metropolitan centers of coal consumption.

In northern Minnesota and Wisconsin, other specialized steam locomotives pulled long drags of stubby ore cars filled with dense, heavy iron ore. Dumped into immense so-called lake boats at Duluth and other harbors, ore moved by water to Gary and other southern ports, then by rail to steel mills. The Duluth, Missabe &

Iron Range, the Pittsburgh & Lake Erie, and other railroads devoted almost solely to moving iron ore attracted little romantic attention. The companies operated few passenger trains and served regions rarely traveled by song writers and other entertainers, let alone the educated elite. Their long trains of hopper cars chugged along at twenty or twenty-five miles an hour, irritating motorists caught at grade crossings. But they freighted the raw bulk material of United States industrial growth. Simply because the spot lay halfway between Pennsylvania coal and Minnesota iron ore, the United States Steel Company sited its mills in the sparsely settled region of Indiana that it named Gary. Steel mills required a steady supply of raw coal and ore, but no one cared how fast the crude cargo rolled through the night—only that it arrived regularly.

Stockholders, however, cared very much about how profitably such bulk cargo rolled, and boards of directors struggled constantly to shave costs. In 1876 accountants employed by the Erie discovered that new locomotives pulling coal trains twice as heavy as those operated in the previous year reduced operating costs per mile from nine cents to five. Railroad companies not only pioneered most business management techniques nowadays accepted as standard but also created sophisticated accounting systems to monitor and suggest innovation. After 1900 number crunching prompted changes in the hauling of coal, ore, and other bulk products, and even produced a new railroad.

Financier Henry Huttleson Rogers built the Virginian in the first years of the twentieth century expressly to move coal across the Appalachians from West Virginia to a brand-new, company-owned export pier at Norfolk, Virginia. Rogers specified heavy rail, massive bridges, gigantic hopper cars, and the most powerful locomotives, but he could do little about the 2 percent grade eastbound between Elmore and Clarks Gap in West Virginia. By 1915 the company operated steel coal cars that each carried 120 tons of coal atop twelve wheels. From 1909 on, the Virginian purchased some of the most powerful steam locomotives American manufacturers built. Its ordinary gigantic locomotives had the equipment of two ordinary heavy locomotives working beneath stupendous boilers. Such engines had two pilot wheels, eight coupled drive wheels, another eight drive wheels, and two trailing wheels; each locomotive weighed 342 tons. To cope with the increased coal traffic following the outbreak of World War I in Europe, the Virginian experimented with a gigantic locomotive three times the size of the heavy locomotives used by most other railroads. Moving seven million tons of coal a year through Clarks Gap required most trains to have three monster steam locomotives, generally one leading and two pushing the long trains. Given a forecast that coal traffic would double within a few years, and knowing that the long coal trains inching over the single track could be neither lengthened or speeded up behind steam power, Virginian management determined to electrify 134 miles of track and replace the steam locomotives.

The box-shaped electric locomotives, each fifty-one feet long and weighing 212 tons, usually operated in groups of three. The Virginian management considered them discrete units—and so publicized them as the largest locomotives in the world. In September 1925, with much fanfare, the Virginian moved an eight-thousand-ton train of sixty-two cars using two of the three locomotives. Powered by electricity generated from its own coal-fueled power plant, the Virginian had a surefire winner in the new motive power.

The boxcab electrics doubled the speed of coal trains over the pass. No longer did the trains roll at fourteen miles an hour. By 1927, the first year of full operation under electric power, the company moved almost 12 million tons of coal. Despite a drop in tonnage during the Depression, coal traffic remained profitable, and during World War II surged to almost 13 million tons. Three years into peacetime, that figure rose to 15.5 million tons, and the company began replacing its first-generation electrics with units that stretched 150 feet and weighed 517 tons. One new electric soon moved a three-thousand-ton coal train up the grade at thirty-five miles an hour: it moved a ten-thousand-ton coal train at forty-five miles per hour on level track. In 1957 the company bought more heavy electrics capable of operating at sixty-five miles per hour, and until 1962 enjoyed immense success.

Merger with the Norfolk & Western ended the Virginian electrification, since most coal traffic shifted to the gentler grades of the N&W. A smoke-choked tunnel nearly three-fifths of a mile long prompted the N&W to choose electrification in 1912, although its grades made electrification a profitable choice too. By 1915 the company was boasting that electric locomotives moved coal trains through Elkhorn Tunnel in three minutes rather than seven and eliminated the danger of suffocation to crews operating smoke-belching, slow-moving steam locomotives in tunnels. N&W electrics performed almost flawlessly, moving fifty-four million tons of coal in the year 1943 alone, and saved vast sums in operating expenses. But immediately after World War II the N&W built a new grade and tunnel beneath Elkhorn Mountain that eliminated the need for electric locomotives. Heavy steam locomotives rolled coal trains through the new double-track tunnel at speed, and soon captured the coal traffic of the Virginian as well.

High-tech innovation in the poverty-stricken Appalachians passed without much comment, but electrification on the Virginian and N&W convinced the management of other railroads that unit trains operating between mines and large clients might be profitable enough to offset the postwar flood of freight to the trucking industry. In 1960, the year the last regularly scheduled passenger train operated behind a steam locomotive (between Durand and Detroit on the Grand Trunk Western), several railroads began moving coal in unit trains that had been operating since the 1850s.

Unit trains originated in the railroad industry's effort to tap the cheaper, low-sulfur coal regions of Wyoming and other western states. Strip-mined coal poured into hopper cars at a lower cost than coal moved from underground mines, and electricity-producing companies, especially those along the Great Lakes and the Ohio River, wanted the cheapest coal possible. The 1970 Clean Air Act accelerated the unit-train concept, since the federal government mandated that all coal-fired power plants switch to low-sulfur coal. From strip mines in Virginia, Wyoming, and elsewhere, unit trains began moving cleaner-burning coal to power-generating customers, supplanting the fading steel industry. The 1973 and 1979 gasoline crises only accelerated the momentum of the unit-train concept.

In September 1966 the first Santa Fe unit coal train left the York Canyon mines in New Mexico on its 1,082-mile trip to Fontana, California, about fifty miles east of Los Angeles. Between a Kaiser Steel coal mine and the sprawling Kaiser Steel mill, the brand-new train shuttled mostly along the main line of a long-established railroad. But the Santa Fe had built fifty-seven miles of heavy track away from its main line at French, New Mexico, to tap the new Kaiser mine in the northeast corner of the state. Only a short time earlier, the Southern Pacific had abandoned its 114-mile Tucumcari-to-French branch line. By pure coincidence, the Santa Fe was thus the only railroad able to reach into York Canyon and the new mines fitted with equipment that loaded each hopper car in sixty seconds. The company bought eleven new locomotives and 101 massive hopper cars for the Kaiser unit-train service, and soon operated one of the first, and longest-routed, precision-scheduled unit trains in the nation.

A unit train moving coal consists of some 100 to 110 identical cars owned either by an individual railroad or by a client, usually a power-generating company. The train shuttles between mine and client, always an integral unit, always full one way and empty the other. The dedicated train moves on a regular schedule and produces a regular, predictable profit from contracts negotiated annually or at longer intervals. It generates income as steadily as it moves, and the more efficiently it moves, the more profitable it proves for both the railroad company and the purchaser of the coal it carries. But just as the long pre–Civil War trains of the Philadelphia & Reading rarely enter university history courses, and the high-tech Appalachian experiments of the Virginian and N&W existed far from the eyes of most express train passengers, coal-carrying unit trains operate from remote mining regions to power plants usually located away from close public scrutiny, often across sparsely settled rural or wilderness regions. If bystanders occasionally notice the ribbonlike trains of silver or yellow or black coal cars, they probably fail to recognize them as both generators of economic value and indicators of spatial and economic changes immediately ahead.

Bulk transport using standardized, integral trains operating over fixed routes on predictable schedules suggested all manner of innovations by 1965. Developments in mainframe computers, software, and integrated logic circuits implied that dreams might come true, perhaps sooner than expected. No doubt union leadership shivered every time the industry adopted another cybernetic component.

Automatic train operation debuted in New York. In January of 1962 a robotic subway train began shuttling between Times Square and Grand Central Terminal. Union opposition delayed the inaugural run: until a motorman manned the robotic train, the Transport Workers Union threatened to close down the entire New York City subway system. Within weeks, however, the shuttle train had begun to prove itself. The prototype for the automatic "people movers" now whisking terminal-changing passengers beneath airports in Atlanta, Dallas–Forth Worth, Pittsburgh, and elsewhere, the New York City shuttle train moved a bulk cargo most railroaders by then ignored. People.

In Canada, far from cities and beyond the gaze of all but the most intrepid hikers, automatic train operation had already proven itself. On the Quebec, North Shore & Labrador, eighteen-car trains of iron ore routinely operated twenty-four hours a day, seven days a week behind robotic diesel locomotives. Over the 5.7-mile route moved four trains. At any given moment, one train moved slowly under loading chutes, another moved slowly across unloading devices, and two rolled along the main line, passing each other at a midway passing siding. The QNS&L saw the robotic trains as short-term experiments, for the company had long-range plans involving automation in a wilderness area beset by harsh winters.

Earlier experiments in the United States, especially the 1955 demonstrations of automatic train operation on the New Haven between New Rochelle and Rye Beach in New York, prompted ongoing research by the Union Switch & Signal Division of the Westinghouse Corporation. By 1962 General Electric had begun demonstrating a robotic trolley car named Tomorrow, one of the prototypes of the cars that now operate on the Bay Area Rapid Transit system in San Francisco. But most research focused on moving freight robotically.

By 1969 the new Muskingum Electric Railroad in southwest Ohio had proven that automatic train control and electrification welded into smooth, extremely economical operation of bulk material. Hauling coal from mines to the Muskingum River generating plant of the Ohio Power Company, the railroad used the latest in 25,000-volt, 60 cycles per second, alternating current power distribution already proven in Europe and Asia. Such electric power simplified the equipment needed in substations and locomotives, eliminated the need for special transmission lines paralleling the contact wire touched by the locomotives, and permitted very lightweight catenary overhead construction, saving initial outlay for copper and subsequent maintenance. Two trains, each with a new locomotive and fifteen cars, operated as automatically as a home washing machine, cruising at fifty-five miles per hour, loading and unloading while moving at slow speed, and easily sweeping up the 2 percent ruling grade.

Not until 1983 did Amtrak change its power distribution system to 25,000 volts, but the lessons of the Muskingum sank deeply into railroad management thinking. In a sealed-off area, with instruments probing the track ahead for debris and other hazards, an electric locomotive operated with less human attention than a toy train moving at the whim of a child adjusting its speed transformer. While ordinary diesel-electric locomotives could operate automatically, as the QNS&L proved, all-electrics moved far more reliably and at lower cost. By 1975 the QNS&L had electrified much of its four-hundred-mile main line and begun automatic train control as effective as the Times Square shuttle subway.

For all intents and purposes, Amtrak Acela trains might operate today without engineers. Passengers might worry about emergencies: despite autopilot equipment that enables an airliner to take off, fly, and land without human help, few passengers would trust their lives in a drone aircraft, and life on the ground seems as valuable as life aloft. Bulk haulage of grain, coal, ore, forest products (especially wood chips), newsprint, and other commodities offers glimpses of what already shapes Oakes in North Dakota, and suggests imminent automatic-operation innovation.

A unit train of a standard length, often 110 cars, loads automatically and proceeds to a single destination for automatic unloading, but an engine crew still operates its locomotive. Standardized train length means standardized length of passing sidings. Precision scheduling means a steady, uninterrupted flow of trains; and fast, regular service means a railroad company needs only a few trains to move gigantic amounts of bulk cargo. Standardized service means reduced costs for shippers. The unit train taught railroad management to think in terms of an industry no longer operating as a common carrier but as a contract carrier to large clients. But in the longer run, the unit train focuses management attention on components of the railroad not yet standardized, including the ordinary diesel-electric locomotive still unable to compete with all-electric units. High horsepower is fundamentally easier to design and build into an all-electric locomotive like the Amtrak Acela.

After the Staggers Act of 1980, railroads began exploring the potential implicit in merging old-fashioned mail and package express service with modern unit-train technology. Among the grain, coal, and ore trains it is easy to miss pioneering unit trains like the Burlington Northern Santa Fe Ethanol Express moving biofuel from the Midwest to a refinery in Watson, California, or the first "grocery" unit trains of raw foodstuffs other than grain. Between Florida and New Jersey the all-orange refrigerated Tropicana Orange Juice unit train rolls like clockwork. Eighty unit trains of coal roll out of Wyoming every day, putting many small towns on superb freight tracks that might one day carry something else. Outside the railroad industry little attention accrues to robotic trains that make the Urbmobile seem antiquated. Quebec and New Mexico are remote, and even in Ohio such trains operate behind chain-link fences and "no trespassing" signs. But many vacationing long-distance motorists note with despair the truck traffic on many interstate highways and the wretched pavement stretching endlessly ahead.

It might be instructive to follow unit trains of grain to the small town of Kalama on the Columbia River in Washington. A thriving, beautiful town in a spectacular wilderness setting, Kalama is home to an ultramodern marine shipping terminal. Unlike the older ports of Elizabeth, New Jersey, and Norfolk, Virginia, Kalama's marine terminal scarcely interrupts daily life and indeed is almost invisible. But it is immensely profitable. Day after day, unit trains arrive and depart at the five facilities loading ships departing for destinations around the world. Kalama, then, is Oakes on a slightly grander scale, with boutiques and marinas and sumptuous mountainside houses blossoming from unit-train-generated wealth.

It is not Crete. Nor is Prince Rupert, in British Columbia, transshipping not only bulk commodities but thousands of containers at the far end of a transcontinental rail line that reaches to New Orleans and to Halifax. Nor is Port MacKenzie, a brand-new seaport two miles from Anchorage, transshipping wood chips, limestone, and coal.

Such ports are the new ends of the line. New container ships, especially the gigantic ones owned by the Danish firm Maersk, which carry thirteen to fifteen thousand twenty-foot-long containers at a time, and bulk carriers transporting coal, oil, and grain are far too large to pass through the Panama Canal, let alone fit into older harbors with low bridges and shallow channels. High-tech and prosperous, the new ports demonstrate the astounding impact of behemoth ships and unit trains rolling bulk commodities on global trade, reshaping investment and the North American landscape. Railroads know that mile-long, slowly moving unit trains frustrate motorists stuck at grade crossings, so they replace crossings with overpasses. As grade crossings vanish, railroads note increased potential for high-speed freight trains, automated operation, and even passenger trains. Innovation may arrive first along routes modified for the oldest cargoes of all, but ones headed from new transshipment points to new deep-water ports.

SOURCES: Babcock, Bunch, et al., "Impact of Short Line Railroad Abandonment," and "Impact of Short Line Railroad Abandonment"; Babcock, Russell, and Mauler, "Study of the Impact of Rail Abandonment"; Colucci-Rios and Yoder, *A Methodology for Evaluating the Increase in Pavement Maintenance Costs;* Drury, "Tank Train"; "Electrification: In the Future"; Fales, "Our Crumbling Interstates"; Josserand, "Tomorrow"; Kansas State Board of Agriculture, *Kansas Grain Transportation;* Middleton, *When the Steam Railroads Electrified;* "Muskingum Electric Railroad"; "Muskingum Electric: Trains on Their Own"; O'Neil, "Quebec, North Shore & Labrador"; Prater and Klindworth, *Long-Term Trends in Railroad Service;* Rose, *Interstate;* Santa Fe Railroad, news release, R-33-2, August 27, 1966; Sonstegaard, "Competitive Access to North American Rail"; Transportation Research Board, *Low-Volume Roads;* J. H. White Jr., *The American Railroad Passenger Car.*

Approaching a grade crossing at 70 miles per hour, the commuter train deflects attention from the unpaved service road paralleling it, but that road indicates space enough for adding another track when patronage increases.

TRANSFER

Predicting sometimes fails. The most meticulous analysis of census data proves no guarantee of future birth or death rates, and the stock market performance over decades may suggest little about its behavior tomorrow. Even demographic and economic data rooted in geography and existing real estate development sometimes trick analysts, and what seems surefire sometimes backfires, as the New York, Westchester & Boston Railroad (NYW&B) learned in the 1920s. Only a few relics remain of perhaps the most visionary, best-built passenger railroad in the United States, one intended to carry almost no freight at all.

The East 180th Street Station of the New York subway system ought to interest patrons, but most rush in and out of the handsome structure, unaware of its clouded history. Its facade fails to intrigue, and inside few glance at the adjacent abandoned platforms and tracks used to store older subway trains. The No. 2 and No. 5 trains pause at active platforms, operating between Dyre Avenue in the North Bronx and downtown, and people bustle in and out. Few notice the caduceus molded into the station facade. But the symbol of Mercury, the Roman god of speed, still dignifies a subway line punctuated here and there by extraordinarily massive, ornate stations built in a quasi-Mediterranean style. The nearby Dyre Avenue station, now housing also a police station and a convenience store, resembles that on East 180th Street. The massive, ornate, timeless, vaguely modern architectural style, and the disused tracks adjacent to active ones, suggest that something special happened in the Bronx, but only temporarily. Fragments endure, reminding twenty-first-century investors that predictions fail.

In early 1929 disaster stalked the Harlem Board of Commerce. It published *Three Plans for the Relief of Traffic Congestion in New York City,* a cogent, assertive, and perhaps disingenuous plea for relief from motor vehicle traffic. The board wanted an end to ferry boats serving upper Manhattan, and so proposed what became the

Triborough Bridge, to "divert thousands of motor trucks away from lower Manhattan," across the upper part of the island, then across another proposed bridge opening on New Jersey. The board hoped to channel rail commuters through the upper end of the island, to which purpose it proposed moving the terminal of the New York, Westchester & Boston Railroad from the Bronx. Trains would operate through tunnels under the Harlem River, then through tunnels connecting with all but one of the Manhattan north–south subway lines, and terminate at a new station near the intersection of 125th Street and St. Nicholas Avenue, the site of the Eighth Avenue Subway Line, already under construction. If suburban trains of the New York, New Haven & Hartford Railroad moved through the NYW&B tubes as well, commuters from Connecticut might reach the upper end of Manhattan as easily as commuters from the Bronx and Westchester County.

Couching the proposals in language that managed to suggest the whole city would benefit, the board obscured its deep interest in attracting office, manufacturing, and commercial enterprises northward. "The present congestion in Grand Central Terminal and 42nd Street will be greatly relieved, the distribution of Westchester County commuters taking place practically the entire length of 125th Street," it concluded. "It would further tend toward the distribution of business and manufacturing establishments, bringing many hundreds from lower Manhattan to the Bronx and other uptown sections, relieving downtown congestion." The Chrysler Building slowly rising toward the sky, the Empire State Building already announced, and other office towers terrified the business community based in the northern end of Manhattan. Unless suburban commuters had a new railroad terminal far north of Pennsylvania Station and Grand Central Terminal, lower Manhattan would prosper as its buildings grew taller. It would prosper at the expense of the rest of the island.

As the board emphasized on the last page, demographic and traffic experts had located the "pivotal point, or hub, of the teeming millions in and around New York" at about 112th Street and Fifth Avenue. For decades the point had been moving northward, but by 1929 it had moved almost three miles north of the northernmost bridge leading onto Manhattan. The two proposed highway bridges would relieve congestion in lower Manhattan and incidentally bring commuters, motor truck traffic, and long-distance motorists across the north end of the island, freeing it from a future as an area of low-income housing. But the key proposal involved relocating a railroad terminal placed where the finest 1900-era expertise predicted commuter traffic would materialize. Something had derailed the predictions on which the builders of the NYW&B invested millions.

Stretching north and east from a terminal at East 132nd Street and Willis Avenue, at the southern edge of the Bronx and adjacent to an expanse of freight yards, the NYW&B eventually reached as far as Port Chester to the northeast and White Plains to the north, branching at Mount Vernon toward its two suburban terminals. Between 174th Street and Mount Vernon, its trains operated on a four-track main line, totally free of grade crossings; beyond the suburban junction, they moved on double tracks. Bridging depressions on massive steel-and-concrete viaducts and burrowing under the Bronx and Pelham Parkway in a four-thousand-foot tunnel, the railroad struck both laymen and experts as extraordinary. Not only did its builders use the finest material, they dignified its route with elegant stations. But most importantly, they electrified every inch of the right-of-way, making possible extremely fast trains, both local and expresses, operating at twenty-minute intervals in off-peak times and more frequently during rush hour.

The NYW&B carried 2,874,484 passengers in 1913, its first full year of operation, and by 1928 moved 14,053,188. However, traffic never grew at the rate its investors envisioned. Although real estate development burgeoned across the suburban region it served, the railroad suffered intense competition. Once the New York, New Haven, and Hartford opened its Hell Gate Arch Bridge in 1917—the gigantic structure Amtrak's Boston–New York service uses today— potential NYW&B riders had yet another quick way to lower Manhattan. Within four years after its inauguration, NYW&B management confronted riders' suggestion that city-bound trains divert at Port Morris from the new right-of-way onto the tracks across the Hell Gate Arch Bridge. Passengers wanted direct service either to

Pennsylvania Station or to Grand Central Terminal, not the subway transfer facility they condemned as inconvenient.

Twenty years later, the NYW&B was still using its original terminal, and its timetable covers explained how to get there. "To reach the New York, Westchester, & Boston Ry. Via Third Ave Elevated Line, change cars at the 123rd Street Elevated Station and use covered passage way direct to Harlem River Station," the directions begin. Via the Lexington Avenue subway, "take express to the East 180th Street joint station with the 'Westchester' or via the Pelham Bay Park extension at Hunt's Point station. Direct connection with 180th St. and Harlem is made via Willis Avenue taxis crossing Harlem River and running through 123rd Street to Fort Lee Ferry." No matter how much New York City improved its elevated and subway lines, NYW&B riders accustomed to spacious, comfortable, high-speed trains found public transit cars crowded, noisy, dirty, and slow. The Harlem River Station seemed a greater abomination with every passing year, and increasingly passengers found ways to commute on other railroads or by automobile. Instead of enhancing commercial activity and property values at the north end of Manhattan, the NYW&B terminal seemed to have no impact at all.

In addition, government intervention condemned the NYW&B to bankruptcy from the start, although at the beginning no one glimpsed the impact of local ordinance. In 1916 New York enacted its first zoning laws, restricting the growth of commercial development north of 59th Street. In the last decades of the nineteenth century and up until 1916, the center of business activity had moved slowly but certainly northward. The inventors of the NYW&B assumed that by around 1950 it would arrive at 125th Street, approximately across the river from the Harlem River Terminal. NYW&B inventors and investors alike envisioned increased patronage as the suburban region grew more populous and the focus of Manhattan commerce moved toward the new terminal. Escalating ridership might pay to extend NYW&B tracks under or over the Harlem River, directly into the new center of Manhattan enterprise. But three years after its trains began operating, NYW&B management confronted the impact of a zoning ordinance that made the upper half of Manhattan largely an awkward mix of residential and warehouse neighborhoods increasingly clogged with trucks. Instead of moving north as it had been doing, white-collar enterprise had begun to build upward, making the area near Pennsylvania Station and Grand Central Terminal thronged with pedestrians, especially in rush hour. In the meantime, in the suburbs NYW&B riders learned to drive their automobiles to competing railroads that operated into the two great terminals of Manhattan.

The 1920s suburban commuters driving to railroad stations other than NYW&B ones behaved almost exactly as grain shippers behave in the High Plains today. They used automobiles as grain shippers use trucks, and they produced the same controversies over highway alignment, improvement, and maintenance. Far more importantly, however, they altered highway planning in Westchester County and transformed real estate investment. A community enjoying high-speed, frequent, comfortable electrified commuter service over fenced tracks isolated from highway crossings discovered would-be residents and businesses moving to similar communities whose trains reached Grand Central Terminal or Pennsylvania Station. By the 1930s suburban real estate developers everywhere in the United States knew the paralyzing lesson of the NYW&B.

The short life of the NYW&B deserves more than passing mention, for it illuminates a profound change in the trajectory of American urbanism. Other railroads deposited Manhattan-bound commuters away from the two great stations. The Erie and the Lackawanna used ferry terminals in Hoboken; and until it built its tunnels beneath the Hudson, the mighty Pennsylvania diverted commuters to the Hudson & Manhattan, nowadays rebuilt by the Port Authority and operating between Manhattan and Newark. The Baltimore & Ohio; the Reading; the New York, Ontario & Western; the Lehigh Valley; and other railroads never swept into Pennsylvania Station and Grand Central Terminal. Social historians, urban planners, and political pundits still ignore parameters imposed by steel-and-concrete investors more than a century ago. Engineers on the payroll of profit-minded investors shaped the public realm in ways that still vex city and regional planners, urban designers, and politicians today and that profoundly threaten the modern real estate development, trucking, and automobile industries.

A year before the Harlem Board of Commerce publicized its concerns about street congestion and the uselessness of the NYW&B passenger terminal, the Regional Plan of New York and Its Environs documented a broader crisis. *Transit and Transportation and a Study of Port and Industrial Areas and Their Relation to Transportation* remains a landmark in urban planning history. The fourth volume of the Regional Plan traces patterns of growth within contemporaneous context, and then predicts likely events. Illustrated with maps keyed to tables and charts, the volume emphasizes that a "policy of drift" has permitted private-directed growth at public expense, producing extremely unbalanced urban and suburban development. More importantly, especially for any contemporary reader musing on sprawl, revitalizing cities, creating high-paying office and industrial jobs in urban areas, or simply caught in automobile and truck traffic near or in New York, *Transit and Transportation* warns that ignoring engineering issues imprisons taxpayers, property owners, and especially politicians. Above all, it demonstrates beyond doubt that late 1920s experts analyzed data that let them see around the curve of time.

"The present serious difficulties in Manhattan exist at a time when only a small proportion of the buildings exceed ten stories in height," warns the foreword. "The real problem is what is going to happen when the land in Manhattan is put to its full use." *Transit and Transportation* is not really a planning document, but it is an analytical one. Decades before the rise of computers, the engineers retained by the Committee on the Regional Plan used desk calculators and pencils to outline what would happen in the immediate and distant future. Theirs is one of the finest early scenario analyses, and one of the last made public in ways that reached special-interest groups and citizens alike.

Retrospect made the analysts skeptical at once. Simple engineering realities produced gigantic social consequences. The Long Island Rail Road, a subsidiary of the Pennsylvania, enjoyed tunnel access beneath the East River into Pennsylvania Station. Direct service, even service requiring changes at Jamaica, caused a boom in suburban residential development in western Long Island, and enriched the Pennsylvania. Commuters reveled in the direct service to lower Manhattan so coveted by NYW&B commuters north of Long Island Sound. But analysts discovered a geopolitical secret buried in Long Island schedules and ticket receipts: the Long Island Rail Road provided such excellent service that New York City had delayed building subway or elevated rapid transit lines in the easterly part of Queens.

Moreover, since the Pennsylvania Railroad realized its massive new Manhattan station would be overwhelmed if New Jersey commuters used it in numbers approaching those from Long Island, commuters from south of the Hudson River discovered fares intended to make them shift in New Jersey to the rapid-transit "tube trains" of the Hudson & Manhattan. The arrangement worked splendidly, not only to eliminate potential congestion in Pennsylvania Station, but to boost revenue on the H&M, which the Pennsylvania controlled. But since Pennsylvania competitors provided free ferry service from their Hoboken terminals across the Hudson to Manhattan, many commuters preferred the ferries to paying an additional fare to the H&M just to save a few minutes. Bit by bit, analysts assembled seemingly fragmentary and conflicting data into a pattern of commuting that linked rising suburban property values on Long Island with New Jersey commuter willingness to use free ferries that took longer than H&M trains. Pennsylvania Railroad commuter tickets offered a glimpse at corporate power skewing the growth of the metropolitan region.

Some data outlined puzzling issues. Certainly, wealthy commuters avoided the H&M transfer and chose Pennsylvania commuter trains operating to and from Pennsylvania Station. Those commuters simply walked to their places of employment, enjoying total freedom from the subway rides that irritated NYW&B riders. Such riders undermined the entire methodology of commuter study. For the Regional Plan analysts, purchase of monthly tickets defined railroad commuters, although in a pinch the analysts applied the definition to all passengers riding trains inside the zone in which railroad companies offered reduced-fare tickets. "Commuted-price tickets," often sold by the week or month, not only gave commuters their name but seemed a simple way of identifying regular riders. But the prosperous Pennsylvania commuters using Pennsylvania Station suggested a new commuter pattern.

In one of its few deviations from hard-data analysis, *Transit and Transportation* stated that there were "quite a number of commuters coming daily from points between the one- and two-hour zones and a few that come from still greater distances." Such commuters merged seamlessly into the larger pool of long-distance passengers, and proved nearly impossible to isolate. The passengers enjoyed comfortable, fast trains, including dining cars and club cars in which to enjoy an afternoon drink, and often walked to both their local stations and Pennsylvania Station. The time they spent aboard trains operating beyond the one-hour zone had to be weighed against amenities and their not having to ride a subway train, trolley, or bus to an urban station, or even a trolley to their local one. Such passengers appear to have included NYW&B commuters who learned to drive to New York, New Haven, and Hartford stations for trains running directly to Grand Central Terminal. Almost all who did not walk used local stations with ample free parking for their automobiles. In 1946 the long-distance railroad commuters produced unending difficulties for planners and real estate developers. Many of these long-distance commuters spent less time each day traveling than people who used subways or a combination of subway and ordinary commuter trains. Typical commuters might spend ten minutes on a subway train to reach a H&M tube train or to reach a ferry leaving for New Jersey; others might spend twenty minutes on a subway train headed for the NYW&B terminal. But such commuters also had to walk to the subway station and then sometimes wait for a train; if they arrived on the platform just as a train departed, they might wait an additional three to eight minutes. The waiting time would vary, but the commuter had to allow for the longer period in order to consistently make the scheduled departure of the commuter train. Some commuters learned to calculate total commute time in each direction, and at least some determined to work within walking distance of Grand Central Terminal or Pennsylvania Station and commute via long-distance train. Higher transportation charges (partially offset by the absence of subway fares) and comfort might tip the scales in favor of such a decision, but the opportunity to live in pleasant and often less expensive places may have provided more incentive. Those places became the exclusive, high-property-value suburbs so evident by 1960.

In 1929 Regional Plan analysts found themselves mired in what had become conventional wisdom. "It is generally conceded that families should be encouraged to live as far as possible outside the congested centers where land is cheaper and where their environment, while it might be less exciting, would be more wholesome," they admitted in a report entitled *Transportation*. Bowing to what women's magazines had concluded forty years earlier and had hammered home with dedication, the analysts glimpsed not only the realpolitik of suburbanization but its engineering implications.

Unless New York built more railroad terminals on Manhattan, upper-middle-class families would tend to locate along the long-distance lines running from Pennsylvania Station and Grand Central Terminal. Corridors of wealth would reach south into New Jersey, north along the Hudson River, and eastward toward Connecticut. For a decade or two, Long Island would accommodate the families of men did not earn quite enough money to commute long-distance. Then the city and its immediate neighbors would confront either impossible congestion or a sort of centrifugal shattering. In 1929 the term *sprawl* was not yet in currency, but undoubtedly there were concerns about an impromptu, unplanned spinning off of downtown capital into diffuse suburban and exurban space. "Excitement" might leave lower Manhattan, jump over a zone jammed with trucks and over a drab residential ring, and take root in a zone of large-lot homes inhabited by the households of long-run commuters.

Between 1914 and 1924, Grand Central Terminal commuter traffic increased by 9.8 percent over each preceding year. In general terms, based on surveys at all New York rail terminals, commuter traffic doubled every nine years, and total railroad passenger traffic doubled every thirteen. Since 1918 the price gap between monthly commuter tickets and regular round-trip ones had been increasing, but by 1928 analysts knew that many riders bought monthly books and used them only twelve to eighteen times before giving them to family members or friends. Ticket sales alone produced only part of a larger picture; passenger counts made clear the inadequacy of ticket sales as indicators. Actual counting of passengers demonstrated that projected growth rates might be too conservative, and that without immediate steps the region would confront, first, traffic jams and flight of real estate capital, then the loss of middle-income families and the businesses dependent on them. Accordingly, the Regional Plan analysts suggested building more railroad terminals on Manhattan and linking at least some of them with a belt line used by commuter trains. Such construction would increase property values away from lower Manhattan, certainly above 59th Street, and would open huge adjoining regions to suburban residential development focused on Manhattan.

The analysts studied the movement of express and freight, too, and paid special attention to the role of piers and warehouses. Transshipment between steamships and barges and railroad cars—and trucks—received as much scrutiny as passengers striding toward Hudson River ferries. While commuter patterns remained relatively stable between 1918 and 1928 as ridership grew, freight movements altered dramatically. Fuel oil began replacing coal, for example, and analysts envisioned scenarios in which coal would become far less important within two decades. Declining coal traffic would free coal yards and other facilities for redevelopment, but it would adversely impact the Lackawanna, Lehigh Valley, and other coal-focused railroads that also provided commuter service. Beyond coal, the chief problem of transportation—excluding "transit" involving people—lay in the movement of food into New York and manufactured goods into, from, and across the city and its region, increasingly by trucking companies that kept inadequate records.

Lack of data complicated the problem. Since 1914 no agency had collected totals on express and freight movements, and only fragmentary data hinted at changes between 1899 and 1924. Imports of hay had dropped as motor vehicles replaced horse-drawn ones, and coal moving to New England did so increasingly by rail, rather than by ships or barges leaving from Hudson River wharves. Throughout the 1920s, building material arrived by all three modes of transport, and the building boom that produced such commuter congestion problems in turn exacerbated the movement of building material into lower Manhattan. The amount of food entering the city increased year by year, but more and more of it arrived as time-sensitive, refrigerated cargo, and much of it moved by truck. Outbound express and freight made up only about a fourth of the total tonnage of inbound shipments, but it proved of very high value, consisting almost entirely of manufactured goods. Most departed as time-sensitive shipments as well. Motor truck traffic increased dramatically year by year, and the city needed to build some sort of airport for the growing numbers of airplanes, dirigibles, and other flying machines that seemed likely to multiply but prove useless in mitigating commuter jams. A lack of data about the movement of material was worsened by vague and sometimes inaccurate information about the transfer of goods. Some food arrived by train and moved from warehouses to trucks to grocery stores, but some moved directly from railroad cars to trucks. Some fuel oil moved from railroad cars to distributor storage tanks, but some flowed from tank cars directly into factory storage tanks. Certainly the movement of express and freight interfered with the movement of people, but it also threatened to overwhelm street traffic, especially away from the skyscraper district. The Harlem Board of Commerce perceived the threat of motor truck congestion all too accurately, as did the Regional Plan analysts.

At some point, Manhattan would suddenly begin to hemorrhage jobs, capital, and especially innovative new companies. Public schooling and other social goods would suffer, gradually at first, then dramatically. One plausible solution emerged from the success of the Railway Express Agency and other railroad industry affiliates. Engineers retained by the Regional Plan suggested building a miniature freight subway beneath Manhattan, with extensions to New Jersey, Long Island, and the Bronx. Trains would bring merchandise to stores and, more importantly, remove ashes, trash, and garbage; they would move purchased items to close-in residential neighborhoods, toward suburban ones, and directly to Railway Express Agency facilities for transfer to high-speed long-distance trains. Subterranean freight trains would eliminate much local-delivery truck traffic, speeding trolley car and bus schedules and making motorists happier, all the while broadening the influence of New York City retail enterprise.

Chicago had enjoyed such a subterranean freight railroad since 1906. When investors in a nascent underground telephone cable company realized that the small construction tunnels might carry miniature freight trains, they began building larger tunnels secretly. After squabbling over franchise rights with politicians, they received the right to operate trains through sixty miles of interconnected tunnels, most below central Chicago. Forty feet below city streets, running in steel-and-concrete arch-shaped tunnels pushed through clay soils, fifteen-car trains pulled by electric locomotives soon linked almost every major building with every railroad company freight house.

Trains cruised at fifteen or twenty miles an hour, exchanged cars in a freight yard beneath a wholesale grocery warehouse, and sometimes operated directly into department store basements. Marshall Field became a major customer immediately, receiving merchandise round the clock and dispatching hundreds of thousands of packages for transshipment—to the Railway Express Agency. Candy manufacturers were delighted with the rapid shipment of product to long-distance railroad trains, especially via the Illinois Central Railroad, whose Central Station stood directly above the narrow-gauge tracks. While Marshall Field had its own spur tracks and loading platforms, other businesses used elevators that plucked individual cars upward from tunnels. In its first decades, the company proved successful and profitable, even trendy.

The Illinois Tunnel Company, later renamed the Chicago Tunnel Company, impressed United States legislators and foreign dignitaries. At hotels such as the august Palmer House, Mae West and other celebrities descended to glimpse high-tech urbanity and perhaps be photographed within it. The company built a special tunnel to serve the Field Museum of Natural History, demonstrating its ability to reach across as-yet-undeveloped land toward valuable customers, and for decades seemed an eminently sensible means of minimizing street congestion.

But while New York Regional Plan engineers were admiring it in the 1920s, the Chicago railroad had begun to confront the impact of fuel oil replacing coal. By the late 1920s its motor truck subsidiary had drawn away much time-sensitive merchandise as underground haulage of coal and ash slipped. Between the late 1930s and 1943 the building of city subways eliminated six miles of Chicago Tunnel Company tunnels, cutting off all access to downtown department stores. As late as 1954 new leadership experimented with moving mail between the main and branch post offices, but the loss of the department store connections ended in bankruptcy and, in 1959, abandonment.

While a few miles of tunnel today carry high-voltage electric lines and fiber-optic cables, most of the system lies empty. In surprisingly good condition for century-old tunnels (despite some water damage caused by a 1992 pile-driving mistake that diverted the Chicago River through it into basements whose owners had long forgotten the trains), the system exists in limbo. Perhaps it waits, as Greenbush waited a half century after the last trains left the salt marsh terminal for Boston. Perhaps it waits in vain, perhaps not. But it does not disappear from urban design thinking. After all, such a system might at least remove trash, garbage, and recyclable products. Even if the system delivered only half or perhaps even a quarter of the merchandise arriving by truck, removing most trash might make it feasible.

Since 1929, urban designers have understood that moving people often collide with moving goods. While 1960s visionaries gobbled up federal funds in studies of automated people-moving devices like the Urbmobile, almost none focused on the goods–people collision depicted so acutely in *Transit and Transportation*. Even the 1970s energy crisis did nothing to stimulate sensible—or even wacky discussion—and today few experts know much about the movement of goods, garbage included, as a modifier of urban life, let alone as a generator of urban design and real estate profits. UPS and FedEx are well versed in the fine points of package moving, but who knows why a single convenience store or delicatessen is serviced by six different bakery trucks every day? Designing a city above a freight, merchandise, and refuse subway railroad still remains an abstraction, although planners studying the movement of people grudgingly admit that goods-transfer congestion impedes downtown people movement.

In 1928 packages dropped down chutes beneath the Marshall

Field store, moved along a conveyor belt, and dropped again onto tables from which men sorted them into the little cars of the Chicago Tunnel Company. After arriving at the proper freight house or Railway Express Agency depot, the packages moved up conveyor belts for sorting. What happened then around the clock happens around the clock now in Memphis, at the national hub of FedEx. Given simple barcode and robotic technology that already routes FedEx and UPS packages and envelopes, the Chicago Tunnel Company activity might function with extremely few employees: perhaps almost none. A robotic underground freight railroad would decongest city streets and dramatically improve urban sanitation. Certainly it would reduce air pollution. But the nature of business, especially wholesale business, still precludes serious planning for such improvements.

While the FedEx driver delivering an envelope at an address may also pick up a package for shipment, the bakery truck driver delivers product and takes orders for more. In hundreds of thousands of small firms, delivery drivers work also as salespeople, and they move goods only one way. Possibly the bakery truck returns at the close of day with a few loaves of day-old bread on board, but most delivery trucks return totally empty of merchandise but with order books on board.

Dedicated delivery trucks are not common-carrier vehicles. Generations of regulations restrict the operation of common carriers open to hire by any shipper. Some of the regulations are starkly simple: an 18-wheeler that carries poisonous chemicals to a factory may not roll down the street and accept a load of cookies for movement a thousand miles away. Health and safety concerns make up only a small portion of regulations; the bulk of government effort focuses on regulating rates and services for the public good, ostensibly by ensuring competition. Thus a bakery-owned truck cannot transport household belongings, apples, or newspapers later in the day. Such items must move either in trucks owned by their manufacturers or purchasers, or aboard UPS, FedEx, or other motor freight common-carrier vehicles.

Just as no owner of an automobile may drive to the end of a queue of taxicabs and begin his own taxi business, no owner of any truck, even a pickup, can set up shop as a trucking company. The metal taxicab medallions and masses of stickers and cryptic initials decorating the sides of cabs and common-carrier trucks attest to the host of arcane regulations governing their use. Politicians who speak glibly of deregulating the motor freight industry know perfectly well that deregulation can proceed only so far before chaos develops. Economists who study the motor freight industry know its remaining regulations as perhaps the most byzantine of any industry.

Regulations govern the cost of trucking dog food, but not other animal food; dog food moves at a cost 10–35 percent greater than cat food. Prepared frozen meals including chicken, turkey, and fish move free of regulation; meals including a hamburger patty move under regulated tariffs that increase costs 20–25 percent. Lobbyists for some trucking companies oppose restrictive tariffs, but other lobbyists champion them. Into the debate move unions and non-union associations, shipper and consumer alliances, and representatives of railroads and other competitors. Always watchful and always proactive, local and state politicians monitor regulation of motor freight rates, for they understand that regulation and deregulation have sharp geographical consequences.

Congress began regulating railroads in 1887, when it created the Interstate Commerce Commission (ICC) to oversee safety concerns and rate setting. Schoolchildren still learn how hundreds of thousands of farmers organized through the Patrons of Husbandry to lobby Congress; the "Grangers" figure prominently in Frank Norris's famous 1902 muckraking novel *The Octopus,* and in other works pitting rural families against rapacious railroad barons charging all the market will bear. Federal regulation of railroad rates not only produced tens of thousands of specific rates for specific products between specific places but also made almost any innovation, from abandoning a line to building a new route, a political issue, almost invariably at the local level. Into the 1970s the railroad industry confronted regulatory ferocity when it tried to abandon money-losing passenger train service or transport truck trailers via express train. The regulation and deregulation of railroads, and subsequently of the trucking industry, prove that national policy often originates in measures as localized as New York City changing its zoning to benefit real estate developers owning property near Grand Central Terminal and Pennsylvania Station.

The Motor Carrier Act of 1935 brought the trucking industry into the jurisdiction of the ICC. From its birth after World War I through the last years of the Depression, the long-distance trucking industry moved over rough roads that produced tough, often rough behavior. Few graduate students read A. I. Bezzerides' 1938 novel of the industry, *The Long Haul*, although many old-film aficionados know the Raoul Walsh film based on it. In the 1940 epic *They Drive by Night*, starring George Raft and Humphrey Bogart, tough truckers in frail trucks blunder off roads into criminal behavior, and into federal regulation. The heavy hand of formal education keeps *The Octopus* in print, but *The Long Haul* has slipped into an oblivion as near total as that of the NYW&B.

From 1940 until the 1960s the ICC stymied motor freight innovation and stifled competition. Any trucking firm that produced the necessary paperwork to demonstrate its pre-1935 operations received a federal certificate permitting subsequent operation, but after 1935 entrepreneurs found creating a new trucking firm almost impossible. Instead, investors would try to buy an existing firm and expand it, often paying hundreds of thousands of dollars for a permit to carry a particular product over the road between two cities. Expansion and merger produced regulatory rate conflicts that drove many owners to distraction. If a trucking firm owning the right to move a product between Pittsburgh and Detroit acquired a firm with the right to move the identical product between Detroit and New York, the ICC required that the product continue to move via Detroit, not over highways running directly from Pittsburgh to New York. As John R. Meyer, Merton J. Peck, and other noted economists pointed out in a seminal 1959 book, *The Economics of Competition in the Transportation Industries*, ICC regulation of the trucking industry restricted national economic growth while guaranteeing the prosperity of some cities and businesses along certain routes. After twenty years the ICC had seemingly lost sight of the motor freight industry as one fundamentally different from railroads. The ICC saw long-haul trucking as railroading on rubber tires, and its view shaped the creation of the Interstate Highway System. Highway designers understood ICC tariff and route regulations to predict future growth in truck traffic, and designed accordingly.

It mostly escapes general notice that interstate highways are situated where they are in large measure owing to an ICC fixation on trucks as de facto trains that ought to follow predictable, unchanging routes—routes that make cities prosperous.

The ICC restricted railroad innovation until the 1970s. Order 321 ICC 582, Grain in Multiple-Car Shipments—River Crossings to the South, a 1963 ICC decision derisively remembered in the railroad industry as "the Big John case" from the nickname applied to the innovative railroad car involved, reveals federal regulator unease over the invention of extremely large grain hoppers that could be coupled into unit trains that would immediately reduce shipping rates and enrich farmers and railroads. Engineering invention was a cause of concern for ICC officials, since any invention offered the potential for making the railroad industry suddenly more efficient than the barge and trucking industry.

Long after the de facto deregulation of the trucking industry—begun in 1975 by the Ford administration and continued by the Motor Carrier Act of 1980 at the insistence of Jimmy Carter—difficulties persist with roads owned and maintained by government, and tariffs involving dog food and other products. Deregulation slashed the power of the Teamsters and other unions. While the industry as a whole still pays higher wages than most others and so attracts many rural young people into a seemingly romantic life on the road, overall its upper-limit average wages have dropped about a tenth over the past decade. Competition not only drives innovation and efficiency but also drives down wages; lower wages have helped keep the trucking industry viable in a time of railroad innovation.

Buying a used 18-wheel truck and becoming an owner-operator common or contract carrier is not a simple process, but neither is it especially difficult or hard to finance; even buying a small licensed trucking firm is straightforward. Entrepreneurs need only the vehicle and appropriate licenses and permits. The road is free, except for road-use taxes, and the road leads anywhere. On the other hand, individuals can buy used railroad locomotives and even learn to operate them, but no railroad company will accept their operation. Even short-line railroads are big business compared with one-truck owner-operators who sleep behind the seat.

The floor of an 18-wheeler trailer sits four feet above the road, a constant reminder that trucks evolved to load and unload from railroad boxcars with a standard floor height. Today, in a quasi-deregulated business environment, scrutinizers of urban warehouse districts, rural crossroads, and exurban parking lots often notice 18-wheel trucks unloading part of some cargo into the beds of pickup trucks backed against them. While railroad companies focus on long-distance unit trains and solid consists of intermodal containers, many very large long-haul motor freight carriers now compete with UPS and FedEx Ground, each of which moves packages up to 150 pounds. But no longer do large-truck drivers necessarily seek out warehouses with loading docks. Often they rendezvous with business people who own only pickup trucks, or who rent a U-Haul box truck and transship freight, or who run businesses in residential districts and ask that truckers deposit heavy freight on front lawns despite zoning regulations. What seems like innovation indicates a fast-deepening poverty, a sort of mercantile scruffiness. Trucks roll everywhere, not only jamming roads and parking lots but defying any rational response by highway and other planners.

The idea of regulating the motor truck industry originated in part through congressional awareness that physical constraints might make trucks the predators of urban prosperity. The Harlem Board of Commerce wanted to improve passenger access to the northern end of Manhattan, particularly via the NYW&B. It and the Regional Plan Association were well aware that truck traffic had begun to strangle much of upper Manhattan, and even parts of the Bronx and Brooklyn. The situation was serious enough to prompt congressional action: the 1935 Motor Freight Act, aimed in part at proportioning truck traffic congestion among cities.

Despite its best efforts, the ICC failed. By the middle 1950s trucking companies had pulled huge volumes of lucrative freight traffic away from railroads, often because railroads either refused to innovate or discovered ICC opposition to innovations it deemed unfair to the trucking and airline industries. Interstate highway construc-

tion at first kept pace with growing truck traffic, but manufacturers, freight forwarders, warehouse firms, and consignees discovered
massive congestion on and abutting their real estate. The ICC set
many rates without regard to regular, predictable traffic delays. The
arbitrary rates assisted established shippers and receivers only into
the 1960s. Then many new shippers and receivers began relocating
to cities and suburbs free of truck congestion, and demanding lower
rates. Trucking firms realized far greater profits from high-speed,
fast-turnaround trips, and so favored rural and exurban clients as
much as they could under regulation. As more shippers and receivers moved away from center city, then even suburban areas, rural-
area congressmen pressured the ICC to set rates based on open
roads and vast, sprawling parking lots and loading docks.

While Kennedy and Johnson administration experts viewed the
lines of 18-wheelers waiting to off-load at single urban freight elevators as an imminent economic calamity, they were only too con-
versant with the power of the Teamsters and other unions. Despite
Kennedy's insistence that the United States needed an integrated
national transportation plan, neither he nor Johnson did much to
anger unions. But Ford and Carter moved with dispatch, and despite the 1982 recession, by the mid-1980s the impacts of the 1980
Motor Carrier Act and the 1980 Staggers Act began to be obvious.
Between 1981 and 1986 intermodal shipment of truck trailers by
railroad companies grew 70 percent.

Unit trains of truck trailers or containers speeding along well-
maintained tracks now pass so frequently through much of the
Midwest and Far West that few locals pay them much attention.
But unlike hopper cars of coal or corn, the containers are individual
items moved and monitored differently. In the late 1960s the railroad industry began experimenting with bar coding all its cars and
locomotives. On January 1, 1970, every piece of rolling stock carried a machine-readable label similar to the bar-code labels nowadays found on every grocery store item. The industry envisioned
the project first as an accounting/information system. Computers
would track the whereabouts of every car and locomotive, reducing paperwork and providing data useful in increasing efficiency.
In some semiautomatic classification yards, the labels might en-

able computer-driven switching and makeup of freight trains. The second projected use of bar codes—never widely publicized—involved automated control of trains: the labels might precipitate a new era in which optical scanners recognized entire trains and fed data into computers regulating speed and routes. But just as supermarket chains have found bar codes useful for inventory control and speeding checkout, yet have so far found the labels useless in automating the bagging of disparate groceries, so the railroad industry found the label system unsatisfactory in the long run.

Dirt, especially rain-washed dirt, and snow obscured the sophisticated labels and eventually prompted the replacement of the entire system with other systems that simply read serial numbers painted on car sides. By 1980 the industry had essentially automated its car-monitoring system, but a decade earlier had discovered that moving truck trailers and containers expeditiously did not guarantee that the trailers and containers *arrived* expeditiously at their final destinations. The trailer, automatically monitored during its rail trip across the nation, moved away from an intermodal railroad yard onto highways and local roads and into an informational black hole. Despite advancements in subsequent years, particularly in Global Positioning System monitoring, truck drivers still determine many short-haul truck movements and often must decide to detour on long-haul routes as well. Just as rural highway commissioners find themselves surprised by overnight conglomerations of heavy grain-hauling trucks, so urban, suburban, and metropolitan planners and real estate investors discover mysterious gaggles of trucks suddenly descending upon particular locales. The lack of data concerning short-haul truck movements, especially following transfer from railroad trains, that vexed Regional Plan experts in the 1920s endures today.

In the absence of information, real estate developers choose boldly but cannily, accepting very high risks. In aging cities such as Boston and Baltimore, New York and Indianapolis, Chicago, St. Louis, Denver, and Seattle, and others with increasingly vibrant downtown business districts generating "excitement," inner ring zones jammed with trucks are now scorned. Passed through quickly by suburban commuters aboard trains, moved across far less quickly by suburban commuters driving their own cars, the ring zones grow more jammed and more rundown by the day. Long-haul truck trips terminate in them, and inside their confines railroads transfer trailers and containers from flatcars to trucks that often jam parking lots. In old coastal cities, such transfer often mixes with transfer between ships and planes and trains, producing the gridlock so evident to I-95 motorists approaching the George Washington Bridge from the south. Almost everyone, from environmentalists to politicians to artists, is enthusiastic about "revitalizing downtown," but almost no one is interested in the ring zones separating downtown from suburbs. No longer the industrial zone of manufacturing, not even a zone of warehouses and freight forwarding firms, the ring caters almost entirely to intermodal transfer and to the transfer of long-haul truck cargo. Among the clogged highways and local streets live the poor, squeezed between gentrified downtowns and high-value inner suburbs easily accessed via commuter trains.

Public transportation means, of course, vehicles that transport groups of people. Goods, however, tend to move privately, and these movements are difficult to track and defy analysis. Real estate developers embrace the dichotomy directly. They assume that where passenger trains once ran, they might, indeed will, run again, and they invest accordingly, especially downtown. Recently the federal government awarded New York City another $150 million for its ongoing East Side Access Project, a rerouting of Long Island Rail Road passenger trains through the new tunnels near 63rd Street in the vicinity of Grand Central Terminal. Renewed passenger train access translates into tens of thousands of people transferring between trains and places of work, shopping, and recreation; such transfer drives up property values, and developers know that. Developers assume, too, that local delivery of goods that conflicts with the movement of people drives people away. In this assumption they are in accord with Regional Plan analysts and the Harlem Board of Commerce. Consequently they concentrate on old passenger train routes into cities and leave the question of freight and trash subways to financiers thinking about automating the transfer of goods. No one knows exactly how people and goods flow into, around, and from cities. It is clear, however, that expediting the flow of people now means segregating the flow of goods to ring zones that will soon strangle downtown expansion.

Real estate developers scrutinize the example of the NYW&B not because they know it offers a window on local zoning ordinance transforming the development of a vast metropolitan region, nor because it demonstrates that commuters will drive from one commuter train station to another they believe offers better service. Instead they examine the NYW&B because it terminated in the Bronx next to freight yards.

Investing in almost any urban downtown, especially one blessed with stable or rising property values, requires significant capital. Property immediately adjacent to downtown usually bustles with trucks, warehouses, and related businesses serving downtown and suburbs. If more and more truckborne freight moved via rail, not beneath downtown but adjacent to it, large quantities of ring-zone real estate might suddenly become available for reuse. From the bottom of the pot in which the stew of the old and new Motor Carrier Acts, the Staggers Act, and other government regulations simmers now bubbles up the example of the NYW&B. Thinking ahead is hard, and scenario analysis sometimes fails. But an extraordinarily profitable real estate investment boom might have happened in upper Manhattan in the 1930s, especially if the locale had been freed of truck traffic and made accessible to commuters.

Many cities have such locales today, laced with railroad tracks to be sure, but also crammed with trucks and truck-dependent businesses. If the trucks might be eliminated or nearly so, and their freight handled more or less robotically in very condensed neighborhoods, developers might be able to transform regions near downtown. Almost all real estate developers realize the short-term consequences of the massive population growth immediately ahead, and they realize that almost all of that growth will occur in metropolitan places. The only sort of space with any potential for solving the coming housing crisis—and at a profit—is the ring-zone warehouse district adjacent to downtown.

Over the past decade, Harvard University has quietly acquired a gritty neighborhood of warehouses, freight-forwarding companies, and even a railroad yard. Few academics—indeed almost no white-collar people—ever visited the neighborhood just beyond the Harvard Business School in Boston. Harvard expects rail and truck traffic to move away from its newly acquired property in Allston, and it intends to build a new campus after it demolishes the old buildings. The truck-based businesses will indeed move away, but now shippers and politicians insist that the intermodal rail transshipment yard remain. Harvard waited too long. It bought the last rail/truck/warehouse conglomeration abutting downtown Boston, at very inflated prices and from investors who knew the long-term property value of a neighborhood most white-collar people found—and still find—invisible, even as they sit in traffic jams caused by trucks entering and leaving its last functioning businesses.

Then Harvard discovered something scenario analysts began studying in the late 1970s, the Grand Junction line. An active freight railroad over which switching locomotives move commuter train cars late at night, the track indirectly connects the northern suburbs of Boston with those to the west and south. This indirect link between North Station and South Station bisects the campus of the Massachusetts Institute of Technology and crosses the Charles River, but the Boston-area intellectual elite scarcely see it. Scholars studying mental mapping discover that few questionnaire respondents even know the bridge exists. News media mention the line annually, when elephants parade from a circus train stopped adjacent to MIT laboratories, but for almost everyone the track proves invisible.

Now it is a nightmare. With almost no modification other than a concrete platform, commuter trains from north of Boston might terminate not at North Station but at a new stop at the southern edge of the new Harvard campus. Even worse, that southern edge abuts a very active commuter rail line whose passengers might choose to detrain in Allston rather than at South Station, a mile east in downtown. Even as the realization dawns that sending passenger trains over the Grand Junction track would link Wellesley College, Boston University, Harvard, MIT, Tufts University, and north-of-Boston beaches, real estate developers close the trap on Harvard. If the university indeed creates an entire new campus across the Charles River from its existing one, if it encourages spin-off commercial and scientific development, might it not create a new locus of commuter train service? Canny developers knew the answer by 1980 and sold only some of the property, at inflated prices, to Harvard. The rest they retained, assuming that the combination of Harvard growth, predicted by analysts anticipating the moves of large institutions, would combine with rail access to shift much capital away from downtown Boston. This is the lesson of the NYW&B. Passenger- and freight-train access to a point near the downtown of a vibrant city can destabilize growth in downtown. But when the moment is right, it can also radically enrich long-term investors by shifting capital to a new nearby location invisible to almost everyone.

SOURCES: Arcara, *Westchester's Forgotten Railway;* Harlem Board of Commerce, *Three Plans for the Relief of Traffic Congestion;* Homberger, *Historical Atlas of New York City;* John R. Meyer, Merton J. Peck, et al., *The Economics of Competition in the Transportation Industries;* Moffat, *Forty Feet Below,* and *The "L";* Mortimer, "ACI . . . Have You Got It?"; New York, Westchester, and Boston Railway, *Westchester Timetables;* Regional Plan Association, *Transit and Transportation and a Study of Port and Industrial Areas;* Westcott, "Midnight Local."

OVERHEAD

In 1979 the Muskingum Electric began proving that General Electric remote sensing technology then undergoing testing on Bay Area Rapid Transit (BART) equipment in San Francisco worked well. The massive coal trains operated under simultaneous continuous and intermittent automatic train control, but not under human supervision. When loading and unloading, and at the ends of the lines, the robotic locomotives received automated radio signals. Only eight commands proved necessary: stop, creep (one-third of a mile an hour), 4, 15, 35, and 50 miles an hour, and north and south. Except when automatically changing speed away from ends of the line, the trains moved under intermittent control. Every five thousand feet one of two paired sensors embedded beneath the rails radioed the locomotive to proceed; if the second sensor received a response from the locomotive within two seconds, the train moved ahead another five thousand feet to the next pair of sensors. While other sensors activated track switches so the trains could pass onto double track from single track, and opened and closed hopper car bottom doors during unloading, the fail-safe electronic sensing system struck all but electrical engineers as NASA-like wizardry. The control system sent messages to the locomotives, but the locomotives actively signaled the sensors too. Automatic train control could move heavy trains in wilderness settings, in all sorts of weather, efficiently and safely.

Such operation made few headlines outside railroad industry journals and magazines read by train enthusiasts, but it affected the long-range thinking of many technically minded real estate investors. Readers of a 1967 *Popular Mechanics* feature article on the new Great Slave Lake Railway operating into the sub-Arctic from Peace River in Alberta, learned that tall microwave towers, radios, and telephones meant no poles and wires marching beside the new tracks. Long trains of lead ore moved behind diesel locomotives operated by engineers, although the wireless communication net-

On rainy days, tourists find the New Orleans light-rail system especially pleasant.

work necessary to automatic train control already existed. Like the cutting-edge subway cars delivered the same year to Cleveland, a city suddenly boasting that its new rapid-transit rail line made it the only city in the United States with high-speed rail service between its downtown and airport, Great Slave Lake Railway equipment still required onboard engineers. But the new Cleveland equipment included the rudiments of far-reaching change. The cars permitted radio-sent cab signals so motormen no longer had to watch ahead for colored light signals beside the track, and sensor-driven equipment that stopped the trains if operators ran past red signals. In 1967 such equipment had been planned for new subway lines in Chicago and Boston, and uneasy unions felt a presentiment that the Muskingum Electric confirmed a dozen years later.

Labor unions stymied automation for decades after 1960. *Trains* editorialized in October 1978 that railroads, like building elevators, had built-in guidance systems: elevators had become automated and railroads might be. Yet after eighteen years of effort, Congress prohibited the railroad industry from adding staffing and work rules to its nationwide contract negotiations. Both the United Transportation Union (UTU) and the Brotherhood of Locomotive Engineers (BLE) successfully lobbied Congress to stymie industry automation initiatives, especially those involving bankrupt railroads. The industry asked Congress to permit bankruptcy trustees to change work rules—but not wages and benefits—on bankrupt lines. Congress refused. The BLE labeled the idea "a time bomb," and in 1978 unions still controlled Congress.

Automation inflected much industry effort after the 1970s energy crises and the success of the Muskingum Electric and other new-built railroads, just as it directed federal research funding. Eventually, it also shattered labor union alliances. The UTU accepted the concept of radio-controlled locomotives directed by conductors, while the BLE rejected the idea. In a last-ditch effort to halt the yard locomotives switching cars remotely (but under the control of a UTU employee on the ground), the much-diminished BLE merged with the Teamsters. Not until the Chicago, Rock Island & Pacific and other huge railroads had entered bankruptcy—often after having been abandoned by trustees unable to make them operate long enough to pay creditors—did Congress finally understand that the greater public good meant changed crew staffing laws and operating rules on all railroads. Cabooses disappeared as crews diminished and conductors rode in locomotives; short lines began working tiny, all-task crews; and dozens of automatic devices, particularly the handheld freight-yard locomotive controller, changed railroading in a multitude of ways.

Urban railroading divided subtly into two categories. As Cleveland and other cities began extending existing subway and trolley lines, and as Calgary and even Los Angeles began building all-new rapid-transit lines, real estate values began changing adjacent to short-ride infrastructure improvement. Not always did upgrades drive up the value of adjacent land; perhaps the examples of the New York, Westchester & Boston and similar lines remained potent. At the same time, Amtrak and urban freight trains were growing shorter and shorter, or sometimes even vanishing altogether. In 1980 the last freight train moved along the old New York Central West Side freight line—the so-called High Line—in Manhattan, abandoning a miles-long, double-track structure. The juxtaposition of modernizing, expanding rapid-transit lines and the withering of long-distance passenger train service and inner-city freight service in the context of railroad automation prompted tremors in real estate investment. In hindsight, 1980s real estate newspaper ads demonstrate the impact of upgrades and other changes along railroad tracks.

By 1990 railroad annual reports began emphasizing the laborsaving advantages of automation. Buses, in contrast, needed drivers. As W. D. Volkmer told *Electric Line* readers in a 1998 article, "Ten Years of Light Rail Progress," urban politicians had realized that light-rail and other rapid-transit rail vehicles needed fewer operators: one person might operate a three-car train. In the immediate future, they reasoned, rail vehicles might need no onboard operators at all, as BART demonstrated. The equation was simple. As the wages and benefits of a bus driver increase in proportion to the number of passengers carried aboard the bus, building an automatic (or semiautomatic) rail-based rapid-transit system becomes more economical, then the only possible alternative for cash-strapped cities and states. *Fixed-guidance systems,* to use the federal term for urban mass-transit systems operating on rails or under permanent overhead power transmission lines, might not be justified in neighborhoods with low population density. As Zachary Schrag demonstrates convincingly in *The Great Society Subway: A History of the Washington Metro,* real estate developers realized that changed zoning laws might make such systems linear generators of higher-density housing stock, office space, and retail development. Against the initial cost of building such systems, especially their protected rights-of-way, investors balanced the wages of bus drivers.

Across most of the United States, trains operate within very permeable corridors. At tens of thousands of grade crossings, automobiles and trucks collide with moving trains, most frequently plowing into the middle of trains, not locomotives. Flashing lights, ringing bells, illuminated gates, and the ear-splitting howl of locomotive horns fail to prevent such collisions. At lesser-used crossings, only signs warn motorists; elsewhere the right-of-way is scarcely protected from wandering livestock and other interruptions. Farmers and hunters routinely move along and across tracks despite signs announcing "no trespassing." When Thoreau said that he crossed the railroad as though it were "a cart path in the woods" he voiced the attitude of subsequent generations of rural and wilderness people. Along unfenced and poorly fenced tracks, automatic train operation proves difficult to implement. Only a traditional locomotive engineer, hand upon the throttle and eye upon the rail, offers safe operation.

But rapid-transit routes typically operate within enclosed rights-of-way. Subways offer the best example of rail routes awaiting automation.

Until just after World War II, only three cities boasted what William Middleton terms "heavy-duty subway operation." In his history of rail-based mass transit, *Metropolitan Railways: Rapid Transit in America,* he explains that for decades Chicago, Hoboken (whose "el" was once considered the largest iron structure in the world), and other cities relied largely on electric-powered trains operating atop elevated structures. Noise and visual blight made els seem old-fashioned in the 1930s, but maintenance costs condemned most by

1940, although some subway lines still operate over short stretches of elevated structure. Only New York, and to a slightly lesser degree Boston and Philadelphia, operated integrated subway systems that shaped urban growth and real estate investment. Throughout the Depression, planners in many transit-poor cities confronted more than financial difficulty. They realized that private automobile ownership reduced transit system ridership, especially in outlying regions feeding downtown rapid-transit systems. Financial strictures and declining patronage led to little construction, but indirectly precipitated downtown automobile traffic congestion, the destruction of buildings to make way for parking lots, and finally the building of highways through central city areas. Heavy-duty subway operations in the three eastern cities molded planning efforts and some construction, but in the end failed as models for smaller, less densely built cities.

Typical small-city subway operation involved trolley cars moving over suburban streets toward cities, then rolling down ramps into tunnels leading downtown. Boston and Philadelphia operate such light-duty subways today, but such systems once seemed an ideal compromise between surface-street trolleys and heavy-duty subway operation. After World War I, many cities choked with trolley cars used abandoned canal beds as the core of light-duty subway systems. Between 1927 and 1956 the Rochester, New York, subway system operated in tunnels located in the abandoned Erie Canal. The present Newark, New Jersey, system, now upgraded to heavy operation, opened in 1935 in tunnels located in the bed of the former Morris & Essex Canal. But the strangest example of subway building endures in Cincinnati.

In 1927, seven years after construction began, the city of Cincinnati had built four miles of tunnels in the bed of the abandoned Miami & Erie Canal, the first of twenty miles intended for immediate completion. But the city made what transit experts now recognize as a classic error: it built a multilane boulevard, now called Central Parkway, directly atop the tunnels. Motorists consequently flooded downtown, and in the Depression worked stopped for good on what might have been a superb light-rail subway. No trains ever operated in the tunnels fitted with rails, station signs, and even benches.

Cincinnati opted to improve automobile access to downtown, and finally located I-75 directly through the heart of the city, along the alignment reserved for future trolley cars moving between suburbs and downtown tunnels.

Eerily, the tunnels remain today. During the Cold War the city debated using them as air-raid shelters, and later its water department located mains on their floors, but few Cincinnatians even know of them. As late as 1946, however, a group of investors tried to use them as a freight subway serving sixteen manufacturers, and the city council passed an ordinance permitting such use. However, when three large potential customers, all breweries, became concerned that diesel locomotive exhaust might contaminate foodstuffs and ended their support, the project died. What Regional Plan experts envisioned in New York in the 1920s, and what Chicago businesses already enjoyed in their electric-powered freight subway, Cincinnati scorned. The result was a "pickled" downtown. The city remains one of the few seemingly unable to break free of automobiles, trucks, and buses, although it persists in producing plans for light-rail systems, often using existing tunnels.

At the opposite end of the spectrum, Newark managed to destroy one of the finest light-rail subway systems in the world. By 1911 trolley cars operating along two main streets that intersected in central downtown brought traffic nearly to a standstill during rush hour. Between 5:15 and 6:15 every workday, 562 trolleys moved through the intersection. When the Lehigh Valley Railroad proposed abandoning the Morris Canal, private interests bought the right-of-way, and amid infighting and chicanery the Hudson & Manhattan Railroad began building its line under the Hudson River to Newark. By 1916, however, Public Service Coordinated Transport, a consolidation of hundreds of small trolley lines carrying 451 million riders annually, had opened its grandiose Central Terminal to reduce street congestion. Each business day the two-level terminal served some 2,600 trolley cars operating to and from Jersey City, Perth Amboy, and other cities within a radius of fifty-five miles. About fifty-five thousand riders poured through the terminal daily, shopping in its grand concourse that never closed, and forcing Public Service to install prepayment fare collection devices. The state-of-the-art terminal attracted experts worldwide, for it demonstrated how meticulous design might create a terminal in which trolley cars moved almost as efficiently as heavy subway trains.

Increased automobile use not only lessened ridership on Public Service trolleys but further jammed streets on which the trolleys operated. Throughout the 1920s Newark debated building a subway, and during the Depression carried forward its Roaring Twenties plans, focusing the system on the new Pennsylvania Railroad station, which served long-distance and commuter trains, including those operating into Pennsylvania Station in New York, and the Hudson & Manhattan electric trains operating under the Hudson River to lower Manhattan. Despite a connecting subway link to the gigantic Public Service terminal, ridership flowed via subway to the new Pennsylvania Station, which became the de facto transit center of Newark almost overnight.

By 1961 only two platforms in the Public Service terminal remained in use, both for buses operating over rails abandoned by streetcars since 1938. Four years later the buses vanished, and the owners converted the lower level of the great terminal into space for air conditioning equipment and other utilities serving offices built onto the upper level. Almost everyone forgot about the tunnel linking the terminal with the city subway. But in 1978 wreckers demolishing the terminal building broke the tunnel roof and discovered streetcars stored in dust, abandoned since the 1930s. A few years later Public Service Electric & Gas had built a new corporate headquarters on the 5.3 acres once covered by perhaps the finest light-rail terminal in the world. Nowadays only transit experts know that the Newark terminal proved the model for the present Port Authority bus terminal in Manhattan. The Public Service terminal disappeared into oblivion.

Buses helped destroy streetcars. Manufacturers advertised buses as flexible. Buses might overtake and pass each other, pull to the curb at the will of drivers, and swerve around double-parked cars and trucks, especially trucks unloading goods in front of stores. Most importantly, buses might operate over different streets in times of severe traffic congestion. Over decades, this flexibility became a trait prized by unthinking Americans, especially in California cities where buses vanquished streetcars. Despite persistent conspiracy theories that bus manufacturers bribed city councils, especially in Southern California locales, to pass ordinances that restricted streetcar operation or forced trolley companies to maintain blatantly unprofitable fare structures, Van Wilkins, whose 1990 *Electric Lines* article, "Who Really Killed the Streetcar?" offers a convincing analysis, and other experts agree that streetcars facing urban traffic congestion simply moved too slowly to please many riders. Those riders who could choose other transit options usually did, eventually leaving behind the poor, whose last-resource vehicle often proved a bus.

Streetcar companies experimented with buses from the 1920s onward, and in the 1930s Public Service tested them in regular service. Between 1934 and 1937 it tried Dodge railbuses that operated over roads on rubber tires; at any grade crossing such a bus could turn onto tracks, lower steel wheels, and proceed independent of trolley-line power. Especially on lightly patronized trolley car routes, the railbus idea seemed attractive, even if the buses provided a bumpier ride than trolleys. The railbus might serve locales away from tracks, might shortcut on and off rails, and might whisk past jammed downtown streets on reserved rail rights-of-way. In the end, it also might eliminate the need for the overhead electric wires that powered trolley cars. As other private urban transit companies experimented with hybrid buses—the Boston Elevated Railway Corporation operated seventy-two generator-electric buses for twenty-two years over city streets, replacing three-inch seat cushions with nine-inch ones to make the ride resemble streetcar smoothness—Public Service abandoned its rail buses. Company accountants argued that a bus might as well be a bus, operate over highways, and avoid expensive private rail rights-of-way.

All-electric buses fascinated operators of many urban transportation systems, and this interest partially explains experiments with hybrid electrics in Boston and elsewhere. In 1913 Merrill, Wisconsin, experimented with buses powered from overhead wires, but the Philadelphia experiment begun ten years later marked the first large-scale effort. Built by Brill and formally christened "Railess Cars," the little buses each seated twenty-eight people, with room for about as many more standees. Until 1935 the buses came with solid rubber tires, but during the Depression a switch to pneumatic tires provided smoother riding and eliminated the need for nine-inch cushions. Trackless trolley operation proved relatively successful in Philadelphia and other cities. The buses, each with two poles reaching up to double electric wires, moved silently, accelerated and slowed as gracefully as any streetcar, swerved around double-parked vehicles, and pulled to the curb for boarding and discharging passengers. In the 1920s Detroit, Salt Lake, New Orleans, and other cities began experimenting with trolley buses.

Westinghouse Electric produced an extensive report on the innovative buses in 1935. As a manufacturer of components used by most builders, it had a vested interest in success, but more importantly, it wanted to demonstrate the efficiency of the buses. *Trolley Coach: Application and Performance Data* makes dense reading: much of the report is highly technical and much focuses on economics. Trolley buses required far less maintenance than those powered by gasoline or diesel engines; they also used little electricity and reduced road repair costs associated with streetcar operation. Trolley buses could swerve around double-parked cars, but they negotiated construction sites just as easily, whereas any road repair work involving streetcar tracks meant streetcar companies paying for overnight effort simply to keep cars in operation across ditches, gravel, and other impediments that trolley buses crossed effortlessly. *Trolley Coach* remains ignored, however, even among transportation historians, although it examines the larger significance of all-electric buses operating under fixed overhead wires.

Westinghouse engineers discovered that abutters loved the silent buses that produced no pavement vibration. Streetcars required heavily built, well-maintained track to move quietly, and usually they squealed around curves. Trolley buses provided passengers with near-silent rides and moved alongside pedestrians, storekeepers, and residents just as silently. The buses accelerated far more quickly than did diesel buses, thus easing vehicular traffic, and their double-stream front doors swallowed and disgorged multiple streams of riders at a time, making stops much briefer. Suburbanites accepted trolley bus installation with better grace than they did the construction of streetcar lines or the imposition of diesel bus routes, because they scarcely heard the electric buses. Urban residents embraced them wholeheartedly, except along streets with high-speed streetcar service. Westinghouse determined that, for economic and environmental reasons, trolley bus lines might serve as feeders for streetcar routes or pioneer traffic creation on new routes until streetcars replaced trolley buses. While the trolley buses could not carry nearly the flow of passengers managed by streetcars, they nonetheless assured merchants and real estate developers of a fixed route.

During the Depression the business community learned the downside of bus route flexibility. Surface-transit ridership did not always shrink or vanish; often it merely changed alignment, sometimes by only a parallel street or two, and often by the machinations of corrupt city councils. A flow of streetcars or even trolley buses along a city street meant a more-or-less assured flow of potential customers. Passengers window-shopped from trolleys, and signaled motormen to stop so they could get off and examine stores featuring especially inviting windows. Except at rush hour, retail streets thronged with slowly if steadily moving trolleys or trackless trolleys became retail gold mines as window displays lured would-be shoppers from streetcars. Merchants invested heavily in so-called trolley-street stores, because they knew trolley and trackless-trolley routes to be virtually permanent. Moving tracks and overhead wire meant extraordinary capital expense, and only rarely did transit companies or transit authorities choose such action.

Buses did not so much destroy window shopping as destroy store owner confidence that their buildings faced a permanent stream of traffic. In order to expedite passenger flow, and sometimes to assuage city councils acting to favor merchants on less-traveled streets, bus companies and transit authorities diverted buses from established routes. Rush-hour commuters often benefited from reduced transit time, but shoppers sometimes preferred slightly longer transit times to moving along streets with unfamiliar stores. In the Depression, as public transit authorities acquired bankrupt street railway companies, more than retail merchants learned how flexible buses made bus routes writhe and bend. Landlords and real estate developers discovered that buses did not necessarily remain on abandoned streetcar routes. Instead they often moved along parallel but low-value streets, making abutting property suddenly far more valuable. Buses might be routed practically anywhere, making entire neighborhoods suddenly bereft of short-distance and commuter pass-through traffic. Just as the 1910-era replacement of clogged downtown streetcar routes by subways transformed real estate values by boosting value around subway stops and lowering it at points midway between stations, so the replacement of streetcars by diesel buses taught urban landowners a nasty lesson.

In Dayton, Columbus, and Toledo, in Rockford and Peoria, and even in Fitchburg, Massachusetts, replacing streetcars with trolley buses reassured abutters that traffic would still flow in the established directions that maintained property values. Where diesel buses replaced streetcars, entire sectors of cities might lose most public transit. Silent-film aficionados might ponder the many sequences in which comics run afoul of Los Angeles streetcars labeled "Watts." Until the late 1930s, Watts enjoyed some of the finest streetcar service in greater Los Angeles, in part because longer-distance routes passed through the neighborhood. New bus routes circumvented Watts, and African Americans found getting to and from work harder by the year.

The jitney fad also hurried the demise of streetcar service, and had an adverse impact on early trolley bus and diesel bus experiments as well. A brief, almost unstudied, and now forgotten fad in the 1920s, jitneying involved automobile owners picking up would-be streetcar and bus passengers and driving them downtown for less than transit fares, then ferrying them home in the evening. Jitneying produced crises in many cities, but the phenomenon has been closely studied only in Birmingham, Alabama. Despite rapidly passed city ordinances forbidding the practice, police in the end did nothing if driver and passengers claimed to be friends. Moreover, city governments often confessed failure if jitney drivers operated across municipal lines, especially when state governments regulated the fledgling motor bus industry as poorly as they did trucking. By 1917 entrepreneurs had bought used motor buses and begun driving their own routes, diverting fares from streetcar lines operating on parallel or adjacent streets. Antijitney legislation endures today—

automobile insurance explicitly fails to cover passengers carried for hire—but transportation historians rarely give the temporary fad much attention. However, many motorists paid for their cars by carrying commuters for pay, and in so doing contributed to the Depression collapse of privately owned transit companies. The latter had invested millions in infrastructure improvements ranging from the Newark terminal to thinly traveled trolley lines reaching across regions not yet suburbanized.

Trolley buses helped private companies and public transit authorities confront automobile ownership, jitneying, Depression-era ridership drops, and suburban sprawl while reassuring developers and property owners that passengers would move along permanent routes. Westinghouse and other firms worked together to build buses that operated under diesel power on the outskirts of cities and under overhead-wire electric power as they neared downtowns. Such hybrid buses eliminated the tunnel fumes that infuriated riders, particularly in summer when ventilator units failed to rid bus interiors of smoke. But diesel-electric hybrids came too late to save many trolley subways. Usually cities that abandoned streetcars late discovered that electric buses might operate well in paved-over tunnels. Cambridge, Massachusetts, began running silent, clean buses in a short subway, but Rochester and Newark abandoned their tunnels just a few years too soon.

A full bus might remove fifty motorists from the highway, and so remove fifty cars, but the bus sat stuck in traffic as did any other over-the-road vehicle. In the late 1960s General Motors Corporation demonstrated a diesel-powered bus that operated on roads and railroads alike. Fluke, however, consigned the new rail bus into the oblivion that consumed its 1930s ancestors.

In the summer of 1967, the GM model SDM 5302, a standard forty-nine-seat, air conditioned, suburban-service (meaning fitted with forward-facing, reclining upholstered seats) bus equipped with vertically movable steel wheels, operated in tests over Philadelphia Suburban Transportation Company tracks in the vicinity of Bryn Mawr, Pennsylvania. Company president Merritt H. Taylor immediately proclaimed it a success, suggested it might restore rail service along abandoned tracks in southern New Jersey and elsewhere, and even interested the Port Authority of New York and New Jersey. Designated the Hy-Rail Test Bus, it made several ceremonial trips with journalists aboard, then made test runs on other commuter railroads, then served as a featured attraction at a national conference of railroad executives. Then, in autumn, the bus rendezvoused with fate in Washington, D.C.

Snow flurries brushed the vehicle as it waited in front of the New Senate Office Building for dignitaries to board. Once full, it cruised easily to Baltimore & Ohio tracks near Union Station and began a demonstration run. Two hours later, in a driving snowstorm, it managed to reach Silver Spring, Maryland, six miles away, where passengers departed in disgust. Not until it reached a grade crossing in Gaithersburg could its driver maneuver it from the rails. Despite being equipped with sanders, the rail bus had crawled twenty-one miles in four hours, delayed an untold number of freight and passenger trains, and convinced Taylor to retain his high-speed electric trains. Americans expected railroad trains and streetcars to operate in bad weather, including the likes of the storm that dumped a foot of snow on the national capital during the Hy-Rail Test Bus demonstration.

Not surprisingly, then, Edmonton and Calgary in Alberta focused on light-rail vehicles (LRVs) in the middle 1970s, only a few years after the Hy-Rail Test Bus debacle. Both cities required fast, reliable rapid transit in snowstorms, and both had learned from the struggles of Boston and San Francisco. In 1959 Boston converted an abandoned commuter rail line to a high-speed trolley line. Conversion of some streetcar routes to trolley buses had left the Metropolitan Transit Authority with a surfeit of trolley cars, and the new Highland Branch proved an inexpensive but amazingly successful innovation. San Francisco, finally moving toward building its Market Street extension of the Twin Peaks tunnel opened in 1917, wanted to buy brand-new streetcars in an era when manufacturers no longer built them. While Toronto determined to maintain its existing streetcar fleet and extend its lines by buying large fleets of used streetcars from Kansas City, Cleveland, Birmingham, and Cincinnati as those cities converted to buses, San Francisco and Boston determined to use federal funds to buy state-of-the-art streetcars from Germany. When the Nixon administration vetoed this idea as exacerbating a worsening balance-of-payments problem, the Urban Mass Transit Administration forced both transit systems to find a United States manufacturer, which they did: a firm that built helicopters. The manufacturer responded by building a prototype car that literally fell apart during testing. United States transit systems officials in Pittsburgh, Shaker Heights, and other cities watched with dismay. The Standard Light Rail Vehicle project seemed only to delay a solution to replacing aging streetcars. In time the firm delivered 170 cars to Boston and 100 to San Francisco (some purchased after Boston refused the balance of its order), but the fiasco delayed innovation by almost a decade. Edmonton and Calgary officials absorbed the lesson and ordered reliable cars from Germany.

Light-rail transit is essentially a euphemism for ultramodern streetcars operating along city streets, sometimes in subways, and usually over reserved but not grade-separated tracks away from downtown. Suspension innovations enable cars to ride only a few inches above the pavement, making entering and exiting easy and fast. Undercarriage design makes cars extremely quiet and able to accelerate and brake rapidly. Multiple-unit control, a century-old invention, enables one person to operate multiple-car trains, even during rush hour. For many cities, particularly small ones with dispersed populations and serious highway congestion, light-rail transit seemed futuristic in 1970 and eminently sensible a decade later.

Calgary opened its first brand-new light-rail transit line in 1981, a second in 1985, and a third in 1987, proving to United States transit officials that people in a small, anything-but-densely-built city would forsake their cars, even on sunny summer days. The German-built streetcars operating largely in expressway median strips and divided boulevards, and along downtown retail streets, transformed urban-design thinking almost overnight. Nevertheless, Americans today often know little of the light-rail revolution that followed the Calgary triumph, and upper-class suburbanites in expensive cars often know the least. Despite subsequent successes elsewhere, electronic news media tend to ignore new light-rail systems as one-of-a-kind experiments or somehow trivial. Newspapers pay more attention. Light-rail riders often read newspapers.

Pie-in-the-sky urban transit efforts ended in Pittsburgh in 1974, when the state of Pennsylvania refused to fund its share of an elevated, automated transportation system called Sky-Bus. Despite the fact that 87 percent of the design work had been completed under federal grants, local citizens argued that the Sky-Bus system would never work in bad weather. Instead, the Penn Central Railroad offered its Panhandle Bridge across the Monongahela River to the city, a consultant reported that streetcars could use the bridge after inexpensive and fast improvements, and in 1985 LRVs began running among older Pittsburgh streetcars. The fifty-five German cars assembled in Pittsburgh advanced the revolution in thinking Calgary and Edmonton had begun. United States urban transit authorities saw success, at a surprisingly low cost.

San Diego's effort built upon the successes of Canada and Pittsburgh. In Southern California, officials abandoned the idea of specialized buses operating between freeway lanes; the futuristic vehicles had vanished before the example of Calgary LRVs. San Diego crated a light-rail system from scratch, bought Siemens-Duewag U-2 LRVs, and by 1981 operated cars between San Diego and San Ysidro on the Mexican border. Patronage grew far faster than anyone expected, forcing the purchase of more cars and, within two years, the double tracking of the main line. In 1986 the system opened a second route to Euclid, and its plans for a 140-mile system no longer elicited "Tijuana trolley" jokes.

Almost unnoticed, the West Coast had become the epicenter of light-rail system innovation. While the San Francisco region emphasized its automated BART system, cities to the north and south moved rapidly toward lower-cost systems using European LRVs. The pace of change flummoxed practicing architects and urban designers and bypassed the curricula of graduate design schools. At a fundamental level, the rapid acceptance of light-rail transit on the West Coast contradicted the commonplace assumption that California, Washington, and Oregon would never abandon the private automobile as the generator of metropolitan design and form.

In Portland, Oregon, grassroots opposition to more freeway building surfaced first in a 1972 referendum. Municipal officials attended a 1976 light-rail conference in Philadelphia, but few other at-

tendees, including would-be United States LRV manufacturers, paid
them much attention. Almost certainly the Portland representatives
gave San Diego participants the courage to proceed with plans for
the line to San Ysidro, and the two cities thereafter supported each
other despite the derision of national and eastern experts. In 1976
Portland determined to rebuild an existing freeway with two light-
rail tracks, and six years later began laying new track on a former
trolley car right-of-way to the suburb of Gresham. Bombardier, a
Canadian company with a plant in Vermont, just across the Quebec
border, provided the new cars, forestalling complaints about public transit authorities "buying foreign." In Pittsburgh and Portland,
citizen opposition to both freeways and high-tech mass-transit alternatives reoriented urban transportation thinking.

Bad weather, especially snow, focused light-rail thinking elsewhere in the country, however, in commonsense ways. In the 1970s
Buffalo embarked on a subway-building idea much like that Edmonton envisioned, hoping that fast, frequent trains would revitalize a stagnant downtown. Common sense and perhaps a desire for
massive amounts of federal grant money nudged Buffalo toward
a traditional subway scheme, but federal authorities insisted that
the project be downsized to focus on light-rail. Once service began
in 1985, low ridership disappointed city officials. Completing the
six-and-a-half-mile-long line in 1987 increased patronage, but the
Buffalo experience caused many other transportation authorities to
wonder at the moderate-weather successes in San Diego, Portland,
and elsewhere on the West Coast.

In 1987 San Jose began service on the first leg of its light-rail system directed toward Silicon Valley, and a year later began operating
vintage trolley cars on dedicated downtown tracks intended to spur
tourist visits. Balancing high-speed commuter and shopping movement and antique trolley cars intended to enthrall tourists immediately changed public and investor attitudes toward central San Jose.
As late as 1991 commentators remembered when downtown San
Jose resembled "Buffalo with palm trees," a cutting remark about
urban blight that in addition emphasized the enduring inability of
Buffalo to make underground light-rail transit a generator of urban
reinvestment. By then, however, Los Angeles had been operating its

Metro Blue Line for a year, providing unnerving information on the long-term impact of light-rail system building in larger, older cities.

The Metro Blue line operates along a right-of-way abandoned by Pacific Electric Company trolley cars in 1961, down the median of Long Beach Boulevard now replanted with palm trees. Part of it runs through a subway tunnel under downtown, and part of it operates over new alignment near Long Beach made available after the Union Pacific built a new intermodal terminal and access track nearby to handle increased ocean container traffic. It ends in the Long Beach Transit Mall. Los Angeles County accepted not one cent of federal money: all $877 million came from sales taxes on local purchases. Into the 1960s the Pacific Electric terminated at Main Street and Sixth in Los Angeles, an area that had become ground zero of skid row by the 1980s, pushing the de facto center of downtown activity to Flower and Seventh. Officials deflected the path of the subway from the old Pacific Electric terminal area to a new station at Seventh, where it connects with the new heavy-duty, third-rail-powered subway line, Metro Red. Much of Metro Blue's open-air route lies through some of the poorest and most crime-ridden neighborhoods in the region. Instead of avoiding the area, the Los Angeles Transportation Commission planned at the beginning to police the line heavily, and to lace it with remote cameras. Fares do not begin to cover operating costs, but the line serves two groups: poor people commuting to low-paying inner-city service jobs, and middle-class passengers commuting between the ocean and downtown. Yet unlike the San Diego, San Jose, and Portland lines, Metro Blue attracts little publicity. Indeed, many Los Angeles inhabitants scarcely know it exists.

The line's obscurity originates in its hidden nature. It neither traverses a well-known, easily identifiable corridor nor seems likely to make one surround its fast, clean, Japanese-built LRVs. Its cars can be coupled together to make long trains at rush hour, it operates safely with low fares, and it most certainly reaches downtown. But it exists in a perceptual limbo in part because it operates along sixteen miles of an existing freight railroad corridor. Close scrutiny by the get-out-and-look method reveals that Metro Blue cars whisk along a corridor evolving so subtly that its present condition is slightly unnerving.

For sixteen of its twenty-one miles, the line shares a corridor with an active freight railroad. In the late 1970s an underutilized freight railroad corridor connecting with an abandoned high-speed trolley corridor seemed the ideal ribbon along which to build a new light-rail line. From the design stage on, however, Los Angeles County Transportation Authorities (LACTA) encountered one difficulty after another, reminiscent of difficulties that had hampered similar efforts in Baltimore and other old eastern cities. The corridor proved barely wide enough for three tracks, two new ones for the Metro Blue system and the still-active one used for freight. Moving the freight track to one edge of the corridor only worked away from stations and bridges, and produced the need for spur tracks to cross Metro Blue rails so the railroad could service corridor clients on the opposite side. Center-platform stations required the most careful design work, since the platforms pushed Metro Blue tracks away from each other. Widening bridges worried highway officials, who saw lengthened bridge abutments as additional obstructions to motor vehicles, and angered abutting landowners who lost frontage. Moreover, along the rail corridor ran dozens of utility system lines, many almost as difficult to move as the water mains weaving through the empty subway tunnels in Cincinnati. Eventually, LACTA negotiated sixty agreements involving relocation of gas mains, electric cables, and other services installed below or above the corridor. About two miles of Metro Blue track rise into the air over heavy-traffic freight spurs. At two locations, the so-called flyovers lift LRVs over crossings of other freight railroads too. What appeared simple to visionaries looking at ordinary maps became extremely difficult to implement once designers began studying existing conditions.

Underlying all Metro Blue design and construction was a scenario understood by the Southern Pacific Railroad and glimpsed by a handful of close observers. In the middle 1980s the "underutilized freight line" carried twelve trains a day, most of them serving the ocean shipping facility but some switching cars to and from corridor customers. As observed by many light-rail advocates, freight traffic in the corridor had been dropping for years. But while the number of trains remained roughly the same, the trains had become longer and individual cars moved more cargo. Sometime in the late 1970s the long-term decline in both numbers of trains and numbers of cars per train leveled off. By 1920s and World War II standards, the line worked far below capacity. But longer trains, and especially longer trains carrying much longer individual cars, tricked many casual onlookers into believing that most of the time the corridor remained idle. Only the railroad company suspected that freight traffic might boom, especially between its Long Beach intermodal facility and the rest of North America.

In the sales and construction agreement signed in 1985, LACTA agreed that its entire construction process would focus on aligning Metro Blue tracks so that the freight railroad might easily double-track its own operation. Five years after Congress passed the Staggers Act, the Southern Pacific understood the potential for massive growth in intermodal shipping to and from ocean terminals. It sold off about half of its sixteen-mile corridor, but it retained almost all its existing use-value and all its potential for growth.

Anyone riding LRVs in Calgary south of downtown discovers that the cars exit the third suburban tunnel into a freight railroad corridor. The LRVs operate between freight tracks: the heavily used ones on one side carrying about ten unit grain and sulfur trains a day on the Canadian Pacific main line from Calgary to Fort Macleod and Lethbridge, the spur one serving local industries on the west side of the LRV tracks. At many places the two railroad routes squeeze tightly, especially at LRV stations sandwiched between LRV and Canadian Pacific rights-of-way. Away from downtown, where short platforms restrict train length, LRVs can operate in five-car trains to speed rush-hour traffic. At the grade crossings south of Calgary, LRVs, especially coupled in multiunit consists, move across highway traffic essentially as ordinary trains. But in Calgary, then in Los Angeles, Baltimore, and elsewhere, LRVs do not share track with freight, commuter, and long-distance passenger trains.

In Sacramento, which designed its light-rail system from the beginning around a philosophy emphasizing minimal cost, trains first operated largely over a single-track route, only part of which was signaled. The system lacked automatic train stop technology, used tie plates salvaged from abandoned freight railroads, and put its first routes in abandoned and disused freight railroad corridors located along a right-of-way purchased for a never-built freeway. The system seems "green" indeed, not only because its builders spent relatively little money, but because it has had scarcely any impact on its corridor environments. At rush hour, lone operators guide trains consisting of four eighty-foot cars; in off-peak hours the same personnel operate single LRVs. Economy guided the creation of the Sacramento system, but the old freight railroad corridors guided its route locations.

Light-rail transit is just that: light rail. Even the heavier rail and roadbed construction used in traditional subway tunnels cannot bear the weight of modern freight and passenger trains, nor can long-distance trains negotiate the sharp curves and narrow tunnels used by LRV and traditional subway cars. Light transit operates in a conceptual limbo only just now beginning to worry and even alarm urban planners, investors, and environmentalists.

Installing light-rail in existing railroad corridors, no matter how disused or even abandoned, usually eliminates the potential of such corridors to carry long-distance trains again. In most metropolitan areas, freight service seems unlikely to return to downtown or adjacent neighborhoods. But where such service exists, it is likely to endure, and perhaps even increase in an era when manufacturing continues to decline but warehousing experts foresee a growing need for urban delivery of valuable goods by rail to eliminate truck congestion. Environmentalists and waste industry experts musing about shipping urban trash by rail pause whenever light-rail advocates ask about using freight corridors, but as yet rail-based solid-waste removal lacks the grassroots support enjoyed by light-rail systems. But restoring passenger service, especially electric-powered commuter rail service operating eighty or a hundred miles outside cities, raises issues simmering since the Muskingum Electric reoriented railroad industry thinking in the 1970s. Once converted to light-rail, corridors lose their potential to serve distant commuters.

Massachusetts recognized the trade-off in the middle 1970s, when the conversion of abandoned commuter railroads to light-rail seemed less and less a good idea. The state benefited from experience most others lacked. The Highland Branch had once transported riders only a few miles from downtown before rejoining a main east–west route reaching far from the city, but its traditional commuter trains operated mostly over main-line tracks terminating on ample capacity South Station platform tracks. In the 1960s trolley cars zipped along its refurbished surface rails, then dove below ground into already crowded trolley subway tunnels. As traffic increased on the upscale Highland Branch, even three-car LRV consists did little to alleviate the tunnel congestion caused by single- and multiple-car consists operating through the tunnels en route to it and other aboveground lines.

Very quietly, the transportation authority abandoned one streetcar route and part of another, trying to free up tunnel space for politically influential Highland Branch riders. The truncated route served a mostly African American part of Boston; the abandoned route served a gritty industrial area that lost value as it lost accessibility, despite being across a river from Harvard University.

Improved LRVs and better signals did little to alleviate light-rail subway congestion, which worsened through the 1980s, forcing thoughtful Massachusetts Bay Transportation Authority riders to realize that the extension of the Red Line heavy subway to Braintree had occupied two of the three available tracks that long-distance commuter trains serving the South Shore and Cape Cod might use. In the 1990s, as the MBTA gloried in the overnight success of two of three long-abandoned commuter routes and planned the opening of another, expert consultants pointed out the limits to further growth imposed by the single track snaking south of the city. At the southern edge of Boston, the lone commuter rail route wends its way between two two-track subway routes, one route on either side. Commuter trains already operate two-level cars to meet public demand. When trains begin operating to and from Greenbush, the lone track will be at capacity, two-level cars notwithstanding. Only electrification will boost its capacity by enabling trains to operate faster.

The only other choice confronting Massachusetts transportation planners seems almost obscene. Part of I-93, notoriously jammed with traffic, will become a railroad right-of-way.

While the situation south of Boston involves the 1970s extension of a heavy subway line into suburbs along an abandoned railroad alignment, light-rail systems pose identical issues everywhere. LRVs prove useful in transporting people, especially commuters, within a radius of about twenty miles from downtown areas. Beyond that zone, however, more-traditional commuter trains prove faster, more comfortable, and in the long run more economical, especially when they share the rails with long-haul passenger trains and, usually in the wee hours of the morning, with freight trains.

Then, too, traditional commuter trains serve well-to-do commuters who like living in leafy suburbs but want very fast access to downtown. However vague and circumspect their voiced desires, they want to travel nonstop through inner suburbs and industrial warehouse zones, and they really prefer to move at speeds above sixty miles an hour. Seventy-nine miles an hour strikes them as a very nice speed indeed.

Looming now as a massive political debacle exacerbated by technical limitations often created by newly built light-rail systems, the coming clash between long-distance and LRV commuters became noticeable in 1977. Federal courts in Pennsylvania and elsewhere determined that all Amtrak trains rolled by definition as intercity rather than commuter trains. Despite the fact that, for example, standing-room-only crowds boarded the Boston-to-Washington Night Owl in Baltimore for the short commute to work, Congress and federal courts persisted in the belief that no commuters rode the system. Amtrak's New York–Philadelphia and Philadelphia–Harrisburg trains precipitated the court cases, simply because the law creating Amtrak specifically prohibits operation of "commuter and other short-haul service in metropolitan and suburban areas." Long-view scenario analysts and real estate investors knew by 1980 that light-rail transit would fail to accommodate long-distance commuters.

Light-rail systems fail under intense ridership pressure, especially when cars fill at the end of the line and irritate would-be passengers who cannot board at subsequent stops. Even operating as multiple-unit trains, LRVs cannot carry enough passengers or move quickly enough to compete with heavy commuter trains. Moreover, LRVs often operate over downtown city streets. While their presence indeed boosts downtown property values, their center-city terminals cannot accommodate large increases in numbers of trains without blocking street traffic. A typical nineteenth-century urban railroad terminal can move many times the number of passengers onto traditional commuter trains usually moving over grade-separated routes and making no stops until they are fifteen or more miles away from downtown. In an ideal world, LRVs would service riders within fifteen miles of downtown and not clog downtown streets, and commuter trains would carry suburban residents. But many cities have planted new light-rail transit lines in disused railroad corridors once used by commuter trains and freight trains. Building light-rail systems often eliminates the option of restoring commuter rail and freight service.

In 1998 the *Economist* produced a special report on commuting that dovetails almost perfectly with a 1978 *Environmental Action* report on Amtrak. In 1978 few experts thought much of light-rail transit; in 1998 the *Economist* scarcely mentioned it. In two decades automobile traffic jams had increased in density and scale, and ridership pressure on urban mass-transit systems had increased dramatically. But in the United States and elsewhere, prosperity had inclined an ever-growing number of individuals and families to buy more than one automobile, and often cars for suburban teenagers. Metropolitan growth covered hundreds of thousands more square miles, and large city downtowns had bolted upward in hundreds of new office towers. In many American metropolitan regions, great numbers of commuters spent at least two hours a day commuting between home and work.

Raw figures are the grist of both data analysts and long-range investors. In Massachusetts alone, 551,000 commuters spend at least forty-five minutes every morning and another forty-five minutes every evening moving back and forth between home and work. For travelers using the Southeast Expressway, forty-five minutes translates into approximately fifteen miles; for riders on the Green Line light-rail routes, about nine miles; for riders on the new commuter rail lines south of Boston, thirty-five miles. Forty-five minutes aboard an Amtrak Acela train operating west of Boston means about a hundred miles, but few commuters can afford to commute via Acela. Yet such time-space equations now shape the bottom line in almost all analyses of downtown Boston commercial real estate ventures and govern housing prices far outside the city. Everywhere around Boston—and around Baltimore, Atlanta, Indianapolis, Houston, Seattle, and dozens of other cities—real estate developers hire analyst firms to recast historic data in scenario-focused ways.

Paradoxically, traditional and brand-new light-rail lines pose serious problems for prospective developers of urban warehouse districts often jammed by trucks but accessible by rail. Redevelopment often depends on reusing railroad tracks as light-rail connectors to downtown. But converting ordinary freight railroad tracks to light-rail means slicing off a section of railroad corridor that formerly extended far from the city center. Thus the warehouse area becomes a profitable zone of residential and perhaps even commercial and office development, but also a blockade that keeps traditional commuter trains from reaching into the far suburbs beyond it. City planners may maintain that some old railroad corridors are wide enough to accommodate single traditional train tracks next to the pairs of light-rail tracks, but most single track strangles commuter train flow.

Light-rail systems isolate downtowns and inner residential, commercial, and industrial rings. Almost invariably—perhaps most notably in Baltimore and Sacramento—they strike taxpayers as necessary and local real estate developers as stable. Only as metropolitan regions choke with highway traffic do municipalities realize that light-rail systems occupy the very corridors essential to reactivating intercity rail routes and the commuter train service that causes downtown and suburban property values to skyrocket. Only when light-rail trains clog tracks at grade crossings at rush hour do riders understand the impossibility of automating light-rail systems in ways that resemble decades-old mining railroad experiments and contemporary airport people movers.

Light-rail systems represent a failure of regionwide scenario analysis. Their opponents often seem fixated on automobiles and buses, but at public hearings it becomes clear that some light-rail opponents want weedy railroad corridors kept open for passenger railroad use in the not-so-distant future. Environmentalists rarely distinguish among opponents of light-rail systems, even as they realize that they misjudged how quickly hiking trails would morph into railroads again. But as Buffalo demonstrated a decade ago, a system without commuter rail links to far suburbs is likely to fail. Light-rail systems only exacerbate the crisis facing metropolitan regions desperately in need of passenger trains.

SOURCES: Baldwin, "Getting to the Trains in Time"; Bente, "The Airporters"; Brownell, "The Notorious Jitney"; "Buses on Rails"; Cheney, "Boston's Electric Buses"; "Commuting"; Comstock, "Slow Train to Great Slave"; Corns, "Ohio's Robot Railroad"; Frank, "Philadelphia Trackless Trolleys"; Gibson, "Rail Transit Returns to Calgary"; Halperin, "The Trolley Coaches of St. Joseph, Missouri"; "Labor, 1978"; Lustig, "Los Angeles' LRVs"; Mannkoff, "The Seventh Wonder of the Traction World"; Matoff, "Sacramento"; McSpedon, "Building Light Rail Transit"; Middleton, *Metropolitan Railways;* Nelligan, "Amtrak Has No Commuters"; Pence, "Cincinnati's Sleeping Subway," and "Dayton Trolley Buses"; "Pittsburgh: One Problem, Two Solutions"; Schrag, *The Great Society Subway;* Transportation Research Board, *Light Rail Transit;* Volkmer, "Light Rail Rolls in L.A.," "Story of Trolley Coaches in the Crescent City," and "Ten Years of Light Rail Progress"; Westinghouse Electric & Manufacturing, *Trolley Coach;* H. S. White, "People Movers"; Wilkins, "Who Really Killed the Street Car?"

CONCLUSION

Contractors work along the old right-of-way leading to Greenbush. Dozens of buildings have vanished to make room for the new passenger train yard and for the huge parking lot adjacent to it. Bridges have disappeared, and some have already been replaced. A lengthy tunnel stretches beneath the seventeenth-century town center of Hingham, and seawall work reaches along part of the right-of-way in Weymouth. Elsewhere along the line, especially deep in the woods, cut brush, surveyor tape, new roadbed, ballast, and rails mark further changes ahead. The train is coming back, and local officials confront demands for realigned roads and zoning changes, shuttle buses, road traffic control, and enduring if now scattered protests from abutters who never dreamed trains would race twenty feet from their back doors.

The county newspaper features a weekly column entitled "Greenbush Update." Every few days the paper addresses problems ranging from floodplain amelioration to the sound of whistles to the demand for condominiums. Activity along the Greenbush line strikes locals as important, and indeed it is locally important. But the route was and will be only a branch line jutting off from a main track that once linked Boston and Cape Cod. Intended to move several thousand commuters a day, and to connect wealthy Bostonians with the marinas and harbors along its route, it will save time and traffic jam frustration for Boston-focused residents of quaint coastal towns and leafy suburbs.

It will transform all sorts of other activities as well. It will enable people to shop in Boston, going and returning after and before rush hour, and it will bring overnight beach guests from the city. Its stations will reorient traffic, shifting much from north–south roads onto east–west routes that end at beaches. It will produce all sorts of minor effects too. Perhaps enterprising high school students or retirees will earn a few dollars driving people to the station if the parking lot fills up before the last inbound rush-hour trains. The prospect of jitney service already worries the handful of taxi cab operators licensed in the towns. Auto repair shops adjacent to stations intend to prosper: commuters will drop off their cars for oil changes and repairs, and pick them up after work. Change floats along across the Greenbush line, sometimes as silently as the sea gulls, sometimes as noisily.

Grasping the scale of the railroad industry in 1930 now challenges more than a few academics. Kansas City Union Station opened in 1914 as the third largest in the nation. Only Grand Central Terminal and Pennsylvania Station in New York surpassed it. Its North Waiting Room alone stretched longer than a football field and nearly as wide. Its restaurants served both grand and simple meals, and its Grand Hall became a place of citywide celebrations. But passengers and visitors never saw its third level. There moved hundreds of carts carrying mail, express, baggage, and food rolling directly to the eight loading platforms, each 1,400 feet long. Through World War II the immense station throbbed with activity almost impossible to imagine today. Approximately half of all military personnel at one time or another walked through its Grand Hall as three hundred trains arrived and departed every twenty-four hours. Then almost overnight its energy began to dwindle, until by 1964 it moved only seventy trains a day, not enough to justify its costs and nowhere near a challenge to its train- and passenger-moving capabilities. In the early 1970s only six trains operated from the station, and Kansas City, along with so many other cities, entered a long era of downtown inactivity.

In Savannah, the joint Seaboard–Atlantic Coast Line depot its owners called a union station vanished to make way for a freeway ramp, and the Savannah & Atlanta station housed an antique business after 1990. The grand Central of Georgia Railroad station became the city visitor center, its tracks bereft of trains, which moved to a little Amtrak station located near the junction of rail lines hauling ever greater amounts of freight. Savannah toys with building some kind of antique trolley car line to attract and move tourists, but as in Kansas City and San Jose, light-rail transit produces little in the way of innovative passenger terminal thinking. Commuter trains might operate into Savannah, but even if they followed the

The engineer sees the long, uninterrupted ribbon of steel, and almost never encounters the equivalent of a highway traffic jam.

tracks of container trains serving the busy wharves, they would have no place to terminate.

Savannah booms in part because of a record trade deficit, one usually reported in billions of dollars but easily calculated visually in the tens of thousands of containers moving from ships in Savannah, Los Angeles, and other port cities. Despite worries about the strength of the dollar and the Chinese trade surplus, moving containers is almost as profitable for railroads as moving grain and other bulk commodities—and sometimes even more so. But containers moving to and from port cities by truck jam highways, especially those used by commuters. Timothy Lomax and other researchers at Texas A&M University assert that between 1982 and 2002 jammed urban traffic went from consuming 700 million hours to 3.5 billion. Even given the explosive population growth in metropolitan regions, especially along the coasts, the figures sober the most optimistic advocates of highway building. The typical Los Angeles motorist spent ninety-three hours stopped in traffic jams in 2002. Around Washington, D.C., the typical motorist spent sixty-seven hours annually. The 187 percent average increase from 1982 to 2002 augurs ill for further highway building efforts, even if cities could find land fit for new highways, since the growth rate surpasses almost any highway building capacity in the country. But no analysts can yet relate booming port-city trade-deficit container movement by truck to details of traffic jams, even in Savannah and similar smaller cities to which upper-income people move in search of high-quality living.

Statistics alert many educated newspaper readers to issues already worrying real estate investors and chain-store retailers, but they prove difficult to analyze against each other. The fact that metropolitan Boston commuter trains board 141,000 passengers every workday and that 225,000 passengers board the light-rail system most certainly matters to someone somehow, but proves almost useless in imagining how an annual growth rate of 10 percent might exacerbate existing highway congestion near suburban stations. How do the 426,000 passengers boarding the heavy-duty subways figure in any analysis of how commuter rail passengers move around Boston after they exit trains? In the end, accumulating mountains of statistics often leads to conclusions similar to those of the Regional Plan experts in New York before World War II.

At a small urban scale, drawbridges offer extraordinary insights into how pedestrians reach train stations. Older cities often replace movable bridges as harbor and river traffic decreases. If some waterborne commerce endures, especially by pleasure boat, highway planners replace drawbridges with fixed bridges arching over water. Motorists transition easily: they push accelerator pedals slightly and cruise over the new bridges. But pedestrians dislike the hills that replace level, albeit intermittently movable, pavement. Replacing a movable bridge with a fixed arch bridge deflects pedestrian flow, especially on streets where rush-hour walkers hurry. Adjacent to South Station in Boston lies a political nightmare, the rusting, decrepit Northern Avenue center-pivot swing bridge pedestrians refuse to abandon for a nicely arched fixed bridge a block away. Distance from South Station or even walking time from South Station no longer suffices to inform real estate developers who know that walking effort often spells the success or failure of real estate development near urban railroad terminals.

At a suburban scale, the parking garages disfiguring small towns in New Jersey and eastern Pennsylvania announce commuter rail success. No longer do ordinary station lots accommodate the cars of commuters. Environmentalists ought to cheer the success of trains, but no one says much about the unsightly garages urbanizing small-town centers. The slightest improvement in schedules causes some commuters to shift allegiance from one station to another on an adjacent line. Automobile traffic to and from suburban train stations confuses public officials. The old suburb–city highways that produced ribbons of tawdry retail development no longer carry most commuter traffic. Often that traffic now moves past the homes of the wealthy, who complain about traffic, noise, and air pollution jamming tertiary roads leading to commuter train stations. Suburban design and planning nowadays prove harder to analyze and practice, even in university graduate schools of design, than urban design. Part of the problem lies in the growing penchant of suburbanites to use any Amtrak suburban stop as a way of reaching another suburb.

Passenger trains operating between eighty and a hundred miles an hour profoundly influence understanding of metropolitan regions and metropolitan lifestyles. Assume the train as a given, and suddenly many small satellite cities, often with very low real estate values, become attractive to real estate investors. Generally, such cities have both operating and abandoned railroad lines, chunks of derelict property abutting underused downtowns, and an inventory of well-built, easily restored period architecture. While increasingly irrelevant as manufacturing centers, such small cities strike investors as ripe for plucking. The most desirable ones—certainly the ones receiving the most careful if camouflaged investment analysis—lie about eighty to a hundred miles between major cities. High-speed passenger train service would transform such locales.

Cities on the edge of wilderness or rural areas might be trans-

formed too. In the 1980s well-educated young married couples discovered Portland, Maine, as a down-at-the-heels but proud small
city boasting not only a fine stock of inexpensive period housing
but also active freight railroads. As much real estate changed hands,
new energy poured into the school system and other municipal
departments, and nonprofits established new museums and other
cultural amenities. Demands for passenger train service to Boston
materialized in ways scenario analysts recognize as predictable, and
not just in Portland, but in cities roughly 120 miles from Chicago,
St. Louis, Atlanta, Houston, and Portland, Oregon.

Massive real estate transformation produces massive investment
return. On a medium scale, Portland provides a fine example. On
a very small scale, New Bedford in Massachusetts offers an example of a run-down but finely built seaport community, but difficult
to access by highways, being discovered by well-educated young
homebuyers and real estate investors. The transformation in New
Bedford mirrors that in Portland: rising house prices, a much-in-
vigorated waterfront and Whaling Museum, and then, suddenly, a
demand for fast commuter train service to Boston. But large-scale
change seems most likely to occur away from coastal New England
and metropolitan New York, in places like Albuquerque.

As railroads improve their rights-of-way by laying heavier rail,
installing sophisticated signal systems, and building double or even
triple tracks, they open the prospect of fast passenger trains linking small rural towns with downtowns. The fast trains might link
the towns with larger metropolitan regions, but far more likely, the
trains will sizzle through warehouse districts and inner suburbs,
perhaps connecting here and there with light-rail systems. The
trains will need downtown terminals, and terminal traffic will gen-
erate business development within the walking distance Regional
Plan analysts recognized in the 1930s. Such trains will operate first
over existing, well-maintained freight lines, exactly as Albuquerque
officials intend to use Burlington Northern Santa Fe tracks north
and south of the city. But almost certainly, urban real estate investors will demand such service on many disused and abandoned
routes as well.

Urban investors recognize that the first cities to reinvent commuter rail operation over a 100- or 120-mile radius from downtown will grab human and economic capital from cities perhaps 150 miles away. Beyond about 75 miles from the seacoast and the shores of the Great Lakes, and away from the arid regions where even cattle ranching proves nearly impossible, cities tend to be about 150 to 200 miles apart, a distance dating to long-vanished steam locomotives and 1890s train travel. Train service once linked them as jewels on necklaces, but the trains moved over vast distances, linking cities in part because they lay on the path to somewhere else. Now investors realize that Amtrak might be supplanted by something less national and less public-spirited. Regional railroads focused on particular cities would cause such hub cities to boom while not necessarily offering service to cities 150 miles or more distant. At ninety miles per hour, commuter trains would focus capital of all sorts, but especially financial, in definable and stable ways. The first city with such service radiating from it would draw riders and capital from within the potential commuting zone of other cities. In the guise of reducing rush-hour automobile congestion, many downtown property owners see radial commuter rail service as a way of gathering in entire populations and reducing the value of inner-ring suburban real estate.

Highway congestion will worsen as the national population increases almost wholly in coastal strips seventy-five miles wide and in perhaps fifteen inland metropolitan regions. Given the worsening congestion and booming population, even the trucking industry realizes that change lies just over the hill. Factories indeed relocate to rural places, in part to benefit from the predictable truck schedules that translate into lower shipping costs, but as manufacturing moves offshore, the great port cities jam with containers moving from ships to trucks. New rail lines now snake away from Elizabeth, New Jersey, and inland from the Port of Los Angeles, but only a few thoughtful observers notice the impact of such lines a thousand miles inland.

The Internet plays an important if shadowy role in the movement of upper-income people to places served by some kind of rail service. Beautiful, trendy, inexpensive-to-live-in places—Leadville, Colorado, is a useful example—that lack high-speed Internet access stumble in the race to prosperity and power. Throughout the 1990s, information technology specialists argued that only when about 40 percent or more of American households enjoyed high-speed cable Internet access would online ordering flex its muscle. The Christmas 2004 shopping season proved the specialists right, but the proof that connection causes change still shapes little news media reporting of people and freight movement. Most shoppers, especially those in metropolitan regions, more or less understand that online shopping has transformed the retailing of everything from books to antiques to DVDs. Often the backroom of a traditional business proves the power of online ordering, as clerks fill orders to be shipped via UPS and FedEx. Sometimes stores close, often suddenly, either in the face of invisible competition or because backroom business has so outperformed ordinary retail that owners locate to cheaper real estate. Scenario analysts tend to agree that the Internet will suddenly transform the national transportation system.

Almost certainly it has, often in negative ways. The difficulties airlines now confront almost certainly originated elsewhere than deregulation, no-frills competition, and terrorism. Business travel began decreasing in the last years of the 1990s, as did the volume of first-class mail: the Internet fueled both revolutions. In positive ways, online shopping explains the proliferation of UPS, FedEx, and other express trucks. FedEx especially distinguishes its services by painting its logo in different colors on different trucks. Online shoppers know the difference between FedEx and FedEx ground, and anyone walking through busy downtown or suburban neighborhoods discovers different FedEx trucks serving adjacent addresses. The combination of online shopping and high-speed express delivery gives shoppers choices undreamed of only ten years ago. But however difficult balancing negatives and positives appears, scenario analysis involves projecting from data and situations known only in fuzzy ways. The Internet, and perhaps cell phones, will transform the landscape by transforming ground transportation. Almost certainly, they will accomplish that transformation by altering railroads.

In September 2006 an Austrian Railways train set a new record for speed beneath catenary. It operated at 221 miles per hour, break-ing the 1955 record of 205 miles per hour set by two French Railways electric locomotives.

Serious money moved in that direction by 1985, and vast amounts of capital move so now. Landownership records remain the last de-centralized, noncomputerized database in the United States. Blind realty trusts own structures and land, but no one penetrates the trusts to the individuals who create and run them. Tracing the changes in ownership of land near a railroad junction means time-consuming work in a registry of deeds, but it usually confirms the argument of this book. While some land remains, decade after decade, in the hands of trusts waiting for something, much has changed hands recently, often for much higher prices each time. Local real estate agents know that some owners simply deflect any buyer, but that knowledge is difficult to extract from strangers. Consulting firms, especially those retained by trust officers of banking institutions and attorneys charged with increasing the value of funds in their care, generally prove close-lipped on the subject.

When the analysts access historical documents, especially those pertaining to the operation of a railroad rather than its financial status, archivists, librarians, and scholars glimpse something of the research effort that focuses so much intellectual energy. Often the analysts must approach railroad enthusiasts and their historical so-cieties to learn the answers to seemingly arcane questions. Gradu-ally, the more thoughtful of these enthusiasts, especially those con-nected in nationwide Internet groups, realize that the inquirers have agendas beyond history, nostalgia, and intellectual curiosity.

Consultants and analysts and investors-at-large may contact their graying professor to ask about lectures they heard twenty years ago. They inquire about my own *Metropolitan Corridor: Railroads and the American Scene,* which appeared in 1983, and often their questions reveal research, at least well begun and sometimes com-pleted. The questions range from purely historical ones to inquiries about my present research, but answers come only when the ques-tions are put in the frameworks that teach the asked. One involves a never-built connector railroad intended to link two metropolitan New York lines. Another involves a half-imagined chain of wilderness inns resembling one along a Swiss railroad. Other questions look forward. If commuter trains run on time, Professor, evening after evening, would commuters use cell phones to order take-home meals from restaurants located near stations? Bit by bit the questions reveal where so much now-hidden late-1990s dot-com-boom money went. It went to wait for the train.

All anyone else can do is look around, especially at railroads and where railroads once operated.

MIT erected buildings over the lightly used Grand Junction line and it owns other air rights above the track. Its buildings rise over trains and are constructed so that the single track can be widened immediately to double track. Such architectural evidence of assumed future change is everywhere along railroads, but only the observant notice it. Across the entire United States trains are moving faster now, and often much more frequently. Where trains rarely operate, or where the right-of-way lies bereft of rails and ties and trains, rewards scrutiny too.

Anyone who stands and looks around may glimpse the signs of railroad resurgence. Often in the quiet, long-ago whistles echo faintly, announcing the train again.

SOURCES: Hamilton, "Savannah Scrapbook"; Hansen, "Give the People a Monument"; Lomax, *2004 Urban Mobility Study.*

NOTE ON SOURCES AND NAMES

While much of the material underlying this book can be obtained from any good public library, some of it lingers in obscurity. The New York State Department of Transportation's *Special Report on Railroads* (April 1976) includes a perceptive article by Raymond T. Schuler, Commissioner of Transportation, about the long-term impact of downgrading the main line of the Erie-Lackawanna Railroad running through the southern half of New York. It is the sort of document only sustained academic inquiry—or great good luck—rescues from dust. Examined over decades, railroad industry press releases often suggest at least the outlines of large-scale change ahead. One 1970 release notes that three railroads, the Seaboard Coast Line, the St. Louis–San Francisco, and the Union Pacific, had organized to operate the longest daily scheduled freight train, 3,311 miles from Florida to the Pacific Northwest. Not for decades did real-estate investors realize the impact of that experiment. Railroad company annual reports offer much data about present operating conditions and intentions for future development. Some source material includes railroad and railroad-related industry data not intended for the public. *Trolley Coach: Application and Performance Data,* an in-house report by the East Pittsburgh Works of the Westinghouse Electric and Manufacturing Company, explains much about the present diesel-engine bus industry. Underlying this book, too, are weekly Internet reports aimed at industry officials and investors. One of the best such reports is *Weekly Rail Report,* produced by David Mears and available free to any inquirer. Valuable unpublished works like "Railroad Postal Routes from 1867 to 1961," by Herbert H. Harrington, a philatelist who mined the archives of the Boston Philatelic Library (now at Boston University) to delineate mail train routes over decades, make sense of ephemeral but critical government documents like *Instructions and Rulings with Reference to Transportation of Mails by Railroads,* a 1938 publication of the Office of the Postmaster General. *Directions for*

Using Fleming Mail Catcher and Deliverer (1898) published by an Erie, Pennsylvania, manufacturer of robotic devices that enabled mail trains to pick up and deposit mail without stopping, describes equipment that changed post office standards from those specified in its 1886 *Mail-Bag Crane*. Such sources the reader may find listed at the end of each chapter and in the bibliography of this book, but many similar ones of extremely narrow significance are omitted. Readers interested in the recent history of the railroad industry might begin with Richard Saunders's magisterial *Main Lines: Rebirth of the North American Railroads, 1970–2002*. Those intrigued by railroad operations that shape larger changes might buy the latest copy of any enthusiast magazine, perhaps especially *Trains, Railfan & Railroad, Model Railroader,* and *Railroad Model Craftsman*. Finally, this book derives from long-term reading of special-focus, non-railroad-industry magazines like *Transmission and Distribution*. The electricity-generating industry has its own agenda concerning electrifying railroads, but that and many other topics are beyond the scope of this book. The best source of information remains close scrutiny of railroad operations and real estate investment along railroad corridors. Railroading is dangerous: it is best to observe from a distance.

Mergers make the use of former railroad company names problematic. Here old names designate companies and routes as they existed, and contemporary names designate present postmerger corporations and lines.

BIBLIOGRAPHY

Abbey, Wallace W. "Railroads and the War." *Railroad History* [Millennium Special volume] (2000), 81-88.

Anderson, Sherwood. "Business Types." *Agricultural Advertising* 11 (April 1904), 39–40.

Arcara, Roger. *Westchester's Forgotten Railway: An Account of the New York, Westchester & Boston.* New York: Quadrant, 1972.

Armstrong, A. H. *The Future of Our Railways.* Schenectady, N.Y.: General Electric Co., 1920.

Babcock, Michael W., James L. Bunch, et al. "Impact of Short Line Railroad Abandonment on Highway Damage Costs: A Kansas Case Study." *Transportation Quarterly* 57 (Fall 2003), 105–21.

———. "Impact of Short Line Railroad Abandonment on Wheat Transportation and Handling Costs: A Kansas Case Study." *Transportation Quarterly* 57 (Fall 2003), 87–105.

Babcock, Michael, Eugene Russell, and Curtis Mauler. "Study of the Impact of Rail Abandonment on Local Roads and Streets." *Conference Proceedings: Sixth International Conference on Low Volume Roads,* 1995, 110–19.

Baldwin, Deborah. "Getting to the Trains in Time." *Environmental Action,* August 26, 1978, 4–9.

Bente, Bruce R. "The Airporters: Cars for Cleveland's New Airport Rapid." *Headlights* 29 (December 1967), 4–10.

Bertolini, Luca, and Tejo Spit. *Cities on Rails: The Redevelopment of Railway Station Areas.* London: Spon, 1998.

"Better Move, A." *Boston Herald,* September 16, 2005, 30.

Bezilla, Michael. *Electric Traction on the Pennsylvania Railroad.* University Park: Pennsylvania State University Press, 1980.

———. "The Electrification That Might Have Been—and Might Still Be." *Trains* 38 (March 1978), 30–34.

Bixler, Herbert E. *Railroads: Their Rise and Fall: A Personal Observation.* Jaffrey Center, N.H.: The author, 1982.

Black, Archibald. *The Story of Tunnels.* New York: Whittilsey, 1937.

Black, W. J. *Santa Fe de-Luxe: Third Winter Season, 1913–14.* Chicago: Franklin, 1913.

Borrone, Lillian. "Sparking the Globalized Trade and Transportation Connection: Supply Freight System Responses to Global Trade Demands." *Transportation Research Record,* no. 1906 (2002), 5–16.

Boyd, Jim. "One Hundred and Fifty Years of the D&H." *Railroad Model Craftsman* 42 (August 1973), 38–45.

Brown, Kevin V. "Build This 'Flying Volkswagen' for Less Than $600." *Popular Mechanics* 129 (May 1968), 120–24, 176.

———. "Build This New 4-Place Cabin Plane for $3500." *Popular Mechanics* 131 (May 1969), 112–17, 208.

Brownell, Blaine A. "The Notorious Jitney and the Urban Transportation Crisis in Birmingham in the 1920s." *Alabama Review* 25 (April 1971), 67–89.

Burr, William, ed. *U.S. Planning for War in Europe, 1963–1964.* NSA no. 31. Washington, D.C.: GPO, National Security Archive, 2005.

"Buses on Rails—a New Concept?" *Headlights* 30 (January 1968), 2–6.

California High-Speed Rail Authority. *Building a High-Speed Train System for California.* Sacramento: CHSRA, 2000.

Canton, Steve. "Fight for Survival: How Long Can Railway Express Stay in Business?" *Railroad* 53 (December 1950), 20–30.

Carstens, Hal. "The Shawangunk Carrier." *Railroad Model Craftsman* 45 (February 1977), 4, 106.

Cheney, Frank. "Boston's Electric Buses." *Rollsign* 23 (October 1986), 10–24.

Cherington, Charles R. *Regulation of Railroad Abandonments.* Cambridge, Mass.: Harvard University Press, 1948.

Christopherson, Ed. "Bold Proposal: A Bridge for Alaskan Oil." *Popular Mechanics* 141 (January 1974), 106–8, 182.

Cole, Henry G. *The Road to Rainbow: Army Planning for Global War.* Annapolis: Naval Institute, 2002.

Collucci-Rios, Benjamin, and Eldon J. Yoder. *A Methodology for Evaluating the Increase in Pavement Maintenance Costs Resulting from Increased Truck Weights on a Statewide Basis.* West Lafayette, Ind.: Purdue University, Dept. of Highway Engineering, 1983.

Comarow, Murray. *The Demise of the Postal Service?* Bethesda: National Academy of Public Administration, 2002.

"Commuting." *The Economist,* September 5, 1998, 1–18.

Comstock, Henry B. "Slow Train to Great Slave." *Popular Mechanics* 128 (July 1967), 110–13.

Condit, Carl W. *The Port of New York.* Chicago: University of Chicago Press, 1980–81.

Corns, John B. "Ohio's Robot Railroad." *Trains* 39 (March 1979), 22–28.

Crossley, Robert P. "Those Fast, New Trains." *Popular Mechanics* 131 (May 1969), 98–99, 205.

Daniels, Wayne M. "From Rumor to Renaissance: The Delaware & Hudson." *Railroad Model Craftsman* 43 (November 1974), 33–34.

DeGraw, Ronald. "Ohio's New Electric Railroad." *Headlights* 30 (January 1968), 8.

Department of Agriculture. *Open-Country Poverty in a Relatively Affluent Area— the East North Central States.* Washington, D.C.: GPO, 1971.

————. *Rural Poverty in Three Southern Regions.* Washington, D.C.: GPO, 1979.

DeViers, Jon B., and Gary Lenz. "Recentralization: Intermodal Shipping Centers Have the Potential to Transform America's Inner-City Industrial Areas." *Urban Land* 58 (June 1999), 69–73, 94–96.

Doughty, Geoffrey H. *New York Central and the Trains of the Future.* Lynchburg, Va.: TLC Publishing, 1997.

Drury, George H. "Tank Train." *Trains* 38 (October 1978), 16.

Dubin, Arthur D. *Some Classic Trains.* Milwaukee: Kalmbach, 1964.

"Electrification: In the Future." *Headlights* 32 (November–December 1970), 10–17.

Ewing, Reid, Rolf Pendall, and Don Chen. "Measuring Sprawl and Its Transportation Impacts." *Transportation Research Record,* no. 1831 (2004), 175–83.

Fales, E. D. "How You'll Drive 120 Mph Legally." *Popular Science* 187 (October 1965), 98–101, 186.

————. "Our Crumbling Interstates: A National Dilemma." *Popular Mechanics* 145 (July 1978), 66–69, 118.

Fantel, Hans. "New Low-Cost System Lets You Tape TV Pictures at Home." *Popular Mechanics* 122 (October 1965), 117–19.

Faulkner, W. D. "The Story of Trolley Coaches in the Crescent City." *Electric Lines* 5 (May–June 1992), 8–12.

Fifer, Valerie J. "Transcontinental: The Political Word." *Geographical Journal* 144 (November 1978), 438–49.

Fitzgerald, F. Scott. *The Great Gatsby.* New York: Scribner's, 1925.

Fleming Mail Catcher and Deliverer Company. *Directions for Using Fleming Mail Catcher and Deliverer.* Erie, Pa.: Fleming, 1898.

Frailey, Fred W. "Blank Bullet." *Trains* 63 (February 2003), 32–43.

Frank, Joseph H. "Philadelphia Trackless Trolleys." *Electric Lines* 5 (January–February 1992), 23–25.

Garrett, Klink. *Ten Turtles to Tucumcari: A Personal History of the Railway Express Agency.* Albuquerque: University of New Mexico Press, 2003.

General Electric Company. "Can Technology and the Environment Peacefully Coexist?" *Wall Street Journal,* September 19, 2005, A10–A11.

Gibson, Alan J. "Rail Transit Returns to Calgary." National Model Railroad Association *Bulletin* 47 (June 1982), 34–39.

Gilmore, C. P. "How You'll Drive the Amazing Urbmobile." *Popular Science* 191 (October 1967), 75–78, 208.

Grant, Bob. "This Car Really Flies." *Popular Mechanics* 136 (June 1975), 87–91, 176.

Grant, H. Roger. "Piggyback Pioneer: Any Idea to Boost Revenues Was an Idea That the Great Weedy Couldn't Refuse." *Trains* 46 (January 1986), 31–34.

Griswold, Wesley S. "How to Drive in a Crisis." *Popular Science* 185 (September 1964), 43–45, 182–83.

Grivno, Cody. "Amtrak's Mail and Express Fleet." *Model Railroader* 79 (March 2003), 71–73.

Gronau, Reuben. *The Value of Time in Passenger Transportation: The Demand for Air Travel.* New York: Columbia University Press, 1970.

Gunnell, Bruce C. *An Atomic Powered Railroad Locomotive.* New York: Association of American Railroads, 1955.

Halperin, R. J. "The Trolley Coaches of St. Joseph, Missouri." *Electric Lines* 3 (September–October 1990), 28–31.

Hamilton, Andy. "Savannah Scrapbook." National Model Railroad Association *Bulletin* 47 (August 1982), 24–29.

Hansen, Peter A. "Give the People a Monument: Kansas City Union Station." *Trains* 59 (April 1999), 62–73.

Harlem Board of Commerce. *Three Plans for the Relief of Traffic Congestion in New York City.* New York: Harlem Board of Commerce, 1929.

Harley, E. Thomas. "U.S. Railway Freight Electrification." *Electric Lines* 1 (July–August 1988), 12–13.

Harmon, Roy L. *Reinventing the Warehouse: World-Class Distribution Logistics.* New York: Free Press, 1993.

Harrington, Herbert H. "Railroad Postal Routes from 1867 to 1961." Unpublished typescript, 1964. Photocopy, Boston University Library.

Hediger, Jim. "New Railbox ABOX Boxcar." *Model Railroader* 56 (September 1979), 58–59.

Hemphill, Mark W. "The Unknown Rio Grande." *Trains* 45 (July 1985), 24–35.

Hicks, Clifford B. "They'll Tell You How You'll Vote." *Popular Mechanics,* 122 (October 1964), 105–10, 116, 122.

Homberger, Eric. *Historical Atlas of New York City.* New York: Holt, 1994.

Howard, F. H. "Piggyback and the Portager Dream." *Trains* 37 (April 1977), 44–51; (May 1977), 45–51.

Hubbard, Freeman. "Nine Hundred Thousand Barrels a Day." *Railroad Magazine* 34 (July 1943), 8–45.

———. "Will 'Piggyback' Make the Boxcar Obsolete?" *Railroad* 69 (February 1958), 28–31.

Hungerford, Edward. *A Railroad for Tomorrow.* Milwaukee: Kalmbach, 1945.

"Italian Electric 'Rapido' Does Amazing 149.04 m.p.h." *The Whistle Stop* 2 (December 1952), 35.

Joachimsthaler, Anton. *Die Breitspurbahn Hitlers.* Freiburg: Eisenbahn-Kurier Verlag, 1981.

Johnson, Stanley W. *The Milwaukee Road Revisited.* Moscow: University of Idaho Press, 1997.

Johnson, Todd. "Rail Yard Infill." *Urban Land* 62 (June 2003), 40–51.

Josserand, Peter. "Tomorrow: Trains with Brains?" *Railroad* 74 (April 1963), 19–24.

Kansas State Board of Agriculture. *Kansas Grain Transportation.* Topeka: Kansas State Board of Agriculture, 2003.

Koester, Anthony J. "The Fun of Finding Yesterday." *Railroad Model Craftsman* 47 (August 1978), 90–91.

Kotkin, Joel. "The Great Plains." *Wall Street Journal*, August 31, 2006, A19.

"Labor, 1978." *Trains* 38 (October 1978), 3–6.

Lambert, Bruce. "More Long Islanders Looking to Move Out, a Survey Finds." *New York Times*, December 1, 2005, A31.

Lamson, Ted. C. "Catching and Throwing the Mail." National Model Railroad Association *Bulletin* 37 (October 1971), 14–15, 41.

Levy, Mark R. *The VCR Age*. London: Sage, 1989.

Light, Jennifer S. *From Warfare to Welfare: Defense Intellectuals and Urban Problems in Cold War America*. Baltimore: Johns Hopkins University Press, 2003.

Lomax, Timothy. *2004 Urban Mobility Study*. College Station: Texas Transportation Institute, 2004.

Long, Bryant A., and William J. Dennis. *Mail by Rail: The Story of the Postal Transportation Service*. New York: Simmons-Boardman, 1951.

Lustig, David. "Los Angeles' LRVs." *Railroad Model Craftsman* 59 (March 1991), 65–73.

Machalaba, Daniel. "Expensive Toys: Private Rail Cars Are Back on Amtrak." *Wall Street Journal*, November 12, 1984, A1, A21.

Machalaba, Daniel, and Christopher J. Chipello. "New Track: Battling Trucks, Trains Gain Steam by Watching Clock." *Wall Street Journal*, July 25, 2003, A1, A16.

Maiken, Peter T. *Night Trains: The Pullman System in the Golden Years of American Rail Travel*. Chicago: Lakme, 1989.

Mankoff, Al. "The Seventh Wonder of the Traction World." *Electric Lines* 3 (July–August 1990), 30–35.

Margetts, F. C. "Trains for Tomorrow." *Trains* 36 (April 1976), 40–45.

Marshall, James. *Santa Fe: The Railroad That Built an Empire*. New York: Random House, 1945.

Matoff, Tom. "Sacramento." *Electric Lines* 3 (July–August 1990), 14–19.

McMurty, Larry. *Roads: Driving America's Great Highways*. New York: Simon & Schuster, 2000.

McSpedon, Edward. "Building Light Rail Transit in Existing Rail Corridors: Panacea or Nightmare? The Los Angeles Experience." *Electric Lines* 4 (January–February 1991), 19–25.

Meikle, Jeffrey L. "Industrial Design Speeds Forward." *Railroad History* [Millennium Special volume] (2000), 62–72.

Menzies, Ian. "The South Shore—200,000 People Within 10 Minutes of an Unused Rail Line." *Boston Globe*, February 11, 1974, 20.

Meyer, John R., Martin J. Peck, et al. *The Economics of Competition in the Transportation Industries*. Cambridge, Mass.: Harvard University Press, 1959.

Middleton, William D. *Metropolitan Railways: Rapid Transit in America*. Bloomington: Indiana University Press, 2003.

———. *When the Steam Railroads Electrified*. Milwaukee: Kalmbach, 1974.

Mierzejewski, Alfred C. "High Speed Motor Trains of the German National Railway, 1920–1945." *Railroad History* 175 (Autumn 1996), 57–68.

Mischke, Charles P. "Pages from the Past: The Pelham Park Monorail." *The Whistle Stop* 2 (December 1952), 34–35.

Moffat, Bruce. *Forty Feet Below: The Story of Chicago's Freight Tunnels.* Glendale, Calif.: Interurban Press, 1983.

———. *The "L": The Development of Chicago's Rapid Transit System, 1888–1932.* Chicago: Central Electric Railfans Association, 1995.

Morgan, David P. "Forget the Gods of Old." *Trains* 38 (October 1978), 58–59.

———. "Mr. Pullman Revisited." *Trains* 25 (January 1965), 20–23.

———. "Ninety Miles an Hour Aboard a 4-6-4." *Trains and Travel Annual* 1 (1953), n.p.

Morris, Bill. "How Copters Can Solve Traffic Jams." *Popular Science* 190 (April 1967), 94–97.

Mortimer, Kenneth. "ACI . . . Have You Got It?" National Model Railroad Association *Bulletin* 33 (April 1968), 7.

"Moving Mail on the MoPac." Terminal Railroad Association of St. Louis Historical and Technical Society *Bulletin* 49–50 (Winter–Spring 1999), 2–31.

"Muskingum Electric: Trains on Their Own." *Headlights* 34 (January–February 1972), 10–12.

"Muskingum Electric Railroad." National Model Railroad Association *Bulletin* 34 (April 1969), 12–13.

Mysak, Joe. *Perpetual Motion: The Illustrated History of the Port Authority of New York and New Jersey.* Santa Monica: General Publishing, 1997.

Nelligan, Tom. "Amtrak Has No Commuters." *Trains* 37 (June 1977), 44.

Nelson, John W. "Look Again." National Model Railroad Association *Bulletin* 49 (June 1984), 39–44.

New York Central Railroad Co. *Fast Freight Schedule, November, 1948.* New York: New York Central Railroad Co., 1948.

New York State Department of Motor Vehicles. *The Safety Sedan: Summary of Final Report.* Albany: Department of Motor Vehicles, 1968.

New York State Department of Transportation. "A Future for Southern Tier Rail Service?" *Special Report on Railroads* 3 (April 1976), 1–4.

New York, Westchester, and Boston Railway. *Westchester Timetables.* New York: New York, Westchester, and Boston Railway, November 1, 1937.

Norfolk Southern Corporation. *Annual Report 2005.* Norfolk, Va.: The Corporation, 2005.

Official Guide of the Railways and Steam Navigation Lines of the United States, Porto Rico, Canada, Mexico, and Cuba. New York: National Railway Publication Co., 1929.

Olson, Mancur. *The Logic of Collective Action: Public Goods and the Theory of Groups.* New York: Schocken, 1965.

O'Neil, Thomas. "Quebec, North Shore & Labrador Railway." National Model Railroad Association *Bulletin* 41 (October 1975), 31–34.

Overbey, Daniel L. "Piggyback: Where Do We Go from Here?" *Trains* 46 (February 1986), 40–47.

Pence, Herbert. "Cincinnati's Sleeping Subway." *Electric Lines* 3 (March–April 1990), 18–21.

———. "Dayton Trolley Buses." *Electric Lines* 4 (November–December 1991), 17–20.

Pennypacker, Bert. "When Steam Achieved Metroliner Speeds." *Railroad Magazine* 61 (May 1970), 21–25.

"Pittsburgh: One Problem, Two Solutions." *Headlights* 31 (September–October 1969), 2–7, 16.

Plous, F. K. "The Flight of the Falcon." *Trains* 39 (February 1979), 22–30.

Poorvu, William J. *The Real Estate Game: The Intelligent Guide to Decision-Making and Investment*. New York: Free Press, 1999.

Prater, Marvin, and Keith Klindworth. *Long-Term Trends in Railroad Service and Capacity for United States Agriculture*. Washington, D.C.: Department of Agriculture, 2000.

Price, C. Grattan. "I Remember." *Trains* 37 (February 1977), 46–47.

Railway Mail Service. *Schedule of Mail Routes No. 294*. Fort Worth: Babcock, 1935.

———. *Schedule of Mail Routes No. 513*. St. Louis: Curran, 1935.

Rand, McNally & Co. *Handy Railroad Maps of the United States*. New York: Rand McNally, 1928.

Regional Plan Association. *Transit and Transportation and a Study of Port and Industrial Areas and Their Relation to Transportation*. New York: Regional Plan Association, 1928.

Reutter, Mark. "Building a Better Iron Horse." *Railroad History* [Millennium Special volume] (2000), 38–61.

"Rising Costs, Falling Ridership Rattles Rural Air Program." *Staunton News Leader*, August 30, 2003, 1.

Rose, Mark H. *Interstate: Express Highway Politics, 1939–1989*. Knoxville: University of Tennessee Press, 1990.

Runte, Alfred. "Yosemite Valley Railroad." National Railway Historical Society *Bulletin* 39–40 (1974), 10–13.

Rushkoff, Douglas. *Coercion: Why We Listen to What "They" Say*. New York: Riverhead, 1999.

Saunders, Richard. *Main Lines: Rebirth of the North American Railroads, 1970–2002*. Dekalb: Northern Illinois University Press, 2003.

Scammon, Richard M. *Study of Population and Immigration Problems*. Washington, D.C.: GPO, 1962.

Schrag, Zachary. *The Great Society Subway: A History of the Washington Metro*. Baltimore: Johns Hopkins University Press, 2006.

Schwieterman, Joseph P. *When the Railroad Leaves Town: American Communities in the Age of Rail Line Abandonment.* Kirksville, Mo.: Truman State University Press, 2001.

Shaffer, Marguerite S. *See America First: Tourism and National Identity, 1880–1940.* Washington, D.C.: Smithsonian, 2001.

Smith, Vernon L. "The Diesel from D to L." *Trains* 39 (April 1979), 22–29.

Sonstegaard, Miles H. "Competitive Access to North American Rail." *Transportation Quarterly* 57 (Fall 2003), 61–67.

Sperandeo, Andy. "The Bi-Modal RoadRailer." *Model Railroader* 49 (July 1972), 62–63.

Stelling, Carl. "Designing for the Ladies." *Landscape Architecture Magazine* 63 (Winter 1958–59), 84–86.

Stephens, Bill. "What to Do with RoadRailer?" *Trains* 62 (May 2002), 32–39.

Stilgoe, John R. *Metropolitan Corridor: Railroads and the American Scene.* New Haven: Yale University Press, 1983.

———. "Onshore Force." *Cambridge* [U.K.] *Architecture Journal* 18 (2006), 92–101.

———. *Outside Lies Magic: Regaining History and Awareness in Everyday Places.* New York: Walker and Co., 1998.

"Super-Highway." *Life,* July 29, 1940, 56–59.

Swain, Stafford. "Scenery of the Canadian Shield." *Railroad Model Craftsman* 47 (January 1979), 56–63.

"Testing 6 Sports Personal Cars." *Motor Trend* 20 (January 1969), 24–42.

Thompson, E. L. "Definition of a Redball." *Trains* 26 (June 1966), 25–27.

Toffler, Alvin. *Future Shock.* New York: Random House, 1970.

Transportation Research Board. *Light Rail Transit.* Proceedings of a National Conference on Light Rail. Washington, D.C.: National Academy Press, 1975.

———. *Low-Volume Roads.* Proceedings of a Workshop Held June 16–19, 1975, in Boise, Idaho. Washington, D.C.: Transportation Research Board, 1975.

Union Pacific Railroad Co. *Map of the Kansas City Terminal Area Showing Junctions and Interchange Points.* Omaha: Union Pacific Railroad Co., 1972.

United States Congress. Committee on Transportation and Infrastructure. *Planes, Trains, and Intermodalism: Improving the Link between Air and Rail.* Washington, D.C.: GPO, 2003.

United States Post Office Department. *General Scheme of Kansas, 1935.* Washington, D.C.: GPO, 1936.

———. *General Scheme of Texas, 1935.* Washington, D.C.: GPO, 1935.

———. *Instructions and Rulings with Reference to Transportation of Mails by Railroads (Steam and Electric) Issued by the Second Assistant Postmaster General.* Washington, D.C.: GPO, 1938.

———. *Mail-Bag Crane.* Washington, D.C.: GPO, 1886.

Urban Mass Transportation Act of 1962. H.R. 11158. Washington, D.C.: GPO, 1962.

Usselman, Steven W. *Regulating Railroad Innovation: Business, Technology, and Politics in America, 1840–1920*. Cambridge: Cambridge University Press, 2002.

Vardy, T. L. "Something for the Freight Yard." National Model Railroad Association *Bulletin* 43 (April 1978), 62–64.

Volkmer, W. D. "Light Rail Rolls in L.A." *Electric Lines* 4 (January–February 1991), 8–11.

———. "Story of Trolley Coaches in the Crescent City." *Electric Lines* 5 (May–June 1992), 8–11.

———. "Ten Years of Light Rail Progress." *Electric Lines* 1 (May–June 1988), 8–13.

Wahl, Paul. "Personal Rapid Transit." *Popular Science* 199 (November 1971), 72–77, 136.

Wakeman, Frederic. *The Fabulous Train*. New York: Rinehart, 1955.

Waller, Margy, and Evelyn Blumenberg, *The Long Journey to Work: Federal Transportation Policy for Working Families*. Washington, D.C.: Brookings Institution, 2003.

Warren, Elizabeth, and Amelia Warren Tyagi. *The Two-Income Trap: Why Middle-Class Mothers and Fathers Are Going Broke*. New York: Basic, 2003.

Westcott, Linn H. "Midnight Local." *Trains and Travel Annual 1953*, n.p.

Westinghouse Electric and Manufacturing Company. *Trolley Coach: Application and Performance Data*. East Pittsburgh: Westinghouse, 1935.

White, Howard S. "People Movers: Mass Transit's Wave of the Future or Just Another Boondoggle?" *Headlights* 35 (November 1973), 3–5.

White, John H., Jr. *The American Railroad Freight Car: From the Wood-Car Era to the Coming of Steel*. Baltimore: Johns Hopkins University Press, 1993.

———. *The American Railroad Passenger Car*. Baltimore: Johns Hopkins University Press, 1978.

Wiley, Aubrey. "Meet the 'Lynchburg Special.'" National Model Railroad Association *Bulletin* 41 (January 1976), 7–10.

Wilkins, Van. "Who Really Killed the Streetcar?" *Electric Lines* 3 (January–February 1990), 20–21, 38.

Wurst, Nancy Henderson. "On Rail's Trails." *Chicago Tribune*, January 11, 2004, 12-2, 12-5.

Young, Andrew. D. "San Jose Light Rail." *Electric Lines* 4 (July–August 1991), 14–15.

INDEX

abandonment, 173–74
Acela (train), 19–20, 250–51; behavior aboard, 122–24
Adams Express, 137
advertising mail industry, 149–50
advertising men, 119
Agricultural Market Service Division, 184
Airborne Express, 134
air-conditioning units, 145–46
airplanes, homemade, 79
airports, 43–46
Albuquerque, N.M., 58
American Express Company, 138
American President Lines, 167–68
American Rail Box Car Company, 150–51
Amtrak, 8, 83, 168–69; commuters, 249
Amtrak Express, 168
Anderson, Sherwood, 53
Armstrong, A. H., 17
Austrian Railways, 260–61
autogiro, 78–79
automatic train operation, 198–200
automation, 229

Babcock, Michael, 182–83
baggage, 136–37
bakeries, 215–16
Baltimore & Ohio Railroad, 192, 240
banana trains, 50–52
barcode technology, 216, 221
Bar Harbor Express (train), 98–99
Bay Area Rapid Transit, 198, 227
Bethel, Maine, 3–4, 87
Bezilla, Michael, 35, 173
Bezzerides, A. I., 218
Blatchford Stack Cranes, 163
blitzkrieg, 66–67
Blumenberg, Evelyn, 77

Bogart, Humphrey, 218
border trade, 159
Boston & Maine Railroad, 99, 193, 235
Boston Metropolitan Transit Authority, 240
Boston University, 225
branch-line development, 186
Brinkley, David, 5
Britain, 160–62
British rail transport crisis, 160–61
British Railways Board, 160–61
Brotherhood of Locomotive Engineers, 229
Bucklin, Kans., 143–47
bulk freight, 177–201
Burlington Northern Santa Fe Railroad, 200
Burlington routes, 60–61
buses, 230–41; trolley, 239–41

cabooses, 155–56, 170
Calgary, Alberta, 241
California High-Speed Rail Authority, 126
California Limited (train), 109–10
Canadian National Railroad, 157
Canadian Pacific Railroad, 165
Canadians, vacationing of, 101
capital, movement of, 261
Caribbean service, 49–52
cars: charter, 106–7; private, 122–23
Casselton, N.Dak., 188
Cedar Rapids, Ia., 174
celebrities, creation of, 113–14
Century Expressway, 81
charter cars, 106–7
Chesapeake & Ohio Railway, 166
Chicago, North Shore & Milwaukee Railroad, 163–64
Chicago, Rock Island & Pacific Railroad, 229

275

INDEX

play-toy-nostalgia

↓

lost
past reality

↓

aforrestation?

CPSIA information can be obtained at www.ICGtesting.com
Printed in the USA
LVOW07s1536090314

376569LV00001B/9/P